Skills and Vocationalism

Skills and Vocationalism:
The easy answer

Edited by
Maurice Holt

Open University Press

Milton Keynes · Philadelphia

Open University Press
Open University Educational Enterprises Limited
12 Cofferidge Close
Stony Stratford
Milton Keynes MK11 1BY, England

and
242 Cherry Street
Philadelphia, PA 19106, USA

First Published 1987

British Library Cataloguing in Publication Data
Skills and vocationalism: the easy answer.
  1. Vocational education—Great Britain
  I. Holt, Maurice
  370.11'3'0941   LC1047.G7

ISBN 0–335–10290–5

ISBN 0–335–10289–1 Pbk

Library of Congress Cataloging in Publication Data
Skills and vocationalism.
  Includes index.
  1. Vocational education—Great Britain. 2. Education
—Economic aspects—Great Britain. 3. Education and
state—Great Britain. I. Holt, Maurice, 1931–
LC1035.8.G7S57 1987   370.11'3'0941   87–11252

ISBN 0–355–10290–5

ISBN 0–335–10289–1 (pbk.)

Text design by Clarke Williams
Typeset by Marlborough Design, Oxford
Printed and bound in Great Britain by Biddles Ltd., Guildford and King's Lynn

Contents

Acknowledgements

This book had its beginnings in a seminar of the Philosophy of Education Society of Great Britain. I am grateful to the society not only for fostering the view that philosophical inquiry has much to contribute to the critique of current issues, but also – in providing a forum for airing drafts of the chapters here by Ruth Jonathan, Richard Smith and myself – acting as midwife to this symposium.

I owe a particular debt to Phil Snelders of the School of Education, Leicester Polytechnic, who organized the original seminar and first proposed that it should form the basis of a book. Without his vision and encouragement it would not have come about.

My discussions with Bill Reid, of the Faculty of Education, University of Birmingham, on the shape and content of the book were invaluable, and helpful comments on an earlier draft were offered by Professor Frank Coffield of the University of Durham and by Clyde Chitty of the University of London Institute of Education.

I am grateful to all the contributors, who have been patient during the protracted business of turning papers into a single volume, and to the support throughout of Naomi Roth of the Open University Press.

Maurice Holt

January 1987

Abbreviations

BTEC   Business and Technical Education Council
CDT   Craft, Design and Technology
CGLI   City and Guilds of London Institute
CPVE   Certificate of Pre-Vocational Education
CSCS   Centre for the Study of Comprehensive Schools
DES   Department of Education and Science
DoE   Department of Employment
DTI   Department of Trade and Industry
EDC   Economic Development Committee
ESG   Education Support Grant
FEU   Further Education Unit
GCSE   General Certificate of Secondary Education
IMS   Institute of Management Studies
IT   information technology
ITEC   Information Technology Education Centre
LEA   Local Education Authority
MSC   Manpower Services Commission
SCDC   School Curriculum Development Committee
SEC   School Examinations Council
TRIST   TVEI-related in-service Training
TVEI   Technical and Vocational Education Initiative
YTS   Youth Training Scheme

Introduction

Maurice Holt

Growing youth unemployment and Britain's faltering economic performance have dominated the political agenda since the start of James Callaghan's Labour administration in 1974. And just as 'short-termism' preoccupies our industries – a word coined by Mary Goldring to describe a preference for quick gains over the short term rather than fundamental reconstruction over the long term – so it does our politicians. Scapegoats and nostrums become the stock-in-trade of ambitious ministers in a television culture. Just as City financiers, seeking a fast buck in a rising market, make it hard for British industry to raise risk capital and invest in the future, so easy answers are more likely to advance a political career than measured inquiries that seek the real causes.

The easy answer, in the case of the economy and unemployment, is all too obvious; blame the schools. This was the solution mapped out by Mr Callaghan in his Ruskin College, Oxford, speech of 1976: schooling must equip children for 'a lively, constructive place in society and also fit them for a job of work'. Thus 'school and working life' became one of the four issues for Mrs Shirley Williams's 'great debate', deftly stage-managed by the DES. Education was not to be sanctioned as a good in itself, but bent instrumentally to the needs of industry. The message had a simple, cracker-barrel appeal: make schools more vocational so that their products may be more employable and our economy more competitive. It was taken up with enthusiasm by David (now Lord) Young as chairman of the MSC in the subsequent Thatcher administration, and the cult of relevance was adopted by Sir Keith Joseph as Secretary of State for Education. Another enthusiast for linking schools to industry soon appeared, bearing the banner of information technology. In response to burgeoning media interest in the silicon chip, Mr Kenneth Baker emerged from the parliamentary penumbra, persuaded Mrs Thatcher to make him Minister for Information Technology, and subsidised the purchase of microprocessors by schools – despite inadequate software, no clear educational rationale and the threat of imminent obsolescence. As successor to Sir

Keith Joseph, Mr Baker is energetically manoeuvring schools down the same vocationalist road with his proposals for 11–18 'City Technology Colleges' and the separation of pupils into academic and vocational streams at the age of eleven or twelve.

The vocational solution to a complex and many-sided problem is not only wrong-headed, it is deeply dangerous. For it allows us to sidestep important questions both about education and training, and about British industry. It is not just the fact that no connection has ever been demonstrated between a particular form of curriculum and economic success; it is the error of shuffling off responsibility for our industrial weakness on to schools, when a moment's thought indicates that the root causes must lie elsewhere. Prominent among them must be:

- the failure of our politicians, of both major parties, to develop a ministry for industrial and economic planning analogous to that of France or Japan; the parsimony of British employers, in investing so diffidently in training;
- the conservative approach of our banks, in failing to offer long-term loans of the kind readily available to industry in West Germany;
- the social divisiveness of British society, reflected in a 'them and us' attitude by managers to their workers, and likely to be exacerbated by a divided 11–18 system of education and training of the kind now advocated by our political masters;
- a philistine disregard for the arts and the nature of design, leading to the production of unattractive goods which fail to find a place in the world market.

These criticisms of our political and managerial culture were commonplace ten years ago: yet they are no less valid today. This represents a serious failure to grapple with the real issues, and a significant indictment of the MSC and its works.

By the same token, the easy answer of skills and vocationalism has diverted attention from the real defects of our education system. By establishing vocational courses alongside a traditional academic programme animated by a nineteenth-century model of specialist education, it has sustained a divisive culture and at the same time propped up a defective, narrowing curriculum which most other developed countries had begun to abandon by the early years of this century.

But the blight of vocationalism spreads further than this. Because it allows central government to intervene, under the guise of restoring economic vigour, it drives out localism and favours detailed control of education by government agencies. The process began with the 1977 Green Paper and subsequent DES circulars: since 1983 the MSC has staked its claim to the school curriculum through TVEI, and in 1986 the Secretary of State announced his intention of installing, in the next Parliament, a national curriculum with specified objectives at every level of schooling. And this is to be accompanied by severe curtailment of LEA powers.

More than that: another unpleasant consequence of linking education with industrial practice is that it introduces the apparatus of procedures, specified outputs, line management and appraisal to activities which are fundamentally social and moral: which respond not to the language of skills and the market economy, but to deliberative inquiry and practical judgement. Improving education is therefore not a matter of central decisions, conveyed to schools by technocratic 'delivery systems': it is a matter of supporting schools, teachers, pupils and their constituencies to arrive at solutions to problems rooted in a particular context and yielding to social and moral inquiry.

The argument of this book, then, is that the lure of vocationalism – and its attendant jargon of systems, modules, and skills – is seductive but unsound. It has led to the extravagant funding of ill-conceived schemes, lowered school morale through rampant centralization, and deflected teachers from a consideration of the real issues. And vocationalism has done nothing whatever to increase the competitiveness of British industry, nor to address the consequences for our children of what may turn out to be a jobless society.

The book explores these issues in the style of a symposium rather than a collection – as befits its origins in a seminar of the Philosophy of Education Society of Great Britain. Its contributors have tailored their papers not to a standard length and format, but to a style appropriate to the issues they examine. It is proper that Bernard Barker's opening chapter should be by the head of a comprehensive school: for it is schools which lie on the receiving end of the vocationalist prescriptions devised by central government. That it has a polemical flavour will come as no surprise to those whose contact with schools makes them familiar with the anger felt by many heads – anger at costly strategies which will serve their pupils ill.

Mike Golby's subsequent chapter sets the scene in a different way. It analyses the defects of our present system of schooling, offers a critique of vocationalist assumptions, and draws hope from current interest in strengthening local representation on governing bodies. Golby notes the present polarized debate between the vocationalists and intellectual elitism, and its cost in terms of neglected issues. He seeks a restoration of curriculum making to the local level 'as a participatory and collaborative activity', and in many ways offers an agenda for the chapters which follow.

By examining the notion of skills in the context of new technology, Jerry Wellington exposes the soft underbelly of the new vocationalism and notes that vocationalism is absent from Japan's schools. Richard Smith shows how disquietingly pervasive the notion of skills has become by examining their use in a different, yet fashionable context: that of the education of teachers and the concept of 'classroom skills' in particular. His critique leads him to some valuable observations on teaching as a professional activity, rather than a craft, and on the dangers of skills-based teacher appraisal.

In the following chapter I attempt an interim judgement on the progress of the TVEI operation. This centralist intervention continues to attract government funding, despite the lack of any considered, independent evaluation. This chapter puts the consequences of vocationalism in a practical setting and takes further most of the issues touched upon here. It is followed by Ruth Jonathan's searching and revealing study of the notion of core skills, which forms the central education-and-training component of the YTS. It is an inquiry of the first importance and throws a stark light on the pretentious rhetoric which characterizes so many vocational aspirations.

Clive Seale looks at the YTS from a different perspective, and bases his study of its concepts of education and training on a survey of actual practice. This involves some scrutiny of the FEU, which comes in for detailed study in Paul Grosch's chapter. Here the deficiencies of the FEU's model of curriculum development are charted, as are the parallels between so much of the FEU's activity and the vocationalist movement in the US, half a century ago. Finally, I attempt to draw together the various strands which run through the book, and offer the view that only a reinterpretation of the concept of liberal education can, as the basis for an 11–18 programme, equip our children for a future which will require rather more from them than the solution of today's problems in yesterday's terms. Yet it is the mark of the vocationalist solution that it can never amount to more than that. A country with our moral and intellectual resources deserves better, and needs better for cultural richness and economic growth.

CHAPTER 1

Pre-Vocationalism and schooling

Bernard Barker

The once secret garden of the curriculum has been manured, watered and artificially heated in the years since Callaghan's 'Great Debate', flowering with manifold pre-vocational blooms. The DES, the DTI and the MSC have sponsored a host of schemes, each of which has taken a variety of local forms. No one TVEI scheme is the same as another. TRIST in-service funding has reached schools through a variety of LEA schemes. Employers and further education establishments have adopted a multiplicity of arrangements for one- and two-year versions of the YTS.

Diversity has not, however, obscured a broad-based movement towards work-consciousness and employment-related education. LEA officers, inspectors and teachers have been as eager for vocational schemes as Lord Young. MSC or ESG money has been grasped for a succession of projects. Schools swiftly introduced CGLI examinations (for students) as a step towards the CPVE. Innovations as different as the GCSE and the YTS exhibit in varying degrees features of the pre-vocational approach.

Pre-vocational education dates from Shirley Williams's 1977 Green Paper rather than Sir Keith Joseph's 1984 Sheffield blueprint and enjoys support from disparate sources across the political spectrum. People believe that youngsters should be trained as self-sufficient competitors in business and industry, ready to fight in world markets. Art and imagination are perceived as leisure pursuits that can be funded only by business; economic success is held to depend on manufacturing. Communications skills are valued as an essential instrument of commerce; the study of literature is perceived as a luxury to be earned. Few realize that the Royal Shakespeare Company can match the export earnings of many an engineering firm. Disinterested scholarship is presented as an effete, gentlemanly irrelevance, almost the cause of industrial decline.

The vocational argument depends on a number of doubtful propositions and there are real risks in so partial a vision of the transforming power of knowledge. Since the days of Harold Wilson's 'white heat of the technological revolution' politicians have searched with increasing desperation for policies to restore the efficiency and competitiveness of British industry. Keynesian expansion and monetarist constraint have in turn failed to rescue the economy from the limitations of an exposed island, vulnerable and dependent on the goodwill of its trading partners. Unwilling or unable to reform British institutions, James Callaghan at Ruskin College proposed an agenda for changing the attitudes of school children. His desire to promote a positive awareness of industry, work experience, school–industry links, enterprise and 'relevance' in the curriculum foreshadowed similar Conservative ideas. From 1979 a sharp rise in unemployment enabled ministers to allege that comprehensive schools had not produced sufficiently skilful workers for changing world conditions. An 'academic' curriculum became a scapegoat for economic failure.

Teachers were equally critical of traditional disciplines and methods. Schools despaired of some of their own efforts, aware that many children seemed alienated from an 'academic' curriculum. Schools Council projects sought alternatives to the didactic approach through the 1970s. Teachers, politicians and the public found themselves in agreement that 'something' needed to be done. Worries about education, industry and modern society at large converged and found a common expression in a new political/ educational agenda for changing people and attitudes rather than institutions or policies. There was silence about public investment or devaluation. Multi-cultural education and 'young enterprise' were offered as solutions to inner city problems such as black unemployment.

An attractive, liberal-sounding vocabulary has been invented or borrowed to describe the aims, objectives and techniques of the movement, emphasizing the personal qualities and attitudes it is intended to develop. Learning is now 'experiential', 'active', 'practical' and 'participatory'. Courses are modular, with a 'core' and 'options'; teaching emphasizes 'processes' and 'skills' rather than 'content' and 'facts'. Pupils are 'profiled' on a 'matrix' through 'continuous assessment', not simply tested or examined. Proposals for new schemes have to be written according to 'criteria' and submitted for approval and 'accreditation'. Teachers and pupils involved in the various initiatives (TVEI, CPVE) are encouraged to feel themselves part of something special, new and exciting, engaged in the task of transforming an outmoded education system through 'changed attitudes'. Pre-vocational courses invariably require staffing, resources, timetabling and facilities more generous than those allowed for old style 'academic' lessons, now dismissed as archaic and 'irrelevant'.

This politicized language defines the terms of a discourse about current social and moral problems, describing desirable behaviour, attributes and attitudes. It establishes a structure of approved relationships, a process through which teachers and pupils may contribute to material progress. Scholars are challenged to give up their ivory towers and engage in the 'real' world. The language of pre-vocational education infiltrates every in-service course or meeting of teachers, washing away ground upon which critics might stand, obliging the sceptical to consider whether or not to endorse irrelevant academicism.

Pre-vocational rhetoric relies upon contrasts useful for social comment and political debate but almost meaningless for education. What do words like 'academic' and 'practical' denote? Is the study of *Othello* an outmoded, 'academic' activity? Does Shakespeare become less 'academic' when he is performed and costumes are made? Is personal writing a 'practical' task? Is class discussion more or less 'practical' than an experiment in chemistry? Do computer keyboards and typewriters have a vocational practicality missing when mathematicians study the formulae upon which electronics is based? Art and music, like most other subjects, depend upon a blend of theory and practice; facts and concepts are no less vital than practical experiments in forming and understanding of reality. Quantum mechanics and Hegelian philosophy are remote abstractions that have changed man's relationship with the 'real' world.

Relevance is a fundamental pre-vocational concept but conveys no precise meaning or intention. Instead it is used as a vague term of approval, implying that direct and immediate economic applications justify some forms of knowledge but not others. No particular topics are prescribed; instead relevance is a criterion teachers are supposed to apply in the drafting of syllabuses. The DES summary of *Better Schools* provides a tautological definition of relevance which illustrates how empty such criteria can become: 'subjects should be taught so as to bring out their applications to the pupils' own experience and to adult life, and to give due emphasis to practical aspects'. On this basis, almost any subject could be taught in whatever manner suited the teacher. Teachers have in fact always chosen topics in this way, seeking to stimulate the imagination and interest of as many children as possible, judging what is appropriate for their pupils. The danger is that pre-vocational education seeks to generalize, moving from a teacher's intuitive sense of what has the best chance of encouraging growth and development towards a narrowly instrumental prescription for whole groups of young people. Learning is too unpredictable a business for this approach to succeed.

Teachers on courses have learned to speak a new language dominated by arcane acronyms (TVEI, CPVE, TRIST) and positive-sounding adjectives without definite meaning. Amongst those in receipt of appropriate funds there is an almost missionary willingness to change the face of school, to foster active, participatory, relevant and practical studies and to use very expensive equipment whenever possible. Unlikely colleagues begin to insist on the need for problem-solving and simulations. When pre-vocational courses are scrutinized in detail, however, their content is disappointing. Too often schemes are no more that a mélange of recycled and familiar ideas, unsupported by suggestions for teaching to achieve the almost moral transformation so earnestly desired. 'Communications skills', for example, resemble the basic arithmetic and business English offered for years on technical college day-release courses or to low-ability pupils in secondary schools. Business studies and information technology do not represent a remarkable development from the standard offering of typewriting and office practice. TVEI has funded a great expansion in the number of computers and electronic devices but it is doubtful whether currently available software is equal to the claims made for micro-learning. Is button-pressing, for example, any more 'practical' or 'interactive' than reading? Nor is there much evidence that the future will hold large numbers of jobs for pupils familiar with keyboards.

By contrast, pedagogy in physics and mathematics has been unaffected by pre-vocational ambitions. Only a small number of students properly master electricity, electronics and control technology. For such pupils TVEI has opened new possibilities, but what of relevance for the majority, who remain as baffled as ever by circuits, whether constructed with batteries and wire or integrated and printed on silicon? Strangely, science has been omitted from many vocational schemes; money has flowed into applications rather than generating ideas for new development.

Work experience and careers guidance support these vocational elements, as they do in almost all schools. Personal and social education is not an invention of the pre-vocational movement. Other ingredients include community service, gardening, environmental studies, art and drama; all areas well developed by schools in the 1950s and 1960s.

Vocationalism has attracted few able students; GCSE is the guarantee of worth ambitious families pursue. Public schools have not complained of their omission from vocational or pre-vocational plans, nor do they enter candidates for CPVE, BTEC or CGLI courses. Parents and able children calculate that worthwhile jobs are not available by this route. 'Practical' training is not a realistic preparation for leadership positions in British society.

On the other hand, the pre-vocational movement has raised important questions, enhancing the status and credibility of work for the less able. It has enabled teachers to revive discarded ideas and approaches, especially from the secondary modern tradition, formerly squeezed into the margin by comprehensive reorganization. Teachers have been stimulated by working on curriculum development with colleagues from other schools. A willingness to experiment with profiles and composite, team-led courses *are* an alternative to deadening habits and routines. Some excellent teaching has characterized the best TVEI and CGLI courses and a genuine effort has been made to address the needs of less than average students. Some YTS schemes have been narrow and open to the charge of exploiting 'cheap labour' but others have offered a sensible introduction to work. Connections with industry have provided 'reality therapy' and significant improvements have been made in post-sixteen vocational training.

A price has been paid, however, for these modest achievements. Work-related training and education has stolen the initiative from schools, encouraging teachers to adopt fashionable, off-the-peg ideas without careful reflection of their own. Political energy from the centre has focused educational debate upon economic questions, establishing a false set of priorities for the system. New initiatives depend on a ruthless slander of previous efforts rather than research and evaluation; argument proceeds by political assertion, not the accumulation of evidence. It is alleged that by the late 1970s schools were irrelevant, offering an inappropriate academic education bleached of all power to stimulate or entertain. TVEI is presented as a saviour, an injection of life-restoring curiosity and imagination at a single, modular stroke. No mention is made of drama, art, music, CDT, Nuffield science, games, swimming, food and nutrition, computing, work experience or a host of other lively activities enjoyed by most pupils in most schools throughout the period of supposed alienation.

Sir Keith Joseph frequently alleged that the 'bottom 40 per cent' emerge from all these experiences without pleasure or benefit. But if lessons were taught so badly in the past that no one enjoyed them, how are such dreary staff to be energized by TVEI? If teachers are irredeemable, why should vocationalism succeed where all else has failed? If the complaint is about teaching methods in so-called 'academic' subjects (e.g. French, history) why were these pedagogic problems not tackled directly? If pre-vocational education simply means giving some children more of what they seem to like (e.g. craft, work experience, button-pressing) the barely concealed implication is that books should be abandoned altogether on the grounds that reading is difficult.

Pre-vocational schemes give the impression of an approach to education based on key principles; that a new practice influencing teaching has been established. The reality is a retread 'package' for slow learners. Vocationalism has not offered a fresh analysis or detailed criticism of teaching methods or content; nor has it explained why some children learn while others grow to hate what should be the tools fo their liberation. Why do some youngsters turn against apparently enjoyable .activities from trampolining to badminton? A preference for short-term goals and 'practical' learning does not amount to an educational philosophy; the idea of some children being 'good' with their hands is old and discredited.

What is offered instead is an unsatisfactory admixture of progressive ideas and behavioural objectives. Lord Young's reliance on the rhetoric of change and improvement and the MSC's dependence on progressive vocabulary indicate the shallow thought underlying so many initiatives. No one is now better placed to teach Henry VIII with greater relevance or to conclude that Tudor politics is irrelevant to life. No one knows how to make science more appealing for less able students or what knowledge will turn out to be the most profitable.

Essential methodological and curriculum issues are now neglected or judged according to a criterion of usefulness drawn from politics rather than education; instrumentalists are unable to distinguish social and educational objectives. Analysis begins with the unemployment queue and imported music centres, not the intrinsic problems of selecting topics or crafting powerful experiences from them. The result is a misleading, circular argument that technical training and enterprise can cure industrial decay. Where decay has already severely undermined education (in Liverpool, for example), new technological colleges are promised.

An edifice of reform has been built upon a presumed connection between the school curriculum and economic growth for which not a shred of evidence exists. No economist has suggested how the adoption of pre-vocational schemes might enhance the performance of British industry, nor have shortages been identified in the areas for which training is provided. YTS is not part of a strategic plan for the economy; it exists, rather, to service an 'enterprise culture' which is supposed to make planning unnecessary. Vocational initiatives are designed to extend factory/industrial disciplines and controls from the workplace into schoolrooms, allegedly suffused with anti-industrial attitudes and an almost aristocratic disdain for manufacturing.

The vocational emphasis is also damaging to the idea of education for citizenship. Teachers preoccupied with market place considerations find it natural to differentiate pupils and subjects according to their presumed suitability and significance for various types and levels of employment. Students are less likely to be seen as citizens who (in Aneurin Bevan's phrase) 'are to be asked to wield the royal sceptre' and should be educated accordingly in the arts of self-government. They are divided, rather, into 'academic' and 'practical' groups, set to work on quite different assignments. Subjects are classified so that aesthetic and moral experiences central to maturity, judgment and citizenship are secondary to the 'skills' that may earn a crust of bread. Applied activities are exalted above the spiritual and the imaginative in a frantic search for usefulness. Information and word-processing are elevated; the creative activity that leads to words and information is passed over.

Local authorities have to submit schemes and proposals in order to qualify for ESG or MSC funding. This has the effect of removing a 'welfare state' basis for education. In the place of a right to a minimum education provision and an entitlement to an accountable, democratic service, there now stands an embryo apparatus of competitive tendering. Young people are coming to depend for their educational opportunities upon the entrepreneurial flair of inspectors and officers. Teachers lose their professional detachment and scramble for resources instead. Headteachers come to measure their success in terms of additional revenue rather than by the quality of relationships within the school upon which the virtues of education once depended.

There is, too, a sad irony in an obsession with the needs of industry that serves only to enhance an already excessive concern with jobs. Radicals have long criticized the self-defeating emptiness of the qualification spiral and the hollow promise of a 'better job' for hard-working pupils. Teachers have tended to stress instrumental rather than intrinsic satisfactions in arguments with recalcitrant students. Pre-vocationalism is another, explicit turn of a very old screw rather than a new departure, a further narrowing of the scope of education for ordinary people. The attempt to anticipate industry's need for computer programmers, graphic designers, plumbers and motor mechanics is inevitably forlorn; within a few years technology moves on and the limitations of job-specific training are revealed. Nevertheless, the constant stress on getting and spending shifts attention from the proper business of education. Education, especially mass education, should be concerned primarily with extending democracy and enabling individuals and communities to exercise power over their own lives. This does not mean that work and industry should be set on one side, only that aesthetic, moral and political decisions should not be neutralized by economic considerations.

Pre-vocational education replaces the ambiguity of a poem with the certainty of production; the tangible virtues of spelling and adding are substituted for the complex symbols of art and music. The interpretation of meaning and culture is discounted as pupils are introduced to specific techinques and skills. The vocational impetus has impoverished education by defining human purposes so narrowly.

Teachers should not seek to escape to a secret grove of academe, cultivating their blooms without reference to an outside world. There is nothing wrong with usefulness and relevance, only their development as instruments of political ideology. Industrial culture is an inescapable and necessary feature of our lives. There is no advantage in a romantic rejection of factories and mills. On the other hand, a democratic vision of education, based on aesthetics, morals and citizenship is more likely to liberate the talent of the people and to provide a secure foundation fo their inventiveness and utility. Literature, for example, engages in a constant dialogue with life. It is not a self-indulgent exercise for an elite. A broad, humane and liberal curriculum is the best guarantee of economic success. Unsuspected and little considered abstract notions will transform human life long after the last grocer's shop has succumbed to an out-of-town hypermarket.

CHAPTER 2

Vocationalism and education

Michael Golby

Education has always been intimately connected with the world of work. Early impulses to provide schooling for the masses contain a mixture of motives but all of them take cognizance of the social reality of employment. On the one hand humanitarian instincts promoted compulsory schooling in the early years of the nineteenth century as a means of liberating children from the heartless depredations of what amounted to little more than slave labour. On the other hand, later in the turbulent years of revolutions and the widening franchise a note of 'education for our masters' was to be heard, schooling as a means of 'gentling the masses'.

In the twentieth century the ideological currents of egalitarianism, notably in the writings of R.H. Tawney, introduce a levelling function into the debate about schooling. Here for the first time in the public sector schooling is not just to follow a religious or secular social order but to act as a reforming force. The invention of meritocracy in the mid twentieth century is a dramatic step towards the fulfilment of schooling as a power of social change. In such social change what work people are to do is at the centre. Harold Wilson's concept of the comprehensive school as providing 'grammar school opportunities for all' – clearly meritocratic in itself – was a step towards a concept of a common curriculum for a common culture.

What this latter formula lacks is a clear recognition of social inequalities pervading the culture, most importantly perhaps in inequalities in access to work and its highly differentiated rewards.

It may well be doubted to what extent we have a common culture, so far are we divided on lines of class, race and region. Our recognition of these factors has been heightened by the increase in worklessness which has been clearly patterned along class, race, gender and regional lines.

In the 1980s, therefore, we are faced with the problem of redefining the relationship between schooling and work. We are helped in this by the legacy of all the experimentations and theorizing that went on through the 1960s. At that time it became possible to articulate a concept of education which separated it from narrow instrumentalism and saw it as an end in itself. To be sure, this was not new to human history, for Dewey had long ago expressed the idea that the only true aim of education was more education – but in an American context where there was no doubt that schooling served a democratic social order, albeit one which was rapidly developing on competitive and capitalist lines.

The question then is not whether schools should serve society, but how. The philosophizing of the 1960s developed a purist conception of education as the pursuit of personal autonomy based on reason. This lacked a responsible account of the social and economic relations necessary for that purpose. In that way it mirrored the separation of the education service, and teachers particularly, from social audit. As economic and ideological stringency set in during the 1970s this separation broke down to the point of mistrust and disillusionment. Two political events may be seen as symbolic of these developments: the abolition of the Schools Council, which was one of Sir Keith Joseph's early measures, and the creation in 1974 and subsequent growth of the Manpower Services Commission. These two developments attacked the values held by the education service and called them to account for the part education should play in the social order.

Unfortunately this accountability, though necessary (for what democracy ought to tolerate vast unaccounted-for expenditure?), has been converted to its own ends by a narrow range of interests from the world of business. Aided by a businessman's government, business and industry have been holding education to account. The next step in the evolution of education as a public service is surely to widen the interests to whom education is to be legitimately accountable. Already, for other reasons, parents are coming to the fore and we may well be seeing the creation of counterforces to the assumptions of industry.

Among these assumptions have been the following:

1 Education principally concerns the pupils' preparation for a world of work.
2 This preparation should concern itself with the 'skills' industry needs.
3 These skills are mainly technical in nature.
4 Schools have perpetuated an anti-industrial culture.
5 Schools have neglected a substantial minority ('the bottom 40 per cent') in favour of an academic group of high flyers.

All of these assumptions, and more, may be called into question by the arrival of new interests on the accountability scene. Parents and governors who get to know the work of the schools intimately will certainly realize that schools can hold out the view that there is more to life than earning a living. What, after all, are we to do with the wealth created by work? As curriculum reform goes on, some of it motivated by criticism such as the above and some of it springing from other sources, the questions will be freshly formulated and we may go some way to asking on what principles an educational curriculum which is also socially responsive may be defined. A suspicion of an answer is that no permanent theory for all this is possible. Instead we should look for a balance of interests in which the recent swings of the pendulum from teachers to industrialists are held more in check by a continuous process of social negotiation in the developing institutions of schooling and government.

The purpose of this chapter is to suggest a broad set of considerations for those concerned with the development of curriculum. Its central theme is that 'education' and 'preparation for work', however broadly defined either or both may be, are not synonymous terms. It will be argued that if there are attempts to convert education to the interests of business or commerce these must be regarded with a critical eye lest other equally legitimate interests in education are consequently devalued. The critique of education from a vocationalist standpoint in recent years has been unhelpful to the improvement of the school curriculum because it has focused attention on too narrow a front. This paper indicates some broader considerations.

It is no part of this thesis that any particular moves are in fact being made, nor that there is any actual conspiracy to bring the education service under the control of business. Those are exceedingly difficult empirical questions which others are addressing. Equally, however, the thesis is not the purely conceptual or linguistic one that the two terms have different 'meanings'. It is not proposed that the content and structure of an 'educational' curriculum can be derived in some *a priori* fashion from an analysis of the terms involved in discussion about it, for example, by contrasting 'education' and 'training'. Though these terms are indeed used to pick out distinctions among practical activities, reliance is better placed upon ordinary human wishes for young people. It will be important therefore that curriculum planning is conducted in such a way that these wishes are not obfuscated by ideology. Centralist tendencies carry this danger and it will be suggested that curriculum planning should be devolved as far as possible to the grass roots level.

In the end, to uphold such a view of curriculum planning is to espouse a value position which has political as well as curricular implications. The message for innovators and curriculum developers will be that personal and professional responsibility demands that full account be taken of the historical and moral dimensions of their work. Relevance to 'work' or 'the economy' must be set against and balanced with the perhaps less easily articulated values contained in the preferences of parents and others for their children. The new school governing bodies – since they will contain a majority of people with a direct personal stake in the curriculum of their school – present an opportunity for this form of resistance to distant dogma.

Rather than philosophically defining terms, it is important for this form of argument to inspect the substantive ends that education may from time to time be called to serve. This is so not only because philosophical analysis tends to carry little weight in the practical world but also for two other reasons. Firstly, philosophers do not agree among themselves on the issues; secondly, and connectedly, philosophy is not value-free enquiry which, if only it could be perfected, would provide the answers to social and moral questions. The work of the philosophers of education in the dominant Peters tradition has been subject to enough scrutiny to establish that a specific educational position is contained within their endeavours. The whole form of work that this genre of philosophy of education represents goes towards reinforcing an academically oriented school curriculum.

The initial question before us in this enquiry is what alternatives may be specified as the ends of education. The bid from vocationalists has to be seen as not the only alternative to intellectual elitism; too much of the debate has been polarized between these two alone. The deficiencies of our secondary education have been exceedingly well rehearsed and practically nobody denies that the secondary curriculum needs overhauling. How far academic values are to retain their central place is, however, a matter of some contention.

A first riposte to the vocationalist thrust, one dismayingly seldom seen, would be to accept the criticism that schooling has failed perhaps the majority of pupils but to say that this is no reason for rejecting the view that school is primarily about the virtues of the considered life. A reformed, well resourced, properly assessed curriculum should be persevered with; it should be detached as far as possible from the ravages of a competitive examination system and the straitening effects of subject-mindedness. This move would preserve the centrality of mind without elevating mere cleverness as an organizational criterion, for example, by rejecting streaming and setting without good reason. General education would be reinstated as the purpose of the compulsory school years. Perhaps the most urgent challenge for such a postiion is to incorporate practical and expressive activities in a tradition of education which is predominantly concerned with the abstract and theoretical.

This move is perhaps too obvious to have achieved much attention yet it is something of the kind the HMI have been propounding in their various publication since *Curriculum 11–16*[1] and *A View of the Curriculum*.[2] These documents have consistently put forward a counter view to that contained in the parallel Ministerial publications. In *A Framework for the School Curriculum*[3] and in the subsequent more muted publication, *The School Curriculum*[4], for example, there resides no discernible overall view of curriculum design. They are concoctions of the obvious, reflecting only an uneasy consensus of the ill-informed and responding to the political preoccupations of the hour. As such, they are of course undefended against the next trend or moral panic to come along. It is noteworthy, too, that despite obeisances in the direction of the world of work such proposals are bereft of specific curricular ideas in that direction. This is surely because the conceptual apparatus being deployed is limited by the rather narrow educational experience of politicians themselves. It is predominately the subject-based curriculum which is assumed in such proposals and this curriculum has the greatest difficulty in articulating a coherent response to cross - curricular initiatives. There is no traditional school subject called 'the world of work' and thus no clear views are forthcoming on what it could represent in the curriculum beyond generalizations of a saloon - bar nature about 'the basics' and the 'will to work'.

As it is, then, the popular rhetoric has it that Britain is an industrial country with an anti-industrial culture; the education service does little to rectify and may even be responsbile for this state of affairs. But these assertions are linked to no historical explanation why Britain became pre-eminent industrially and otherwise in the first place, nor to the role of the education system in that ascendency. If there were some such analysis we might have more confidence in the capacity of education to contribute to prosperity as well as benefit from it. The suspicion must remain that, historically, the origins of industrial success lie well outside the education system, in factors such as maritime access to imperial markets. By the same token it might be thought that the seeds of late twentieth-century economic renewal may well lie equally distantly from the schools, for example, in the movements of international capital. If in the nineteenth century the contribution of the schools was to provide a docile labour force in trubulent political times, then perhaps today's role for the schools is, minimally, in being seen to respond to economic crisis and unemployment. In regard to schools, politicians can be seen to be doing something, sometimes with the added frisson of censoriousness.

But these are big ifs and it is not to the present purpose to claim they are true. They are raised only to suggest that the relation between the schools and the economy is both multi-faceted and essentially contested. Because it cannot be contended that this relationship is clear in a causal, or in any other, way it makes litle sense to claim that the schools are responsible for economic decline or that the economy can be turned round principally by educational reform. Nevertheless, the educationists are in receipt of regular accusations that they subvert the aims of industry, from pre-school to university, mainly by failing to emphasize technological subjects, by failing to foster the entrepreneurial spirit and by indulging the luxury of individualism at the expense of discipline and team work.

The effect of this undifferentiated mass of complaint is to imply that the alternative to the curriculum as it is – and we have acknowledged its defects – is a curriculum geared to the 'real' world of work. And this despite the poor theoretical background and the paucity of thoroughgoing suggestions for curriculum reform – apart from spectacular but essentially marginal assaults on the system such as TVEI.

But these are not the only alternatives. Indeed, at a time of high unemployment, and unemployment among the young in particular, it would seem logical to contemplate an education for a workless future. This, however, is plainly not a political possibility and no political party has dared to mention it. Because it is so inconceivable we have hardly any indication what such an education would look like. It would certainly not be the same sort of thing as education for leisure, for leisure constitutes a range of activities defined as such by contrast to work in precisely the same way that holidays make sense only when there is something to go back to afterwards. A workless culture will necessarily redefine what it takes seriously as constituting the essential tasks of life and what it takes less seriously as perhaps being recuperative or playful. Since we cling to paid employment as the source of social identity, financial sustenance and personal dignity, we are unable to contemplate a workless future whether for ourselves as individuals or for us all socially. Thus education cannot be conceptualized in this dimension and is apt to degenerate into education for leisure. Education is indeed a vision of the future and curriculum plans can only be made on the basis of what we are able – and willing – to see of the future.

If education for worklessness is a more logical and education for leisure a more likely response to the modern situation we should not be ignoring other aspects of adult life for which education should be preparing. It is predictable that the vast majority of pupils will become parents. Yet despite James Callaghan's emphasis on the family at the outset of the great debate a decade ago this aspect of the responsibility of the education service has received scant attention in the ensuing rush to vocationalize. It is tempting to ascribe this neglect to some deep intuition that the family is potentially at least a centre of resistance to social engineering. What close-knit family would be prepared to see its members dispersed nation- and Europe-wide in fulfilment of the supreme imperative of work? But the family itself is in crisis, a crisis certainly in part due to an undermining social, political and economic environment. Education for parenthood ought to equip people to understand their predicament as parents in such terms, enabling them to act in defence of the family as an institution as well as in the interests of their own family as a unit. As it is, of course, education for parenthood degenerates to child care without reference to its social context. It is hardly likely that there is need of a conspiracy to suppress the family in this subtle way, by reducing it to hygiene and sentimentality, when we are all in general so limited in our understanding of what the family could represent in the social structure and in our personal lives.

For much the same reason community education also fails to gain a real grip on the mainsprings of curriculum development which remains torn between academic and vocational emphases. Much energy and ingenuity has been expended on community education but these endeavours have consisted mainly in attempts to share school facilities. There is little sense of what communities might become; and insofar as efforts remain at the technical level there is little prospect of educational action pragmatically clarifying possibilities.

As well as exercising the role of parents and as well as inhabiting a local community, all pupils wil also be members of a political form of life we call democratic. Citizenship, equally with parenthood and community membership, has been a much neglected and misrendered goal of the curriculum development movement in recent years. There are few attempts to relate a knowledge of the forms of government to the levers of political power. So in schools the old civics and British Constitution survives; there are picturesque role playings in the shape of school councils and moots; but the skills of participation and the exercise of personal and community rights receive scant attention. To go beyond the cosily descriptive is for schools to court the charge of mixing education with politics. Here the academic tradition of neutrality is seen as a disease preventing the positive engagement of young people in the political culture. The proposal in the 1986 Education Bill to bar pupils from membership of their own school governing bodies is a symptom of that fear of political activity among young people and in or near schools that has nullified even the most legitimate of programmes such as that proposed Crick and Porter[5]. It seems that in this most crucial of areas the fear of responsible political activity is greater than the fear of the consequences of ignorance. Political breakdown and disorder is surely a more likely eventuality than economic bankruptcy; moreover, it is an area where appropriate teaching could directly affect the quality of judgment the citizen deploys. This is certainly a more likely educational contribution to the collective quality of life than the purveying of dubious employment-related 'generic skills'.

In the closely-related field of economics it is truly significant that calls for education to prepare pupils for 'the world of work' include only nostrums of the 'there are no free dinners' variety and contain no invitation to a critical economic literacy. That there are a number of theoretical ideas about economic growth, all with different policy implications, is to be forever unknown to the majority of people who will make their political choices on the basis of personalities and slogans only. School, which for very many will be their only exposure to a critical consciousness, will have been in dereliction of an educational duty. The conflict between education and vocationalism will have claimed another casualty in the middle ground.

The educational imperatives from the family, from the community, from citizenship and from economics have all suffered neglect or suppression as a result of the vocationalist assault on the curriculum. These modern concerns threaten to go the way of those older curricular aims – Christian salvation and gentlemanly cultivation – in the struggle between ideologies. For it is important to recognize that no bid on the resources of the education system can be free of social and political assumptions concerning the distribution of power and the nature of the good life. When national economic survival is postulated as an overriding priority it will be important to ask 'survival in what form?' Which distinguishable interests will be advantaged and which disadvantaged in any new settlement? Reference to Raymond Williams's[6] threefold classification of educational interests – the industrial trainers, the classical humanists and the public educators – may be complemented by Salter and Tapper's[7] state bureaucrats as a basis for such enquiry. There is an urgent need for research in the real politics of educational policy. Such research, of which Broadfoot's[8] is the best recent example, could help us to discover the centres of educational influence at national and local levels and thereby to learn how deliberation might be opened up to wider constituencies.

Such is the overwhelming strength of the vocationalist impulse that deliberation over the curriculum has been severely curtailed in recent years. It is surely now time to review the direction education is taking, and a start should be made by considering the adequacy of the forums within which educational policies and initiatives are generated.

Since the demise of the Schools Council there has been no independent body wherein curriculum development could be promoted. Despite its well documented shortcomings, its labyrinthine committee structure, its failure to produce a 'whole curriculum' policy, and its apparent lack of 'take-up' in the schools, this was the nearest we have seen to a research and developemnt agency holding the ring between the many diverse interests in education. Its successor bodies, the School Curriculum Development Committee and the School Examinations Council, are not representative of those diverse interests and respond principally from the centre to the political imperatives of the day.

The proposal in the 1986 Education Bill to do away finally with the old Consultative Committees which contributed so much intelligence to policy making over the years is perhaps another symptom of the flight from independent advice which has characterized the centre over the past few years.

In this situation the professional vogue for school-based curriculum development is likely to be restricted to the realm of technique against a backdrop of structural decisions on the curriculum taken centrally. If curriculum is to be rescued from the truncations of vocationalism it can only be hoped that the LEAs will exert themselves and set up their own curriculum development agencies. These should be based on a genuine collaboration of local interests using a disciplined form of enquiry and resulting in clear statements of policy for the whole curriculum. Such statements are not to be confused with prescriptions for detailed curriculum content. It is rather a matter of establishing an agreed working rationale against which practitioners, governors and education committees themselves may make judgments on future developments in the light of experience. The power of the LEAs has been greatly diminished since local government organization in 1974 but they could surely redeem their educational souls by taking seriously their responsibility for the curriculum in concert with governors and teachers.

In doing so there would be a strong tide to swim against. The flow of events is increasingly in one direction, from central to local and then to school level. Centralization is of course a separate question from that of the desirability of the messages that are sent. In the professional mind, though, centralization is inevitably bound up with the vocational trend of recent years. Given the central government's legitimate interest in the economy and in manpower planning it is likely that only the coarser-grained messages will come through that channel. All the more reason, then, for LEAs, governors and teachers to mount their own curriculum initiatives, preferably in concert at the local level where they can be enacted, monitored and improved.

The urgency of this is not simply in defending more sophisticated and locally responsive curricula. More, it is a matter of preserving and furthering the art of curriculum making at the scene of its transmission. If teachers are not to become a mere 'delivery system' of curricular goods defined at the centre (and this is very much the language of the White Paper, *Better Schools*[9]), local exertions are necessary. The new machinery for INSET will need to be used not solely for short-term system maintenance or so as to be seen to be applying central priorities, but also to research more distant goals and more adventurous possibilities. The contractual relationships implied in new forms of teacher appraisal will need to be moderated by a spirit of collegiality. 'Honeypot' or 'goldfish bowl' forms of financial management where competitive bidding for public monies may drive out more experimental and reinforce more conservative proposals will need to be handled with care. Objectives-based planning will need to recognize the creativity involved in innovative work not all of which can pre-specify its outcomes. Above all, the deleterious effects of rush must be minimized. Of course there is urgency; but the strongest impression left by the last ten years of curriculum initiatives is one of too many answers chasing too few questions. This form of educational inflation has depleted energies throughout the system and eroded reserves of educational commitment which badly need renewal. The kind of local activity suggested here, albeit having to work against a prevailing climate, would be a means of introducing a desperately needed and greatly desired quantity of deliberation into a curriculum development process marked of late by destructive haste.

Curriculum making restored to the local level as a participatory and collaborative activity would discipline the rampant and ideological vocational-ism proposed by elites for the children of others. It would achieve this by setting employment prospects in their proper context, namely as important considerations among the full range of desires we all have for our children. We wish them to become good parents, full members of the community, thinking citizens and critical participants in an evolving democracy. We wish them to be happy. Set in this context all sorts of employments themselves stand a chance of being revalued for their contribution to a well-lived life.

References

1 DES (1977). *Curriculum 11–16*, HMI publication.
2 DES (1980). *A View of the Curriculum*, HMSO.
3 DES (1980). *A Framework for the School Curriculum*, DES publication.
4 DES (1981). *The School Curriculum*, HMSO.
5 Crick, B. and Porter, A. (eds.), (1978). *Political Education and Political Literacy*. London, Longman.
6 Williams, R. (1965). *The Long Revolution*. Harmondsworth, Penguin.
7 Salter, B. and Tapper, T. (1981). *Education, Politics and the State*. London, Grant MacIntyre.
8 Broadfoot, P. (1986). 'Power relations and English education: the changing role of central government', *Journal of Education Policy*, January.
9 DES (1985). *Better Schools*, HMSO.

CHAPTER 3

Skills for the future?
Vocational education and new technology

Jerry Wellington

The rhetoric of skills is much in evidence. We here of 'skills for the future', 'relevant skills', 'the skill demands of new technology' and the 'skill needed to survive in the modern world'. The aim of this chapter is to examine the notions behind the rhetoric, and to consider whether an education based on skills has either intrinsic worth or economic utility.

The chapter contains what might be considered an unlikely mixture. Examples of the use of the terms skill, vocational and pre-vocational education are followed by a critical discussion of these terms, particularly the notions of specific and generic skills. This use of language is then related to the needs of employers and the langauge in which those needs are phrased. In particular, the demands which will be made of Britain's education and training systems from the field of information technology are examined by considering both British initiatives and the Japanese approach. Is the rhetoric of skills of value in meeting the educational demands of new technology?

The growth of the language of skills and pre-vocational education

Surely it was James Callaghan who started it all. Callaghan's so-called Ruskin College Speech of 1976 contained an attack on informal, modern teaching methods, a 'concern for standards', and a criticism of the poor relationship between schools and industry. In short, he questioned the very function of schooling by suggesting that schools were not providing the *necessary skills*. Two statements from the Ruskin College speech serve to illustrate this point:

> I am concerned ... to find complaints from industry that new recruits from the schools sometimes do not have the basic tools to do the job;

and later:

> There is no virtue in producing socially well adjusted members of society who are unemployed because they do not have the skills[1].

Thus began 'educational newspeak'. Educational objectives were being defined in terms of *skills* – not a new strategy but one which served Callaghan well and, more importantly, provided a framework for the language of Government White Papers in the 1980s. The language of skills, skill-deficits, skill-shortages, skill centres, skills training and skills in new technology is now firmly embedded in educational parlance.

Two points of major importance emerged from Callaghan's speech which have had a potent (though ofetn tacit) influence on discussions of education ever since. The first point, by implication, is that one of the key factors in the rise of unemployment is the shortage of relevant skills. This can be called the 'skills-deficit' of unemployment. It is a model which is adopted implicitly, and sometimes explicitly, by the Government White Papers discussed shortly. In adopting this model Callaghan was suggesting that one of the key functions of education is as an instrument to provide 'necessary skills' and thereby reduce youth unemployment. The second implication is that a set of 'relevant' or 'necessary' skills exist which (if acquired) would make students more employable and, in Callaghan's words, provide the 'basic tools to do the job'. Callaghan made no attempt to outline what these necessary or relevant skills are – he simply implied that they exist.

Since Callaghan's speech (though not as a result of it) unemployment has risen from 1.2 million to somewhere between three and four million. This steady increase in unemployment has led, paradoxically, to a strengthening of the bonds between education and *employment*.

The impact of unemployment on education can be crudely, but usefully, divided into four sequential stages[2]:

1 The implicit promise in schooling (i.e. 'work hard at school to get a job after it') is undermined.
2 The direction and traditional function of schooling and education are questioned.
3 Education, training, and 'pre-vocational education' are increasingly seen as an instrument to respond to youth unemployment.
4 The bonds between education and employment are tightened.

The latter stage is perhaps the irony in the influence of rising unemployment on education. It seems a paradox that the main effect of unemployment has been to strengthen the bonds between education and employment, and lead to the growth of *pre-vocational education*. This is the area where skills as educational objectives are most in evidence.

The two key White Papers which helped to develop the notion of 'pre-vocational education' were entitled *A New Training Initiative* (1981) and *Training for Jobs* (1984). The former was one of the key documents leading to the YTS. The aim of the paper was to provide 'better preparation for working life in initial full-time education' (paragraph 3), a reflection of the fourth stage described above. The paper therefore aimed to ensure that 'the school curriculum develops the personal skills ... needed for working life' (paragraph 12). The reader is left searching in vain through the remainder of the paper for a clarification of which skills *are* needed for working life. In paragraph 24 reference is again made to useful skills:

> It (the YTS) will aim to develop basic and recognized skills which employers will require in the future.

Some mention is made in the following paragraph of specific skills: literacy, numeracy and communication skills are listed. However, these could hardly be said to lie outside the realms of general education. Nowhere in the paper is an attempt made to specify the skills required for a truly vocational education, or the skills which 'employers will require in the future'.

The question of whether these skills exist, how they can be specified and if so what they are, is one of the issues I would like to raise in this paper.

The 1981 White Paper also contains three key paragraphs which reveal two implicit models of the *causes* of unemployment and its relation to education:

> The skill shortages which have held back our economic progress in the past could reappear when the economy recovers. (paragraph 48)

> For the immediate future the Government sees an increase of public expenditure on this scale as the only way of plugging the gap in the training provision required if we are to be ready to meet the skill needs of the economy as trading conditions improve and to offer adequate opportunities to the current generation of young people. (paragraph 58)

> For many years now our system of training has failed to produce the numbers of skilled people required by a modern competitive economy. (paragraph 61)

These paragraphs are interesting for two reasons. Firstly, they tacitly rely on two models of unemployment. The skills–deficit model comes through strongly in all three paragraphs. The second model of unemployment, which can be called the 'cyclical model', suggests that an upturn of the economy is 'just around the corner' and that unemployment will decrease as trading conditions and the economy recover. This model is now more than five years old but recovery is not yet in sight. Both models have been attacked by established authors since 1981[3]. Stonier (1983), for example, argues that unemployment patterns are caused by structural changes within society in undergoing a revolution from an industrial to a post-industrial era. Unemployment patterns are not fundamentally altered by skills shortages or by cyclical changes in trading conditions. Stonier's argument is supported by raw statistical data. Japanese labour trends indicate that structural changes are indeed occurring in their rather advanced industrial society. There has been a clear trend, which is still continuing, towards service industries and the so-called 'information sector'. The Japanese have even coined a word for it which cannot be printed here but means roughly 'servicization'. Similar, though more depressing trends, can be seen in the statistical data on Britain. Primary and secondary industry have both declined sharply while only service industries have grown.

The reliance of the 1981 White Paper on the skills-deficit and cyclical models of unemployment clearly determines its views on education and training. This comes through most clearly in its references to 'skill needs', 'system of training', 'skill shortages', and the suggestion that unemployment can be tackled by tightening the bonds between education and employment i.e. by 'pre-vocational education'.

Three years later the 1984 White Paper, *Training for Jobs*, seemed to be offering similar explanations of unemployment and the failure of education – despite the published warnings of Stonier, Toffler (1981) and even of Daniel Bell (1973) a decade earlier. The skills-deficit model of unemployment comes through clearly:

> It (vocational education) will enable many more people to be trained and improve their prospects of employment by placing greater emphasis on equipping them with skills that are currently required. (paragraph 41)

As in the 1981 paper, no attempt is made to investigate or even clarify the notion of 'skills that are currently required'. References are again made to 'skill shortages holding us back' but no suggestion is made as to which skills are in short supply. One reference only is made to the effect of new technology upon training and employment:

> The main objective of this strategy (training programmes) is to secure an adequate supply of people with up-to-date skills to meet the demands of new technologies upon which economic growth must be based. (paragraph 39)

This reference to up-to-date skills meeting the demands of new technologies will be investigated later in the paper. The main aim of this section has been to trace the rise of the rhetoric of skills, and alongside it the notion of pre-vocational education. The twin notions of 'skill' and 'pre-vocational education' will now be examined.

The concepts of pre-vocational and vocational education

The notion of *vocational* education is in itself difficult to interpret. 'Vocation' is usually associated with training so that the idea of 'vocational training' makes perfect sense. Training is linked to specific job, career, skill or vocation. when discussing training, it always makes sense to ask 'training for what?' Indeed the notion of training makes no sense at all unless it is a training *as* or *for* 'something'. A person can be training as a car mechanic, training for a Judo competition, or training as an accountant. To say that someone is training always begs the further question *as* or *for* what. Education is a very different concept. Education, unlike training, can stand on its own without being linked to some other aim, goal or vocation. This is perhaps why the concept of "vocational education" is almost a contradiction to certain purists. But, given the instrumentalism or 'new vocationalism' (a phrase coined by Bates *et al* 1985) set in motion by James Callaghan it has now become increasingly commonplace to ask of education, 'education for what?' Hence, the notion of vocational education has become more widespread and perhaps more palatable as 'education' is interpreted as 'training'.

But the notions of *pre*-vocational education still remains an enigma to translate. Can you imagine a teacher trying to explain the idea to a worried parent?

> *Teacher*: Well, it's the education that your child gets before he(she) starts on his(her) vocational education.
> *Parent*: Well, what's vocational education, then?
> *Teacher*: Well, it's the education your child gets once he(she) has finished his(her) pre-vocational education.

The concept of pre-vocational education remains a mystery to me, and (in a most cowardly fashion) I will give up any further attempt to translate it.

Dearden (1984), with his usual rigour and clarity, analyses the notions of vocational education and training in a valuable way (though he sheds no light on the notion of pre-vocational education, so at least I am in good company). Dearden's main general point is that education and training are 'different but not necessarily mutually exclusive'. In other words, the same learning experience may qualify to be called either education or training, or perhaps both. One such area at the intersection of the two concepts *may* be vocational education, which could therefore equally be called vocational training. This would be in sharp contrast to other experiences where the labels 'education' and 'training' imply totally different activities. Sex training and sex education (which Dearden quotes as an example from Peters 1966) will provide totally different experiences – if the former were adopted on the school curriculum, for example, I believe it might cause far more parental anxiety than the latter.

However, vocational training could only be worthy of the term 'vocational education' if it were 'liberally conceived', and included 'learning about the nature of work, discussing its forms and contexts: a version of careers education in fact'. (Dearden 1984, page 65). If it were conceived in this way then the notions of 'vocational training' and 'vocational education' might indeed be synonymous, and there might also be some meaning for the notion of pre-vocational education in terms of the wider, more liberal conception which Dearden descibes.

In practice, however, the notion of vocational training is almost always translated in terms of 'skills' which can be specified and stated. If we use Dearden's perfectly acceptable view that education should involve 'the development of knowledge and understanding in breadth and depth' and a 'degree of critical reflectiveness and corresponding autonomy of judgment'

(Dearden 1984, page 63) then learning experiences involving only skills cannot possibly be called 'vocational education'. This assertion rests on the analysis of 'skills' which now follows.

The language of skills

The interpretation of vocational education, used synonymously with vocational training, is given almost entirely in terms of skills in the White Papers cited above. Similarly, the aims and content for the YTS are based firmly on a Core Skills Programme, consisting of a set of 103 identified skills. This approach is in turn based on the influential IMS report (no. 39), *Foundation Training Issues*. The language of skills is also employed in the 1985 White Paper, *Better Schools*, which talks of the 'skills and attitudes needed for adult and working life' (paragraph 47) and 'the issue of how best to fit work-related skills within full-time education'. In addition, the documents of both the FEU and the MSC have relied heavily on the notion of skills in describing aims and content[5]. I do not propose to analyse any of those documents in detail here. A detailed and rigorous analysis of the documents on which YTS is based, for example, can be found in Ruth Jonathan's Chapter 6 in this volume.

This section will examine briefly the notion of a 'skill' and then go on to consider its father-figure, the generic or transferable skill. In so doing, I hope to show that a worthwhile vocational education can never be defined solely in terms of skills. The language of skills may be *necessary*, but it can never be sufficient.

In addition, a skills-based education may not be very valuable to employers, particularly those involved in new technology. The final sections of this chapter examine the value of the language of skills in matching education and training to the needs of employers in new fields such as information technology. My contention is that a narrow skills-based definition of education makes neither conceptual nor economic sense.

The notion of a skill

One valuable document summarizing many of the publications which advocated a re-definition of education in terms of skills is entitled *Skills for Schools* (Perry and Barnett 1985). This booklet bravely tackles the challenges of defining 'skill' by separating three aspects of human activity:

> Any human activity requires three elements: *knowledge* to understand the context of the activity and predict outcomes; *skills* with which to act; and the *attitude* or motivation to act. (p. 12)

This attempt to analyse human activity into three components may be brave, but conceptually it is crude and confusing. Can the three elements really be separated in this way? Can a person acquire a skill without knowledge, or any worthwhile knowledge (other than what A.N. Whitehead called 'inert ideas') without exercising and acquiring some degree of skill? Knowledge, skill and attitude are both conceptually and practically inseparable.

The rigid knowledge/skill/attitude division is reminiscent of Bloom's three domains of objectives: cognitive, psychomotor and affective. But, as Rowntree (1985) points out, 'skill can be cognitive or affective as well as psychomotor' – the skills of literary criticism, violin playing or counselling a patient are given as examples. This broadening of the notion of skill to include cognitive and affective aspects brings the notion much nearer to Ryle's (1949) concept of *knowing how* as opposed to knowing that. Unfortunately, this broader and more aceptable notion of skill is not applied in the *Skills in Schools* document, or the previous FEU, IMS and MSC publications on which it relies. This is clear from its definition of a skill: 'A skill is the ability to undertake an action under given circumstances to a defined degree of expertise'. (p. 12)

That definition clearly relies on a psychomotor notion of skill and a behaviourist-based view of education. Is skill necessarily tied to action? Can skill not involve 'mental action'? There seems to be no *logical* connection between a skill and a physical action. Can all skills be governed by a 'defined degree of expertise'? If so, where does this leave the mental processes in the exercise of a skill? ·

The bias towards behavioural and psychomotor skills is shown in the lists of skills which are given as part a possible 'core' of identifiable skills required by school leavers. Included in the list are such skills as:

Read and write numbers   Count objects

Pull, push, lift and carry   Cut materials with scissors, shears etc.

In fairness, however, many of the 'core' skills are on a higher level and are listed as:

Give answers   Deal with complaints

Advise   Explain something

Decide job priorities   Describe or give information

But surely not one of the latter group of skills makes any sense or carries any meaning without a *context*. How can a person possess 'advising skill' which is context and knowledge *independent*? This is the first major point that I would like to propose in discussing the notion of a skill. A skill cannot exist except within a certain context, and within a framework of prior knowledge and understanding. How can a person 'decide on job priorities' without an adequate understanding of the relevant context, the necessary information and the prior knowldege of either facts or general principles?

This, in my view, is the essential mistake in the rhetoric of skills i.e. the belief that a worthwhile skill can be separated off and defined in isolation from the context of understanding and knowledge which surrounds it. That mistake is made in both science and technology education. Lists of scientific skills are given for example, which include 'observation skills', 'the ability to hypothesize', 'predicting and informing', 'controlling variables' and so on[6]. Yet not one of these science skills has any sense or meaning in isolation from the knowledge-base, framework or paradigm (Kuhn 1970) which forms the foundation of science. As Popper (1959) is so often quoted as saying, observation is theory-laden. The same is true of hypothesizing, inferring, controlling variables and all the other skills involved in science. A science or technology education which is biased totally towards skills will be as meaningless and empty as one which concentrates soley on content or propositional knowledge (Ryle's 'knowing-that').

In short, skills without knowledge are empty. This will be particularly true in 'new industry', as I will argue later, which is by its very nature *knowledge-intensive* (Alvey 1982).

Generic and transferable skills

Two criticisms of a skills-based approach to education and training are:

> 1 That it often produces lists of skills which, although easily definable, are often trivial and demeaning.
> 2 That a narrow, and specifically-stated, skills-based approach to training is hopelessly vulnerable to changes in society and in technology.

As Ruth Jonathan (1983) puts it, 'the more specific the skills, the shorter their useful life'. These twin criticisms of trivialization and vulnerability to change have pushed forward the notion of 'generic' or 'transferable' skills. These higher level skills are 'fundamental to the performance of a number of activities carried out in a range of contexts', and are significant for vocational education because they are 'generic to a wide variety of occupations and are transferable between vocationally specific areas' (Perry and Barnett 1985).

I would like to examine some of these generic skills and show that, as with specific skills, few of them carry meaning if seen as context and knowledge independent. To hold them up as educational goals in themselves, therefore, is both vague and conceptually unsound. Lists of generic, transferable skills often include the following:

problem-solving	information-handling
planning	decision-making
diagnosis	communicating

Take 'information-handling', for example. This is often put forward as one of the key skills for the future, and who could doubt this is an age where information is said to be vital resource (Stonier 1983) and where the possession of propositional, factual knowledge ('knowledge that') can only decrease in importance as an educational goal. Information skills will involve the ability to collect, prepare, code and retrieve information, in conjunction with the endless capability of new information technology to process and communicate this information. But information skills, vital though they may be in *serving* education, can never provide an educational goal in themselves. Information skills alone, without ends and purposes, have no meaning or value. They cannot exist in a vacuum. Education does not involve the *passive* handling and acquisition of information. Active and meaningful education involves selecting, interpreting and transforming information according to the learner's previous experiences, present needs and purposes, and prior knowledge. Information skills are, to caricature Popper, knowledge and context laden (a point fully argued in Wellington 1984).

Similar points can be made about an equally valued generic skill, 'problem-solving'. Can such a skill be knowledge and context independent? In other words, can the ability to solve problems in one domain *transfer* across to another? The question of generic skills, therefore, rests squarely on a debate which is totally unsettled and indeed has occupied psychologists for much of this century: transfer of learning. This issue, like the heredity versus environment debate, is by its very nature unlikely to be decided conclusively. Perhaps the belief that skills can be transferred from one area to another is, like pseudo-scientific hypotheses, incapable of falsification (Popper, 1959). Yet the bulk of the literature which puts forward generic skills as the aims of education and training totally ignores the question of transfer. (See, for example, Bradshaw 1985).

The same question mark can be placed over the generic skill of 'decision-making'. Is there any evidence to show that decision-making in one domain, e.g. the art of Cordon Bleu cooking, is transferable to another domain, e.g. car repair and maintenance? Indeed how could such a belief ever be falsified let alone confirmed? Dearden makes a similar point in discussing 'good judgment':

> ... simply because good judgment can be exercised in both the stock market and in landing a hot air balloon, it does not follow that there is some general skill of 'good judgement' which is common to both and in which we could be trained free from any particular context. (Dearden 1984, p. 60)

My contention, therefore, is that the language of generic skills can be criticized on two related counts. Firstly, skills of any kind are context and knowledge dependent – skills without knowledge are empty. Secondly, the belief that there are genuine, transferable skills which are the proper aim of education and training ignores the contentious question of transfer.

A third objection to the language of transferable skills, which is based on political grounds, is given by Cohen (in Bates *et al* 1985, p. 113). He argues that many of the new initiatives in training are based on 'a hidden agenda for redeploying the notion of skill itself'. By dissociating skill from specific practices and defining it in terms of 'certain abstract universals', a pool of 'abstract labour' can be created thereby undermining the control by skilled manual workers over conditions of entry and training in their own trades. This may well be as much a consequence of new technology, however, as a political ploy – a point which Cohen acknowledges:

> What 'transferable skilling' corresponds to in reality is the process of deskilling set in motion by new information technologies. (Cohen 1985, p. 113)

The question of the relation of skills to the problems posed by new technologies will be returned to later.

A similar attack on the redeployment of the notion of skill is given by Ann Wickham in Dale (1985). She suggests that the notion of skill has been redefined which, in turn, has given 'training' a new meaning:

> In the past the notion of skill had been associated with craft work, with a combination of mental and physical dexterity in a particular area of work. Under the aegis of the Special Programmes Division (of the MSC) a much wider definition of skill came into use. Skill was regarded more as a way of organizing activity and involved a combination of what are now regarded as individual skills and general skills, that is numeracy, communication and practical skills, together with social and life skills, attitudes to work and a knowledge of working life. Training was ... given a new meaning which was removed from that traditionally used. (Wickham in Dale 1985, p. 104)

This redefinition of the term 'skill' can be seen in its recent broadening to include 'social and life skills', 'employability skills', 'communication skills', 'attitudes to work', 'preparation for life skills', and so on. It is as if the concept of skill has ascended to a new level to embrace not only competencies but also abilities, aptitudes, dispositions, and attitudes. It needs only to subsume the concepts of knowledge, thinking, understanding and motivation to have taken over as the umbrella term covering the whole of education. We may soon be talking of the skills of understanding and knowing just as we already talk of thinking skills, reading skills, social skills and even moral skills.

Hart (1978) argued with emotion against such distortion of language:

> If you don't hold out against talk of 'skills', if you don't see that 'skills' only account for part, and that the less important part, of what we learn, you are driven to conclude that there is nothing for which a man can be held responsible or in which he can see himself mirrored. (p. 215)

Hart's paper makes two valuable points. Firstly, that talk of skills 'is simply a kind of incantation, by which one creates the illusion that one is actually saying something about education'. In other words the addition of the label 'skill' actually adds nothing descriptive. How, for example, does 'reading' differ from 'reading skill'? The same is true of the language launched by Callaghan's great debate. Much talk was, and *is*, heard of 'relevant skills'. Those terms have yet to be give any concrete, descriptive meaning. Indeed the noun 'relevance', and the adjective 'relevant', have no meaning on their own.

Like the term 'skill', they are almost always used as terms of incantation, a seal of approval, having no descriptive but only emotive meaning. To describe a skill as relevant is meaningless. We need always to ask the questions 'relevant to what?' and 'relevant to whom?'. This confusion over relevance is particularly important in considering the 'skills relevant' to new technology.

Hart's second main point, as I interpret it, is that the acquisition of skills is, in a sense, an activity of tackling on or appending skills to bodies. It is a largely *impersonal* process. In contrast, truly educational processes will profoundly affect and alter the person involved. This is not true of skills, as they are traditionally conceived:

> ... education, whatever else is involved in it, is about the individual person and his development; and it's been my contention that only that which is more than simply a skill can contribute to that development, the continual forming and reforming of the person. So that when receiving an education is conceived of, as it is so often today, in terms of acquiring skills, it is conceived of as something superficial. (Hart 1978, p. 213)

This point leads in to the next two sections of the chapter. Does industry want bodies with skills 'appended' to them? Do employers in fact phrase their requirements in the language of skills? Does it make either practical or conceptual sense to discuss the needs of new technology in terms of 'relevant skills' and 'skill shortages'?

The language of skills and the needs of employers

An important article by Gilroy (1983) discusses the value of conceptual analysis in clarifying the work done in empirical research – similar points are made by Barrow (1984) in *Giving Teaching Back to the Teachers*. Gilroy implies, however, that it is not *only* the 'philosopher' who is 'competent to identify and resolve linguistic confusion'. There is a role for the 'empiricist as philosopher', as he expresses it, in direct contrast to John Locke's under-labourer conception of philosophy (Locke 1690).

This is surely the case in examining the language of skills. Armchair analysis may be necesary but it is not sufficient. Valuable progress can be made, in my view, by interviewing employers in depth to probe their 'needs' and requirements and in particular (in this context) to examine the language in which their needs and demands are actually framed. One such study, albeit on a small scale, is reported in Wellington (1986), and is summarized below.

It is clearly a huge task to identify the 'needs' of employers in terms of the skill which they require of school-leavers and trainees. The range of employers will be so vast in terms of numbers employed, on-the-job skills, and the nature of employment that there may be no common ground. With this proviso in mind, a pilot research project was carried out which involved detailed interviews with a small sample of employers from service industries to so-called high-tech employers.

The interviews were conducted in a fairly unstructured way, although some specific questions were asked of all the staff involved. The person approached and interviewed was in each case the 'development and training' or personnel officer of the company. In fairness to those interviewed no specific comments and quotes will be included here – I will simply sum up some of the general principles which came through strongly, and also select some of the more interesting remarks on skills and specific training which relate to earlier parts of this paper.

The strongest message which came through in this pilot study is that the needs of these employers are not framed in terms of *skills* required of school leavers – their requirements are always stated in the language of *attitudes* and *dispositions*. This is perhaps the most important message as a response to the 1981 and 1984 White Papers – they are making a basic 'category mistake' in framing the needs of employers and therefore of vocational education in terms of skills. What employers seem to be demanding of school-leavers and YTS trainees, is a collection of general attitudes and dispositions. The 'attitude' which came at the top of the list was 'interest and motivation'. This was felt to be the most important quality in a school-leaver. Other attitudes and dispositions considered important were: initiative, confidence, self-belief and maturity (particularly in the service industries).

In none of the interviews were skills specifically mentioned. Each of the employers interviewed was asked which skills they required of new employees – none listed skills other than numeracy and literacy, which (incidentally) they felt were of the required standard in the young people they appointed anyway. The so-called high-tech employers were asked specifically about 'computer literacy'. Did they want their employees to be 'computer literate' before joining the company? This notion was dismissed. The kind of 'computer literacy' (a virtually indefinable notion anyway) they might receive before employment was not felt to be of use once they had joined the firm. To be capable of programming a microcomputer was *not* felt to be of prior value. Perhaps the only useful skill in connection with computers was felt to be in the use of a keyboard.

One rather depressing comment was made by a national high-tech employer. They suggested that school-leavers were not likely to be taken into the high-tech side of the industry at all. Recruitment to this facet of their company would be entirely at graduate level and above. Even then (incidentally) the graduates appointed would not necessarily be in Computer Science, who were often receiving training in the wrong computer language e.g. Pascal rather than Cobol.

Some of those interviewed did comment, of their own volition, on the Youth Training Scheme. They saw YTS largely as a grading or interviewing system which enabled them to 'have a good look' at a prospective employee. They felt that it was an ideal opportunity to see if that trainee had the right attitudes and dispositions, such as those already mentioned. One described

YTS as a 'year-long interview', a comment which has since been used by many employers.

I would not suggest that this small empirical enquiry with its small sample could be used to form any definite conclusions on the requirements of employers. However, I would suggest that the study does indicate a gap between the language used in statements and documents on pre-vocational education and the language in which employers and industry couch their requirements. In particular, the study posed the following questions. Should discussions and statements on vocational education be framed in the Callaghan language of 'skills', 'relevant training' and 'tools-for-the-job'? Or should the aims and philosophy of vocational education be couched in terms of attitudes and dispositions? Is there any sense in the notion of 'relevant skills' or 'skills for the future' in a society which may be entering a new phase? If not, then what meaning does the very notion of 'pre-vocational education' hold? With an increasingly uncertain future for employment, depending more and more on the rapidly changing field of information technology, does the notion of *vocational training* make economic, let alone conceptual snese?

These questions will be discussed in the final two sections of this paper, firstly by considering the likely 'skill demands' of new technologies, and then by sketching the response of Japan to the education and training needs imposed by technological change.

Skill demands and the new technologies

The 1981 campaign to instal microcomputers in all of Britain's schools was accompanied by a wave of uncritical enthusiasm and a flood of rhetoric regarding its vocational significance. Kenneth Baker, the new Minister for Information Technology typified the political mood of the time:

> ... I want to try and ensure that the kids of today are trained with the skills that gave their fathers and grandfathers jobs. It's like generals fighting the battles of yesteryear ... And that is the reason why we've pushed ahead with computers into schools. I want youngsters, boys and girls leaving school at sixteen, to actually be able to operate a computer. (Quoted by O'Shea and Self 1983)

That optimism for the vocational significance of the computer permeated into many of the two million or more households which subsequently acquired computers, and largely caused the unprecedented growth of Computer Studies as an examination subject (analysed in Wellington 1985b). The unquestioned connection between computer education and the world of work also surfaced in the plethora of books discussing the use of computers in schools. Mullan, for example, even drew a connecton between primary children's use of the microcomputer and the use of the computer in the world of work which they must experience:

If children meet the microcomputer in an exciting and pleasurable role in school
then one could argue that there is a greater likelihood of them accepting it as an
aid in the world of work which they must experience in the future. (Garland
1982)

The unquestioned belief in the vocational significance of information
technology also affected deeply both the thinking and the publicity associated
with the two key innovations in vocational education: the YTS and the TVEI.

Finn, writing in Dale (1985), discusses the publicity at the launch of the YTS
which 'attempted to associate it with the new technologies at the forefront of
employment creation'. This publicity has continued in the same vein with the
advent of the two-year YTS, a publicity drive which is analysed in the
following section. Similarly, the drive behind TVEI depended to a large extent
on its perceived links to new technology and in particular to IT. Dale (1985), in
discussing the background to and inception of TVEI, diagnoses one of the key
factors behind the initiative as the continuing emphasis on 'high-tech' industry
in the early 1980s. This in turn led to the belief 'that future employment
prospects are likely to be most propitious in IT-based industry and commerce'.

This is a belief which requires thorough and critical investigation. The links
between information technology in education and information technology in
employment have never been fully and critically examined. There is simply an
implicit and unquestioned belief in the minds of many people (parents,
children, teachers and policy-makers) that IT education at any level will make
its recipients more employable. That belief has provided the main impetus for
much of the information technology education in schools, colleges and ITECs.

The purposes of an ITEC have been described in Smith (1985). Their aim is:

> ... to provide young people with the *new skills* necessary for Britain to take a
> leading part in the technological revolution.

But what are these 'skills', and at which levels of education are they
required? The question can be explored in two ways. Firstly, by considering
recent documents and reports on the links between IT in education and
industry. Secondly, by a full scale empirical investigation into the perceived
'skill demands' of employers in IT, their current recruitment patterns at
various levels, and the relation of those demands to the range of IT education
currently offered in our education and training schemes. An empirical
investigation along those lines was launched in April 1986 at the University of
Sheffield[4], and its findings will be published in full elsewhere. However the
first method of tackling the question will be discussed briefly here, by
considering two recent publications. A crucial document was published in
August 1984 by the Economic Development Committee (EDC or 'little
Neddy'), entitled *Crisis facing UK Information Technology*[6]. This publication
described the critical skill shortage in Information Technology which is
apparently holding back the UK industry:

> Too often contracts are being lost, and employment opportunities lost with
> them, because of the lack of a few key engineers. (p. 10)

But at what level *are* these skill shortages? The answer given by this document is that the shortages occur at *graduate level and above*. For example:

> The problem is critical even before the effects of the University Grants Committee cuts have really shown in graduate output. (p. 10)

In other words (according to this document) the critical skill shortage holding back the UK 'Information Technology industry' is clearly not at the level of 16- or 17-yar-old school leavers who are likely to opt for the YTS. It is at the graduate level, of a 'few key engineers'. Skill shortages at this level, according to the document, are resulting in a lack of demand for the employment at *lower* levels. This is perhaps a more *subtle* version of the skills-deficit model of unemployment, i.e. lack of the right skills at graduate level leading to a lack of demand for labour at lower levels. This more subtle version of the skills–deficit model, however, is not even hinted at in the 1984 White Paper.

The EDC report also includes a passing criticism of vocational education and training:

> The UK has a multitude of institutions and agencies engaged in education and training but they appear to have difficulty in responding to the now very insistent signals from the market for skilled people and developing a consistent response.

But what 'signals' are being sent from the market for skilled people? What skills do employers actually require, or at least *say* that they require? This is clearly a case where the rhetoric of skills and skill demands needs to be transated into reality. Clear signals are needed from employers so that education can be expected to develop a 'consistent response'. There can be no substitute for empirical investigation here.

A second key publication in predicting the 'skill demands' of new technology is the report of the Alvey Committee on the future of IT and so-called fifth generation of computers. This vital report is given further consideration in the next section, but its major themes can be introduced here. A large proportion of the report was devoted to the education and training which would be needed to provide the human resources for Britain's advanced information technology programme into the 1990s. Perhaps the crux of the whole report for the future of education in IT is contained in one short statement: 'Information Technology is knowledge intensive' (Alvey 1982, p. 59). In other words, IT industry is *not labour intensive*. The addition of skilled personnel for Britain's advanced IT programme is quantified by Alvey in terms of *thousands*, not even tens of thousands. At what level are these personnel required? Alvey suggests that 'urgent action is needed in the higher education sector':

> Restrictions on expenditure in higher education, whatever the intentions, have tended to fall across the board. It has not escaped. (Alvey, 1982, p. 60)

So what action can be taken for students in the 14–18 range of education and training? Alvey's response is one of the most quoted sections of the report:

... it is no good just providing schools with microcomputers. This will merely produce a generation of poor BASIC programmers. Universities in fact are having to give remedial education to entrants with A-level computer science. (Alvey, p. 62)

Where does this leave the emphasis on 'information technology skills' and 'computer literacy' at the heart of YTS schemes, the ITECs and the new TVEI? My own view, which I have argued elsewhere (Wellington 1985a), is that *education* (not training) in and through information technology should be seen as a valuable end in itself. It can enhance traditional educational aims but should never replace them. The vocational significance of IT has for too long been overemphasized or, indeed, 'hyped up' by the media, by politicians and even by parents. The best way in which education can support the essential growth of IT in Britain's economy is by providing a sound general education for all pupils. This is precisely the pattern in the education system of Britain's Eastern competitor in IT, Japan.

Lessons from the East: the Japanese approach to skills and vocational education

A full-page advertisement began to appear in the newspapers early in 1986, from *The Mirror* to the so-called quality dailies such as *The Guardian*. The advert warned the Japanese of the advent of Spikey Dodds, Tracy Logan, and others with names like Joe Bloggs, about to embark on the new two-year Youth Training Scheme. Spikey Dodds, for example, will 'begin his course by trying out several different skills before he chooses the one he'll train through to the end of the second year'. By the end of his course he will have 'a skill, a certificate to prove it, and a better chance of getting a job'. This may well prove true, though as yet there is little evidence to support such optimism. But the point I would like to take issue with comes in the next paragraph of the advertisement:

Our competitors in the Far East and Europe have been training their young people like this for years.

Presumably, one of the countries implicitly referred to here is Japan. The suggestion, therefore, is that Japan's education system has been training youngsters by allowing them to 'try out several different skills' before choosing the *one* which they will train for and obtain a certificate in. This is patently untrue, and I will not need to exhume publications from university libraries to prove it. A series of articles on the evolution of Japan's education occurred in *Look Japan* from May to December 1983[7]. These articles, written by leading Japanese economists and educationalists, indicate that the skills-based vocational training alluded to in the YTS advert may have taken place in the 1960s and early 1970s but has now been superseded by a totally different educational drive.

An indicator of Japanese misgivings over narrow skills-based training came in the 1981 publication *Japanese Industrial Relations, Series* 7 (p. 31):

> School education now provides both general and vocational courses at the secondary level, but the general public tends to regard the former as preparing intelligent youths for university entrance and accordingly for better employment opportunities and the latter as accommodating the less intelligent who are to enter lower level occupations. Industry generally expects schools to turn out youths with a good level of academic achievement and adaptability and does not attach much importance to pre-employment training designed to prepare young people for specific occupations.[7]

The first sentence of this paragraph gives an early warning of the potential divisiveness of vocational curricula, discussed five years later in *Times Educational Supplement* articles on studies of the new TVEI (see, for example, 'TVEI: very good and very bad', TES 15/11/85). The second sentence indicated that the world's most successful industrial nation would encourage its youth to follow a general education rather than vocational training in the 1980s. This view is made crystal clear later in the document:

> ... the emphasis (in school education) is on developing general intelligence rather than specific skills.

The 1981 statements have since become reality. In 1985, no less than 94 per cent of Japanese students stayed on for 'senior high school' after leaving the compulsory junior high school. Of that 94 per cent, only 10 per cent enrolled for specialist industry schools. Judging from a recent TES article (7/2/86, 'Books first for industrial pacesetters', attitudes have changed little in five years:

> Despite Government efforts to make work-related courses more attractive to students, the vocational high schools are still generally viewed by pupils, parents and employers as being second-best. The demand for places at vocational schools has declined, and many entrants are students who have failed to gain entry to a general high school.

Such enduring attitudes are coupled (both as a cause and as an effect) with the huge growth in Japan's higher education, sometimes called its 'transfer to a higher education society'. The proportion of the relevant age-group staying on for higher education in 1985 was just under a remarkable 40 per cent compared with just over 20 per cent in the United Kingdom.

An important part of Japan's higher education in ensuring its industrial success was, of course, the high-level engineering education provided. At the start of the 1980s Japan's total output of graduate engineers was between five and six times higher than ours at about 75,000, compared with Britain's 13,000 (relative populations approximately 120 million to 56 million). This poor comparison still continues at a time when Britain's information and manufacturing industries are desperate for electronic, electrical, mechanical and software engineers at graduate level.

Britain's principal area of competition with the Japanese in the next decade will almost certainly be in the area of information technology. The Alvey Report indicated Britain's needs for the future:

> ... there is a requriement for a new breed of 'information engineer' with a wide understanding of the potential applications of IT to industrial needs. The supply of graduates with skills relevant to IT must be increased. The undergraduate output is currently some 6,500 per year. This is wholly inadequate to meet our future requirements. (p. 62)

How has Britain answered Alvey's plea?

The central response to the keenly felt need for IT education has been to provide every school in the country with at least one computer and some with as many as thirty or forty. Britain's populace now has the largest number of home computers per head in the world. This is in direct contrast to the Japanese approach to computer education. The 1984 *Japan Educational Journal* reported that only 0.1 per cent (i.e. on in a thousand) of its primary schools had microcomputers at that time. Less than 2 per cent of its lower secondary schools had computers, though the figure reached 45 per cent in its upper secondary schools. However, the computers in the latter area were used largely as an administrative and management tool. The notions of 'computer studies', 'computer literacy' and 'computer-related skills' so widespread in this country, have no place in the Japanese approach to education:

> The school curricula in Japan are designed to give children a broad and basic knowledge which is necessary in order to grasp and enjoy a wide range of ideas and activities. In the field of science and technology, Japanese children are taught concepts, principles and laws of basic science and mathematics, which are the basis of industrial technology. Computer technology is not yet considered to be part of the required 'basic knowledge'.[7]

It seems that the abacus is a more common learning tool in Japanese schools than the computer.

I am not suggesting that we should attempt to copy Japan's approach to computer education, or its education system in general. Britain's culture, its hidden curriculum and its material resources are too vastly different to make that a possibility. I *am* suggesting that we should radically re-think our approach to vocational education (not least in the IT field) in the light of lessons learned from the Japanese, and in view of our need to compete with Japan in the development of new 'knowledge intensive' industries.

It makes little sense to base a new and expensive programme of skills-based vocational training on a view of a system 'in the Far East' which is at best out-dated and at worst purely fictional.

Conclusions

My main aim in this paper has been to examine the rhetoric of skills and the languae of vocational education, and then to begin to compare it with the needs of new technology and the contrasting approach to education for industry in Japan. My first conclusion is that the language of skills so often used in publications on vocational education is frequently biased towards a behaviourist, psychomotor conception of skill. That conception involves, in a sense, abstracting skills from any particular context or knowledge base and describing them as if (firstly) they exist *per se* and (secondly) they can be appended, attached or tacked or to an available human being by the appropriate form of training. In an effort to make that 'training' more akin to 'education' 'the notion of general, generic, transferable skills has been brought forward. My argument is that both specific skills and generic skills have little meaning in a total vacuum. *Skills are knowledge and context dependent.*

Further support has been given to the language of skills by claims that Britains's education system must provide 'relevant skills', skills which related to 'the technological aspects of working life', or skills which can respond to 'the needs of new technology'. My own view is that no reliable evidence yet exists either to indicate precisely what these skills are (specific or generic) *or* even to show that the needs of employers in new industry are actually phrased in terms of sklills. Existing evidence, both from British publications and reports on the needs of IT industry and from a consideration of Japan's educational response, indicates that a purely skills–based approach will not enhance new technology. However, a substantial amount of empirical work needs to be done in this area in relating the needs of employers to the future provision of vocational education and training (see note 4).

Recent attacks on the 'new vocationalism' (Bates, Dale, Fiddy, Varlaam etc.) are rightly directed at vocational training with a narrow skill–based emphasis. But they should not also be seen as a condemnation of a satisfactory and economically essential concept of vocational *education* which has yet to be fully worked out, let alone implemented. That notion of vocational education would involve education for technological change and progress, though it would not involve the appendage of skills deemed necessary and 'relevant' onto the available 'manpower'. The notion would involve the ability to critically evaluate technological change and the future quality of life – it would not see vocationalism as providing a 'skill resource for a Brave New World of technological change' (Jonathan 1985).

A balance of critical evaluation, knowledge, understanding and the skills involved *in those contexts* must form the ingredients of a future vocational education which will provide the human resources for Alvey's programme of advanced information technology. That balance is hinted at by David Young in discussing a philosophy of the vocational which unfortunately has never been put in practice:

> What our education should be is a balance between the vocational and the academic, between the theoretical and the pragmatic, between knowing how and knowing that. There is no correct balance, the depends on the individual, but balance there must be. (Young 1984; p. 14)

Yet the balance between theoretical and pragmatic, general and technical, liberal and vocational, has become less rather than more stable since Young's 1984 speech. Gulfs and divisions between the two extremes have grown worse throughout the education system – in schools, colleges, polytechnics and universities. Indeed the gulf is in danger of being increased by new initiatives, which many (for example, Holt 1983) feel will divide rather than unite the curriculum. But balance must remain the overriding aim, particularly in science and technological education.

This was Aldous Huxley's major concern almost fifty years ago in *Ends and Means*:

> ... both the existing kinds of education, technical as well as academic or liberal, are unsatisfactory. The problem before us is this: to amend them in such a way that technical education should become more liberal, and academic education a more adequate preparation for everyday life in a society which is to be changed for the better. (Huxley 1938 p. 195)

Change is surely needed in an education system fifty years on which, on the one hand, is failing so many young people yet, at the other extreme, is failing to supply the human resources needed for technological growth. But the necessary change cannot lie in either the 'new vocationalism' or the pleas to retain the liberal, general education which is rejected by so many school students. A synthesis of the vocational and the general, the technical and the liberal, the theoretical and the practical must form the basis of the future curriculum at all levels of education. A curriculum divided between the two opposites, with some students opting for one pole and some for the other, can only lead to further divisions within society and the 'inappropriate' development of technology[7].

A course must be steered between two fictional extremes: the technological desert of Huxley's 'Brave New World' based on a highly trained but uneducated elite making progress at all costs; and a nation which cannot advance into the information era because it lacks the human resources in new technologies. That course can be achieved by establishing a new tradition of liberal technological and scientific education in which people learn to consider *ends* as well as means. The 'language of skills' is totally inadequate in describing such an education.

Notes

1 Reported in The Times (19.10.76), *The Times Educational Supplement* (22.10.76), and printed in full as 'Towards a National Debate' in *Education*, 22.10.76, pp. 332–3.
2 A full discussion of the impact of unemployment on education is given in Wattts, A.G., *Education, Unemployment and the future of work* (Open University Press, 1983).
3 See for example: Jenkins, C. and Sherman, B., *The Collapse of Work* (Eyre Methuen, 1979) and Stonier, T., *The Wealth of Information: a profile of post-industrial society* (Methuen, 1983).

4 *Skills for the Future: information technology in education and employment*, a project funded by the Manpower Services Commission based at the University of Sheffield, Division of Education, 1986–7.
5 Beginning, for example, with *A Basis of Choice* (DES, 1979) and *Skills for Working Life* (MSC, 1981).
6 Listed, for example, by *Warwick Process Science* (Warwick University/ASE, 1986) and *Skills in Schools* by Perry, J. and Barnett, C. (Longman, 1985).
7 The following sources have provided all the data on Japan's approach to vocational education:

    1 *Look Japan*, May to December 1983
    2 *Japan Industrial Relations Series, No. 7* (1981
    3 *Japan Education Journal*
    4 *Japan 1985* (Japan Institute for Social and Economic Affairs).

8 A notion discussed fully by Burns, A. (1981) in *The Microchip: appropriate or inappropriate technology?* (Chichester: Ellis Horwood).

References

Alvey Committee (1982). *A Programme for Advanced Information Technology*, London, HMSO.
Bates, I. *et al* (1985). *Schooling for the Dole? The New Vocationalism*. London, Macmillan.
Bell, D. (1973). *The Coming of Post-Industrial Society*, New York, Basic Books.
Bradshaw, D. (1985), 'Transferable intellectual and personal skills', in *Oxford Review of Education*, vol. 11, no. 2, pp. 201–216.
Dale, R. (1985). 'Education and training', in *Westminster Studies in Education*, vol. 7, 1984 pp. 57–66.
Dearden, R. (1984). 'Education and training' in *Westminster Studies in Education*, Vol. 7.
Fiddy, R. (ed.), (1985). *Youth Unemployment and Training*. (Lewes, Falmer Press.
Garland, R. (1982). *Microcomputers and Children in the Primary School*. Lewes, Falmer Press.
Gilroy, P. (1983). 'The empirical researcher as philosopher', in *British Journal of Teacher Education*, vol. 6, no. 3, pp. 237–50.
Hart, W.A. (1978). 'Against skills' in *Oxford Review of Education*, vol. 4, no. 2, pp. 205–216.
Holt, M. (1983). 'Vocationalism: the new threat to universal education', in *Forum*, Summer 1983.
Jonathan, R. (1983). 'The manpower serivce model of education'.
Jonathan, R. (1985), 'Education, philosophy of education and context', in *Journal of Philosophy of Education*, vol. 19, no. 1, 1985, pp. 13–25.
Kuhn, T.S. (1970). *The Structure of Scientific Revolutions*. Chicago, Chicago University Press.
Locke, J. (1690). *An Essay Concerning Human Understanding*. ed. A.D. Woozley, (1964), London, Fontana/Collins.
O'Shea, T. and Self, J. (1983). *Learning and Teaching with Computers*. Brighton, Harvester Press.
Perry, J. and Barnett, C. (1985). *Skills in Schools*. York, Longman for the School Curriculum Development Committee.
Peters, R.S. (1966). *Ethics and Education*. pp. 32–34, Unwin, London.
Popper, K. (1959). *The Logic of Scientific Discovery*. London, Hutchinson.
Rowntree, D. (1985). *Educational Technology in Curriculum Development*. London, Harper and Row.
Ryle, G. (1949), *The Concept of Mind*. London, Hutchinson.
Smith, D.J. (ed.) (1985). *Information Technology and Education*. ESRC.
Stonier, T. (1983). *The Wealth of Information*. London, Methuen.
Toffler, A. (1981). *The Third Wave*, London, Pan Books.
Varlaam, C. (ed.) (1984). *Re-thinking transition: Educational Innovation and the Transition to Adult Life*. Lewes, Falmer Press.
Wellington, J.J. (1984). 'The knowledge we have lost in information', *Times Educational Supplement*, 31/8/84.

Wellington, J.J. (1985a). *Children, Computers and the Curriculum*. London, Harper and Row, 1985.

Wellington, J.J. (1985b). 'Computers across the curriculum – the needs in teacher training', in *Journal of Further and Higher Education*.

Wellington, J.J. (1986). 'Pre-vocational education and the needs of employers', in *The Vocational Aspect of Education*.

Young, D. (1984). *Knowing How and Knowing That: a philosophy of the Vocational*. Birkbeck College, Haldane Memorial Lecture, 1984.

CHAPTER 4

Teaching on stilts:
a critique of classroom skills

Richard Smith

Processions that lack high stilts have nothing that catches the eye.
W.B. Yeats, 'High Talk'

In E.M. Forster's novel *The Longest Journey* the experienced schoolmaster
Herbert Pembroke and his new assistant Rickie make their first entrance of the
school year into the preparation-room to meet their house of boys. The two
men take their seats.

> Each chair had a desk attached to it, and Herbert flung up the lid of his, and then
> looked round the preparation-room with a quick frown, as if the contents had
> surprised him. So impressed was Rickie that he peeped sideways, but could only
> see a little blotting-paper in the desk. Then he noticed that the boys were
> impressed too. Their chatter ceased. They attended.

Such pedagogical devices are familiar enough: we may remember similar
examples from our own schooldays, perhaps with amusement and affection,
as forming part of a particular teacher's personal set of routines and
eccentricities. But it would be odd, we might think, to see them as anything
more – as defining what competent teaching is, for instance, so that a good
teacher would be one who had mastered the raised desk-lid technique and
similar tricks. This kind of temptation however does make itself felt when
sophisticated accounts of the supposed skills and devices of teaching are
available. For a list of skills, since it appears to spell out what a teacher can be
expected to *do*, meets the fashionable demand for accountability by promising
a relatively clear-cut way of distinguishing competent teachers – and courses
for training them – from incompetent ones. It accords well with the spirit of
a time which has largely lost confidence in the less tangible idea of specifically
educational ends and so in educationally worthwhile learning as the criterion
of the quality of teaching.

Elaborate analyses of teaching skills have existed in the United States for some while. Programmes of competency- or performance-based teacher education (CBTE or PBTE), an approach underpinned by the assumptions of behaviourist psychology and involving the specification often of many hundreds of skills and sub-skills, have been widely adopted there. This movement has not gained much of a foothold on this side of the Atlantic in its original form[1], but there is now an influential literature here with certain affinities to it. I refer to the material produced by the Teacher Education Project (hereafter simply 'the Project'), mostly in the form of 'workbooks' published for the Project by Macmillan. These cover topics such as mixed ability teaching, questioning, explaining and class management. The Project was based in the universities of Exeter, Leicester and Nottingham. It was sponsored by the DES and the workbooks, intended for both trainee and practising teachers, are described on their covers as 'DES Teacher Education Project Focus Books'. This does not of course mean that they bear *imprimatur* from Elizabeth House, but a suggestion of at least semi–official status is conveyed to the impressionable and is likely to increase the Project's influence. The Project also employs a rhetoric, similar to much other recent propaganda for skills, that speaks of the teacher as a craftsman, one who plies a trade analogous to that of a plumber or joiner and who should take pride and pleasure in honing his or her skills.

My purpose in this paper is to offer a critique of the skills approach with specific reference, especially in Part I, to the Project's material. In Part II I consider the idea that it is a source of satisfaction and well-being to teachers to work at their skills like craftsmen.

I must emphasize that I have not chosen the Project for my critique because I think it is in any general way misguided or pernicious. I have no quarrel at all with much of its philosophy of teaching and teacher training. It would be hard to disagree with its emphasis on the importance of classroom practice in training and I share the belief that an inductive approach which starts from students' own experiences as teachers and learners is the best way to raise 'theoretical' questions on initial training courses. I am concerned here only with the way the Project conceives of 'teaching skills', though, as I shall try to show, the ramifications of that are extensive enough.

Even to raise these issues, I have found, can provoke surprise and outrage[2]. Let me make it clear that I am not denying that teaching requires ability or skilfulness, nor imagining that almost any adult can stagger into a classroom and do the job. This is so far from being what I believe, that my position could actually be summarized by saying I think teaching is more complex and difficult than can be expressed by calling it a craft or collection of skills. Confusion arises here when we shift between two different senses of 'skill' and its cognates ('skilful', etc.). At the risk of being laborious I will spell these out. The first sense is that in which we can all agree we want skilful teachers in our schools, where this simply means we want ones who can do the job well instead of those who cannot. Accepting this does not commit us to the view that a good teacher is one who has mastered a number of separate and specific skills. This is the second sense of the term, and it is on this that my criticisms are intended to bear.

It is worth emphasizing at this point that wider issues are at stake than simply how teachers are to be trained, how their jobs are to be conceived and (for this is a possible implication) how they are to be assessed. Our whole understanding of the nature and function of education is involved here. To put 'skills' at the heart of our conception of a teacher is to come close to conceding that teachers have nothing to say about the ends of education, no vision of human potential or of the way life might be lived to communicate to their pupils, but are experts in means only. For that is what a skill is: it is know-*how*, not understanding of or insight into that for the sake of which the know-how is exercised. It is not fanciful to see the view of the teacher as a craftsman as a necessary concomitant to the increasing shift towards central control of the curriculum and the growing introduction of vocationalism into schools at the expense of those activities sometimes thought of as truly 'educational'[3]. Thus pupils will be trained in the skills that supposedly answer to the needs of industry and commerce: what is worth teaching will be decided by higher authority, and the role of teachers will be simply to implement those decisions.

I

The Project offers no explicit discussion or defence of what it understands by a 'skill'. There are some suggestive remarks in *Classroom Teaching Skills* (Wragg 1984), a book partly intended to explain and justify the work of the Project. The minute analysis into hundreds of skills and subskills characteristic of competency and performance-based programmes is repudiated, not so much on principle, however, as because the skills that have been distinguished in these programmes are often faintly ludicrous. What the Project regards as a skill can be judged to an extent by the examples given. One of the more recent workbooks, *The New Teacher*, lists what it calls 'skills and attributes of student teachers' (p. 7). Here are the first six of the seventeen skills named:

- Expresses ideas effectively
- Reacts favourably to criticism
- Has a good educational background
- Comprehends subject matter
- Assumes responsibility
- Plans carefully

In the same workbook we find (p. 32) that 'the skills model of teaching is characterized by these assumptions':

1 Practical teaching consists of skills
2 Skills can be identified and isolated
3 Skills can be broken down into component parts

    4 Skills can be studied and taught
    5 Skills can be learned
    6 Skills can be reflected upon and refined with practice
    7 Skills can be evaluated and assessed

Some of the examples, it is immediately noticeable, do not sit comfortably with the 'assumptions'. For instance, it is not obvious that assuming responsibility is something which you can learn as a general skill (if this is what is meant), as if someone might learn to take responsibility as captain of a sports team and could then be relied upon not to shirk their responsibilities as a captain of industry. The best and fairest procedure seems to me to address the 'assumptions', since these give us the most clearly articulated picture of the Project's understanding of a skill.

    I shall take the 'assumptions' in the order that lends itself to most coherent discussions, and start with (3), 'Skills can be broken down into component parts'. Why should we want to break them down like this? The answer Wragg (*op. cit.*) suggests is that although we need to beware of analysis into minute items of behaviour the unanalysed notion of 'teaching' is simply too broad to be of any use. If people want to be better teachers we have to reduce what that involves to manageable units if we are going to help them. The question remains, however, exactly what it is that is to be analysed. Is it 'teaching', or, as Wragg implies a few lines further on, *areas* of teaching such as class management and questioning and explaining, or is it elements of these areas, like 'Selects and organizes a variety of materials' (from the list of skills in *The New Teacher*)? Whether you end up with sub-skills so minute as to be trivial depends on the level on which you start your analysis. Breaking down *skills*, rather than *teaching*, into component parts risks precisely the trivial outcome Wragg wanted to avoid.

    Even where a skill can be broken down logically – for example, the skill of driving a car can be analysed into such sub-skills as making smooth gear changes and looking out for unwary pedestrians – what is logically a component part may not be a psychologically useful component, one that can helpfully be separated for the purpose of learning. No driving instructor takes a pupil out on the road with the instruction 'Never mind the pedestrians today – we'll concentrate on the gear changes'. These sub-skills have to be practised *together*, as is often the case with sub-skills, and it is getting the relationship between them right that is the problem for pupil and instructor. In *The New Teacher* 'understands children and how they learn', 'is effective classroom manager' and 'keeps satisfactory discipline' are listed as separate items. No doubt these are logical components of 'being a good teacher' in that understanding children and how they learn and so on are part of what we mean by being a good teacher. But again this does not necessarily mean that it is helpful to separate them for learning purposes. Student teachers who do not grasp that good discipline is to a great extent achieved *through* understanding how children learn and managing the classroom properly often get themselves into difficulty. Of course it might be replied that there is no intention that these sub-skills should be acquired separately, yet in that case, and in default of any account of the relationships between them, what is the point of the analysis? The next two assumptions, (4) 'Skills can be studied and taught' and (5) 'Skills can be learned' certainly suggest the analysis is made for learning purposes.

Perhaps at least part of the point is to be found in (7) 'Skills can be evaluated and assessed'. I take this to mean that the breakdown into skills and sub-skills has the function of facilitating evaluation and assessment. That is, while it is difficult to say whether someone is a good teacher there is less of a problem with whether he or she possesses a number of skills and sub-skills. This must be doubtful when the skills are of the order 'Has a good educational background' and Exhibits professionalism' (*The New Teacher*): these are every bit as opaque as 'is a good teacher'.

But why ever should it be supposed that skills, particularly, lend themselves to assessment? It is possible, without stretching ingenuity very far, to think of three reasons. Such assessment appears eminently *objective* since it relates to things which people can actually be seen to do (supervise pupils' entry into the classroom, employ visual aids), *fair* since everyone can be assessed against the same list (rather than on different assessors' notions of what 'a good teacher' is) and *scientific* in that qualitative judgments are eliminated, often in favour of ticking boxes on a checklist. But of course objectivity in this sense and the related pseudo-virtues are achieved only by reducing skills to mechanical routines (Did student remember to bring chalk to lesson? Did he/she arrive at classroom before pupils?). Once we expect visual aids to be used *appropriately*, discipline to be kept *satisfactorily* or records and reports to be kept *adequately* (the last two examples are from *The New Teacher*, p. 7), an element of interpretation quite properly enters and the assessment loses the straight forwardness and 'objectivity' that appeared to recommend it.

In the field of education it is perhaps always tempting to list detailed behavioural objectives since these appear to guarantee that the educator has some definite goods to offer. The temptation and the accompanying dangers are especially acute at present because of the search for criteria of performance by which to reward and promote 'effective' teachers, and because of the move towards criterion-referenced assessment of pupils, where an examination grade is associated with competence in a named range of skills. The Inspectorate's booklet *English from 5 to 16: Curriculum matters 1* is a recent example, rapidly becoming notorious (and now to be redrafted) of what happens if you break down the development of literacy, oracy and literary sensibility into a host of sub-skills. It should stand as a reminder that the convenience of those who organize, manage and assess is not a value that overrides all others, least of all in schools, for children are quick to sense what their elders' order of priorities is. If the first priority appears to be the sorting of sheep from goats it is little wonder if children are slow to perceive any intrinsic value in the education they are offered.

What makes it very hard in practice to make firm assessments of teachers, to conclude that one teacher has a certain skill while another does not, is the complexity of the context in which teaching skills are exercised. That complexity appears to be denied by the Project's second assumption, 'Skills can be isolated and identified'. I believe I am not alone in finding that the fears and difficulties young and student teachers experience arise at least as much in the context of their relationships with other teachers as in their dealings with classes. The head of department, it emerges, feels threatened by Peter's first-class honours degree and would rather like to see him fall on his face. Julia's school is still split into factions by the merger that took place over a decade ago. In John's several members of staff, including the two he is supposed to work most closely with, are hoping for the post of senior teacher which carries responsibility for supervising students and probationers: they studiously ignore him, presumably for fear of seeming to advertise their supervisory abilities too blatantly. And so on. (I forebear to give examples of the way the training institution can muddy these waters still more.) This is the minefield in which the Project appears to believe teachers can treat their skills as if they were clinically isolable and work at them like a craftsman.

It seems obvious to me, on the contrary, that working in a school requires a continual awareness of the institution's history, of political and other pressures such as those caused by the recent pay dispute, and of colleagues' sensitivities, to mention only three factors. The Project deals with these complications briskly. *The New Teacher* recommends senior teachers with responsibility for staff development to identify and compile a list of 'those who might need and be prepared for some self-training', to help them devise suitable activities and discuss the results with them. What are likely to be the feelings of a teacher so identified? Anyone implementing the Project's advice here will be confronted with a most difficult and subtle problem in human relationships. The way to deal with it is covered by a crisp sentence in parentheses: 'At all stages, remember to be tactful and non-threatening' (p. 33), as if the complication introduced by other people's feelings were a minor one we all knew how to cope with and only needed to be sure not to forget. Nor are the teacher's own feelings to be allowed to make things untidy. If you find it anxiety-provoking for others to watch you practise your skills, well, don't. 'Do not feel threatened when these observers offer you advice' (*Handling Classroom Groups*, p. 19, and elsewhere). Is it simply a further skill, that of not feeling threatened, that is required on these occasions? What a person experiences as a source of anxiety is, to put it briefly (I return to this in Part II), usually bound up with his or her whole way of perceiving the world, with a wide range of dispositions and attitudes. Learning not to find authority figures intimidating, say, requires a reorientation that may take a lifetime and a change of attitude to much else. That is why it cannot be regarded as 'isolable' and, if skills are characteristically isolable, as a 'skill'.

It is not so much that the Project's conception of skills learning is unsophisticated as that there appears to be a positive determination to view it as superficial, a process that makes minimal contact with the learner's values and feelings and involves little contact between persons. Though scattered remarks suggest learning to teach is a cooperative enterprise ('What the present workbooks provide is a series of starting points for a younger teacher and a more experienced one to begin to explore together', *The New Teacher*, p. 32) the nature of the cooperation is left hazy, and at one point it is clearly spelled out that picking up teaching skills is essentially a solitary exercise in which little help is to be expected from others. *The New Teacher* (*ibid.*) tells us that 'In a profession which makes decreasing provision for in-service training, the emphasis must shift to what the practitioner can do to improve his own performance' and talks of 'self-analysis' requiring 'minimal support or guidance' (*ibid.*). In this picture of learning the role of other people is reduced to that of models for imitation and skills become items to be acquired, so many pieces of cargo to be 'taken on board' and unloaded onto others with no lasting effect on the agent of transport, just like the inert facts of the more academic tradition that skills training is often held to have superseded.

The sixth assumption, 'Skills can be reflected upon and refined with practice', if charitably interpreted as 'Reflection and practice both have an essential role in acquiring skills', does seem to make room for the deeper and more personal assimilation whose absence I have criticized. Here it appears to be acknowledged that without some degree of thoughtfulness skills acquisition risks degenerating into rote and routine. Most of the Focus Books do find a place for reflection, to the extent of having an entire section called 'Reflections', but the size of the gap between this and the acquiring of skills is shown by such comments as that the first two sections are 'directed towards the acquisition of the sub-skills and their combination into an appropriate whole' while 'Part 3 is best undertaken by students at a later stage in their training' (*Mixed Ability Teaching*, pp. 4 & 35), and by the suggestion that 'Reflections' might in concurrent (e.g. B.Ed.) courses be studied a year after the 'skills workbook' (*Class Management and Control*, p. 5).

In any case 'Reflections' does not always appear well designed to stimulate reflection. (There are exceptions, notably, I would say, *Class Management and Control*). Part 3 of *Teaching Bright Pupils*, for example, consists of four topics. The first, 'School provision for bright pupils', is largely descriptive; the other three, 'Some possible teaching strategies', 'Practising skills of questioning' and 'Managing bright pupils in the classroom' are, as their titles suggest, prescriptive in content. This particular workbook ends with four tables, including thirty tips for 'managing bright pupils in the classroom' and thirty-eight 'behavioural criteria' by which bright pupils may be recognized. Nowhere is there any encouragement to consider the educational wisdom of labelling some pupils 'bright' and others, by implication, not.

There remains only the first assumption, 'Practical teaching consists of skills', which I have left until last since it is the most fundamental. What reasons are offered for making this assumption? The line of thought runs: teaching is a 'stagnant' profession offering decreasing opportunities for such extrinsic rewards as promotion. 'One way for the new teacher to maintain job satisfaction is to feel that he is still progressing. Two factors go together to make this ideal realizable. First, there must be a fundamental belief that teaching is about skills ...' (*The New Teacher*, p. 32). So feeling you have mastered skills brings job satisfaction: it is the need for job satisfaction that warrants the first assumption, on which all the rest depend.

II

In this section I speculate on the effects of skills acquisition on the acquirer. As we have just seen, the Project thinks the effects are essentially beneficial, but it is possible to hold otherwise, (There are elements of the dissenting view in Hart's lucid paper 'Against Skills', 1978, and in Lasch's book *The Minimal Self*, 1984). For regarding capacities as 'skills' may be a way of insisting on their separateness from personality: the 'real me' is not put at risk by rebuff or failure if it is only my skills that are found wanting. On a sensible conception of skills, my skills (ability with chisel or computer) do not testify to the kind of person I fundamentally am. You do not know much about me as a person when you have learned that I can or cannot use a word processor. Once I regard *all* my capacities as skills, however, nothing, I may imagine, gives away the kind of person I am and the 'real me' – its profile low to the point of invisibility — is in the ideal condition to survive the contingencies of a hostile world.

Our skills do not say much about who we are because they make no reference to our dispositions, our wantings and valuings, and it is by virtue of these that we are persons of one sort or another. 'It is in what we value, not in what we have, that the test of us resides', Forster writes (*op. cit.*), explaining how Herbert Pembroke was 'stupid in the important sense: his whole life was coloured by a contempt of the intellect. That he had a tolerable intellect of his own was not the point'. The test of us, we might say, lies in our virtues rather than in our skills. And skills can be distinguished from virtues precisely with reference to disposition. I can be skilled with the chisel without wanting to exercise that skill, or without wanting to use it in the right way or for the right ends. But I cannot have a virtue and not be disposed to exercise it. It is part of what we mean by attributing a virtue to someone, calling him frank and open, for example, that he is strongly disposed to be so, not that he can be so when he chooses (that would make him something else altogether).

It is so obvious that personality and character are crucially important in teachers that the point would not be worth making were it not that too much emphasis on skills is effectively a denial of it. We want teachers who are receptive, flexible, patient, willing to take risks, supportive of each other. These are qualities of persons, not skills to be brought into play when you enter the staffroom or classroom. To think of them as skills is immediately to think of them as entered into less genuinely or whole-heartedly. Some sense of this, I think, enters into many teachers' reluctance to exchange better pay for a tighter definition of duties. Rather than be paid for lunch-time supervision, say, they would prefer to be acknowledged, in salary and other respects, as the sort of persons amongst whose merits it can be counted that they are *willing* to do these things. In this they recognize the importance of the kind of person a teacher is and the central place in that of what the or she is disposed to do.

It looks as though 'virtues' rather than 'skills' should be at the heart of our conception of a good teacher. This is awkward, because 'virtue' and 'virtuous' have unpleasant connotations of smugness and self-congratulation. That, as Bernard Williams (1985) points out, is because discussion has taken place too much in the context of the *cultivation* of the virtues, and there is something very suspect about deliberately cultivating a quality because it is a virtue. A brave person does not act under that description: he or she does not dive into the icy river *because* this is the brave thing to do, but because he or she is determined to save the child that has fallen in. People whom we call kind act in order to alleviate suffering, not because they want to perform an act of kindness. We find very unattractive those individuals who act out of a consciousness that such-and-such counts as virtue, and we have a special word for them: we call them prigs.

Because we dislike priggishness and the notion of virtue reminds us unpleasantly of 'character-training' we react against talk of the virtues altogether and are inclined to prefer the unpretentious down-to-earthness of skills. What we fail to notice is that skills can be pursued in the wrong spirit just as much as virtue. It is one thing to learn skills, to acquire know-how in various practical matters, but something entirely different to cultivate skills under that description, *because* they are skills. The two are related as priggishness is to real virtue, or as the love of hill-walking is related to being in love with a picture of yourself as the outdoor type. One involves absorption with the task or activity in hand, the other concentrates on the image you present, both to yourself and the rest of the world. It must be emphasized that it is this second version, the self-regarding cultivation of skills as skills, that the Project recommends, with its repeated injunctions to 'think of yourself as a craftsman' and to seek the satisfaction of feeling that you have mastered skills.

This attitude is at home in a world where it is widely held that people are no more than the sum of the roles they play, so that the 'presentaion of self in everyday life' is seen as inevitably and properly an overriding concern. Self-consciousness is the central factor here, a watching of yourself as it were from the outside, and through the eyes of others. This passes for normality to such a degree that proponents of the Project's sort of approach to skills see nothing odd in proclaiming practicality as amongst its chief merits, and dismissing as self-centred or unduly introspective different philosophies which encourage a greater depth of reflection and admit the importance of the trainee's fears and feelings. Usually the idea seems to be that although such skills training may begin by being self-conscious and awkward, eventually trainees will come to perform tasks smoothly and unself-consciously. But may it not be (to put it paradoxically) that it is the self-consciousness, rather, that ends up being unconscious? Where we begin a routine or activity in a spirit of concern with ourself and our image perhaps it continues coloured by that founding motivation, but we, for our self-respect's sake, cannot allow ourselves to perceive this or remember our original motive. For we were hoping to be craftsmen, after all, not people merely posing as them.

So the teacher who sets out to be a craftsman may come to be like Sartre's famous waiter in *Being and Nothingness*(1958). His movement is exaggerated, 'a little too precise, a little too rapid' (p. 59): his walk imitates 'the inflexible stiffness of some kind of automation while carrying his tray with the recklessness of a tight-rope walker' (*ibid*). The waiter is in what Sartre calls 'bad faith' (*mauvaise foi*) because he has allowed the world's cruder expectations of a waiter to constitute his identity. In acceding to this he denies his freedom. 'He is playing *at being* a waiter in a cafe', Sartre says (*ibid.*); less a 'waiter'. I think we are familiar with this phenomenon from a different context: teachers who have become 'teachers', caricatures of the species. Like ham actors their gestures are too expansive, their vocal inflections too marked, their poses too contrived. Children have sharp eyes for this theatricality. They capture it in nicknames and burlesque it in imitations of cruel accuracy. Many of the trainee teachers I meet fear almost above all that they will turn into the sort of career teacher they see in the staff-room: that such responsiveness and humanity as they possess will vanish forever behind the professional mask[4]. They are the sort of people Wragg (*op. cit.*) contrasts unfavourably with experienced teachers who, he says with what appears to be approval, 'Did not hesitate to come on strong, be larger than life by exaggerating their authority, their preciseness or even, in some cases, their real or feigned eccentricity'. Unfortunately, as happened with the waiter, the mask may set and prove difficult to remove. After years of performing we become uncertain what is feigned and what is real. A student quoted the following confession from a teacher whom she had just observed 'coming on strong' with a class:

> You have to be an absolute monster sometimes, otherwise they'll walk all over you. The trouble is that after years of doing it, it starts to get you like that inside. I sometimes stand back mentally and I think, 'Are you going mad?'

To climb on stilts to teach, reverting to Yeats's imagery, may increase your stature and impressiveness in the short term, but over a longer period there is likely to be a price to pay. Standing aloof holds out the promise of invulnerability but in the end delivers only a growing sense of remoteness and emptiness.

We would do teachers an injustice if we came to think of what I have described as simply an occupational disease to which, mysteriously and rather comically, they are liable as a profession. It is essential to remember that it is a way of coping with certain of the typical experiences of teaching. The strain of continually dealing with reluctant or rebellious pupils brings, naturally enough, the temptation to stand above it all or to retreat behind some kind of mask. Further pressure may come from the pupils themselves: 'Children demand daddy long-legs upon his timber toes' (Yeats), for such a teacher is usually moderately entertaining and conforms safely to stereotype. Then too the current state of teachers' morale and loss of faith – in education as an ideal and in their ability to contribute to it – clearly play a major part, since the Project can recommend the satisfaction of skills acquisition specifically as a solution to this problem. (Not that the craftsmanship model will do much for teachers' declining status if they want teaching to be regarded as a *profession*. Might not the representation of the teacher as a kind of technician, an expert only in means and not ends, be partly responsible for that decline?)

The solution to loss of faith, however, is not to be found in the cultivation of *bad* faith. If bad faith in teaching consists in self-consciously playing at being a teacher then perhaps good faith lies in drawing on a deeper sense of what teaching can be: in working out for yourself a philosophy of education with the capacity to justify and reinvigorate the actions and procedures that it underpins. At the heart of such a philosophy would be an understanding of what learning involves: not merely superficial acquisition, whether of facts or skills, but (amongst other things) taking risks, entering into dialogue with other people, and accepting where appropriate the experience of uncertainty instead of clutching at firm and definite answers. This understanding would go beyond theoretical assent to touch the teacher's own experience as a learner, for only one so in touch can help others towards significant learning. You must, for example, be able to bear uncertainty yourself before you can help others to do so. This is the respect in which your teaching is not inappropriately described as a matter of *faith*: not in any specifically theological sense but in being connected to courage and commitment. To teach in good faith is to be personally committed to the kind of learning you encourage in your pupils, and to acknowledge and accept the accompanying risks, from which the person who insists everything can be reduced to 'skills' hides. It is to have the kind of courage that is a part of unselfishness, in putting your teaching to the service of the growth and well-being of your pupils, rather than to use them as props or foils to meet needs of your own. It is therefore properly to *educate* them, where this is a business of helping them to take responsibility for their own learning and lives. .

The Project remarks strikingly (*Handling Classroom Groups*, p. 44) that there are 'a number of circumstances where pupils may profitably accept a degree of responsibility for the functioning of classroom groups to which they belong, *on a temporary basis* (my italics). This turns out to mean that they are to be allowed to play at being chairman, organizer, spokesman or 'expert': taking responsibility is seen as something done by authority figures, real or pretended, not ordinary learners. The stilted teacher puts his or her own needs foremost, and leaves the centre of the stage only to make room for those who will flatter by imitation. So education becomes turned into one more spectator sport, one more confirmation of the passivity and dependence of pupils, instead of being the means of their achieving autonomy and self-respect.

The professional development of teachers, then, if it is conceived too narrowly in terms of the acquisition of skills, may turn out to be damaging both to the personal development and well-being of the individual teacher and to the educational development of the pupil. It is worth adding that the skills approach is no help, and is likely to be positively destructive, in the development of better relationships between teachers themselves. The Project appears tacitly to acknowledge this in making light of the difficulties in this area, as we saw. Thinking of teaching as a collection of skills and single-mindedly perfecting your own often works effectively as a way of evading the business of supporting your colleagues, for, of course, if they have problems they should simply go off and acquire the skills to deal with them, with the assistance of the relevant experts where necessary. Giving support makes demands not on such specialist skills as we may happen to possess but on our virtues, notably courage and commitment again. For support must be unconditional, and others' doubts and anxieties remind us of our own. What good we are to other people if we can cope only by hiding our fears behind performance or persona is vividly shown in another incident in Forster's novel. Herbert Pembroke has to break to Rickie the news that his baby is born, deformed, lame like her father:

> 'She – she is in many ways a healthy child. She will live – oh yes'. A flash of
> horror passed over his face. He hurried into the preparation-room, lifted the lid
> of his desk, glanced mechanically at the boys, and came out again.

Acknowledgements

Versions of this paper were read to the Leeds and Edinburgh branches of the Philosophy of Education Society and benefited from criticism and discussion. Frank Coffield suggested a number of improvements, most of which I have incorporated. One of the lines of thought that have come together here was prompted by an unpublished dissertation by Jane Bond, sometime student of the Durham University School of Education: 'Teaching – a Dickensian Perspective'.

Notes

1 But see *Competency in Teaching* (Tuxworth 1982) for an attempt to transfer American programmes to the British context.
2 See the correspondence in the *Times Educational Supplement*, 9 July 1982, after a group of lecturers at the University of Bath produced a booklet criticizing the Project. I have not been able to see a copy of this booklet: I believe it was withdrawn from circulation.
3 Worse still – since it compounds utilitarianism with cynical manipulation of language – is the claim that vocationalism and education are the same thing. This is the tenor of, for example, Lord Young's assertion that 'All training means is, that you're educated in skills which you apply' (as reported in the *Guardian, 25 February 1985*).

4 My attention has been drawn to David Hargreaves's remarks on the same phenomenon (*Interpersonal Relations and Education,* p. 210): 'Is it right for the teacher to "act a part"?... The contrived performance is a means to an end, namely the establishment of his dominance. It is essentially a *temporary* measure ... he will soon be able to drop his mask. The only danger is that of permanently "playing a part" where the contrived performance becomes an end in itself. A few teachers do become life-long classroom actors, dreary cardboard caricatures ...' Where I disagree with Hargreaves is over how easy it is to 'drop the mask', particularly if the teacher adopts the Project's sort of approach.

References

DES Teacher Education Project, *Class Management and Control* (1981), *Handling Classroom Groups* (1982), *Mixed Ability Teaching in the Early Years of the Secondary School* (1982), *The New Teacher* (1984), *Teaching Bright Pupils in Mixed Ability Classes* (1981) (all published by Macmillan, London).

Hargreaves, D. (1975). *Interpersonal Relations and Education.* London, Routledge & Kegan Paul.

Hart, W.A. (1978). 'Against skills', *Oxford Review of Education,* vol. 4, no. 2.

HMI/DES (1984). *English from 5 to 16: Curriculum Matters 1.* London, HMSO.

Lasch, C. (1985). *The Minimal Self: Psychic Survival in Troubled Times,* London, Pan.

Sartre, J.P. (1958). *Being and Nothingness* (trans. Barnes, H.). London, Methuen.

Tuxworth, E.N. (1982). *Competency in Teaching.* London, FEU/DES publication.

Williams, B. (1985). *Ethics and the Limits of Philosophy.* London, Fontana.

Wragg, E.C. (ed.) (1984). *Classroom Teaching Skills.* Beckenham, Croom Helm.

CHAPTER 5

Vocationalism on the hoof:
observations on the TVEI

Maurice Holt

In November 1982 the Prime Minister, Mrs Thatcher, announced that £7 million was to be made available to launch a series of 'pilot projects' for the 14–18 age range, 'to stimulate the provision of technical and vocational education for young people'. LEAs would be invited to bid for the projects, for which guidelines would be provided by the funding agency, the MSC.

The MSC is a quasi-autonomous body (or 'quango') administered not by the DES – the department of state with responsibility for education in schools – but by the DoE[1]. Funding a course of pupils completing mandatory schooling from a wholly different department represented an unprecedented shift of policy. So also did the means of devising the policy, which appeared to take DES officials by surprise, and involved no prior consultation with educational bodies.

The first projects began in fourteen LEAs in September 1983. Although this initial phase was described by the Secretary of State for Education, Sir Keith Joseph, as 'an experiment', the second phase was announced immediately the first was under way. The scale of funding for what became known as the 'Technical and Vocational Education Initiative' (TVEI) was lavish by any standards, and overwhelming to schools whose budgets had been severely cut as a result of government policies. In the year 1984–1985, the TVEI cost over £27 million – more than the Schools Council (abolished by Sir Keith Joseph in 1982) spent in its twenty years of existence, from 1964 to 1984. This sum was spent on some 3 per cent of the secondary school population, amounting to more than £17 per pupil per week. Average LEA capitation expenditure per pupil is £0.75 per week. Moreover, as Dale[2] points out, TVEI funding is additional to LEA funding (and cannot be used to supplement non-TVEI activities), is contractually linked and is therefore much more secure than general capitation, which varies unpredictably with cuts and rate-capping. Dale suggests that

TVEI's operation at the margins of the school, like the intensity of its monitoring, provides it with disproportionately greater influence than might be assumed from the level of the funding and the number of pupils involved.

A summary of the aims and criteria for TVEI, framed by its National Steering Group, is given in the appendix to this paper. It will be seen that while these general guidelines specify a vocational orientation in some detail, it was necessary to allow a measure of flexibility to LEAs and schools in their interpretation, so that schools could adapt the TVEI to their existing curriculum arrangements.

A useful survey of the political and educational background to TVEI is offered by McCulloch[3], who summarizes the various attempts that have been made, for a century or more, to reconcile vocational education with the academic interpretation of liberal education which became the preferred form of secondary education in England as the Victorian public schools grew in influence. This phenomenon is of great importance in considering not only how the secondary curriculum got the way it is, but also why it is particularly resistant to change. It requires more space than is available here[4], but some of the issues will be discussed in the last chapter of this book. MuCulloch notes two factors of importance in the run-up to the TVEI. First, there was the appointment of a 'minister for information technology' in 1981, which 'probably fostered greater enthusiasm among Conservatives for technological education'. The subsequent appointment of this minister, Mr Kenneth Baker, as education secretary in 1986 and his swift announcement of plans for 'City Technology Colleges' (CTCs) seems to confirm McCulloch's point. Second, McCulloch suggests that the 1982 recapture of the Falklands emboldened the Prime Minister.

> to give full rein to the rhetoric of change with which the Conservatives had swept to power in 1979. Thatcher seemed indeed to offer a radical alternative to the failed policies of the past which led to Britain's decline.

This gave the TVEI a bias in keeping with earlier Conservative approaches to technology:

> A direct link was assumed between technical education on the one hand and capitalist growth, material wealth and economic competitiveness. The TVEI was highly characteristic of this Conservative tradition in technical education.

It is clear that the party's further 1986 commitment to CTCs reinforces this tradition and the dubious assumption on which it depends. The key issue in appraising TVEI is to examine the influence of this functional and instrumental bias – very evident in the aims and criteria for the scheme – on its subsequent practice. McCulloch concludes with the hope that:

> whether or not the TVEI is maintained in its present form, the narrow and divisive vocationalism of its early rhetoric will continue to be undermined in favour of a broader vision ...

This chapter will attempt a judgment on the state of affairs so far.

Responses to the TVEI

The centralized nature of the TVEI scheme, under a Conservative administration, inevitably gave it a political aspect. Even so, several Labour-controlled authorities tendered for TVEI projects, although the country's largest LEA, the Labour-controlled Inner London Education Authority, declared its opposition to TVEI. The projects were oversubscribed at each phase, and in 1985 the Chancellor of the Exchequer announced a further £25 million solely for in-service education and training in the TVEI, to be administered to LEAs via the MSC. The infiltration of TVEI into the curriculum of all secondary schools is the intention of a third phase of funding announced in 1986. But LEAs accepting this offer will find it much less generous: in Devon for instance, the amount to be provided by the MSC is some £85 per student per year, compared with over £300 in the first-phase Devon scheme of 1983. In order 'to provide a coherent TVEI experience', the Devon Education Committee accepted the recommendation that an additional £65 per pupil should be provided from county funds, bringing the total to £150 per pupil. In this hard-pressed LEA, this commitment will require a total of £22 million expenditure on TVEI extension across the county over the period 1987 to 1995. It should be noted that although the scheme aims to offer 'young people aged 14–18 ... access to a wider and richer curriculum based on the lessons emerging from the pilot schemes', it is the case that 'MSC do not require all young people to be included in the plans'. In its conception, therefore, TVEI remains a technical and vocational programme for *some* pupils[5].

The announcement of the TVEI brought swift and unfavourable comment from some educationists[6]. Others, while expressing doubts about its employment-led aspects, were able to grant it qualified support[7]. Some saw no difficulty in reconciling its provisions with their philosophy of comprehensive education[8].

The MSC was slow to fund TVEI evaluation schemes, but this was soon corrected and higher education institutions now compete eagerly for evaluation assignments. In due course, an avalanche of evaluations of TVEI schemes will doubtless appear at much the same time. Some interim reports have been made available[9], but these are inevitably cautious, largely descriptive statements more inclined to hedge their bets than offer bold analysis. There is a general lack of documents which give an insight into the approach of schools, or a challenging view of the issues involved[10].

The TVEI, in any event, has a 'now you see it,now you don't' quality; it does not define any particular course or curriculum, neither is it linked to any particular form of examination. As an example of a national, official curriculum initiative it must, in this latter respect, be perfectly unique. The traditional approach to curriculum reform – a rare enough event for the DES, in any case – is to introduce a new examination; central government almost always sees curriculum change as assessment-led. Both GCSE at 16-plus and

CPVE at 17-plus are associated with curriculum change, as was CSE in 1964 and GCE in 1950. Both, in the event, reinforced the traditional grammar-school style of curriculum and there is no historical reason to suppose that GCSE and CPVE will be any more successful in promoting innovation.

The response to the TVEI from schools must, however, have owed something to the 'foundation courses' established in 1976 by the City and Guilds of London Institute:

> a new range of courses for young people in full-time education who (are) vocationally uncommitted and to whom the existing provision of academic courses (is) unsuited[11].

The CGLI, as an awarding body operating in further education, had in mind students staying on post-16 in colleges and who needed a less explicit vocational focus than their abler peers for whom the CGLI offered a range of qualifications. The foundation courses, in eight broad areas like engineering, community care and commercial studies, were packages leading to an award, linking subjects together under broad headings, and capable of flexible interpretation by colleges to meet varying demands and resources.

The CGLI, as a market-oriented body on the lookout for new business propositions, discovered quite quickly that the foundation courses were a nice little earner in schools as well as FE and tertiary colleges. At first, enterprising 11–18 schools ran them as one-year, post-16, sixth-form courses, as an alternative to the usual unsatisfactory ragbag of O-level retakes. But by 1980 the courses could be found in 14–16 option schemes, alongside CSE programmes and, of course, the traditional 0-level acedemic choice. In due course the CGLI was to develop its '365' courses – combining general education and broadly vocational elements – with this sector of the market very much in mind.

The appeal of these courses in comprehensive schools lacking any worked-out philosophy of an 11–16 common curriculum is pretty evident. Such schools have usually managed, by the end of the third year, to create a disenchanted underclass – sometimes, and very distastefully, referred to as 'the grey area' – who are reluctant, for a variety of social and educational reasons, to identify with the academic ethic of hard work, O-levels, and generally submissive roles. Traditional CSE courses have little appeal for them. For such pupils 'link courses' 14–16, offering involving attendance at nearby FE colleges on vocational courses, were already popular.

At a stroke, the CGLI had made it possible to retain these pupils wholly on the school timetable (with some work experience and perhaps FE linkage) and provide for them a qualification which, with its aura of the vocational, seemed to promise jobs and, therefore, motivation. The price to be paid was a genuine curriculum innovation: a willingness for staff normally labelled up by subject specialism to plan together cross-curricular programmes. This was not a novelty in FE, for whom the courses had originally been designed. But for schools reared on a grammar-school, subject-based model it meant new thinking (and harked back, of course, to some of the post–Newsom developments of the late 1960s[12]).

Have we here, then, an example of assessment-led innovation which really worked, where all those curriculum-led Schools Council projects failed? Not really. What made the CGLI courses attractive was the combination of three factors, of which the inbuilt assesment was but one. Equally important were the provision of a curriculum framework which offered schools enough support, yet also enough adaptability; and the motivating factor of vocationalism which could be used to sell the courses to pupils and their parents. Although the courses offered a stigmatized, non-academic curriculum, they fitted in well with the rhetoric of joblessness and skill acquisition which was already strong by 1978 (when the Youth Opportunities Programme began).

With hindsight, one could say that the CGLI softened up schools for the TVEI, and also for the FEU with its emphasis on 'vocational preparation'. It planted the vocational rhetoric in schools, linked it to the idea of curriculum innovation, and attracted the support of a wide ability range of pupils. There was also the agreeable suggestion of greater employability. Schools wishing to view the 11–16 curriculum as a continuum, however, could hold no brief for a scheme which divided pupils at the age of 14. They would share, with Tawney, a distaste for:

> the fundamentally vicious doctrine that the education of children during the period of adolescence should be determined by the requirements of the employment which they will eventually enter [13].

I would argue that at root, what underlay enthusiasm for the CGLI courses at age 14 was not a desire for innovation, but a need to deal with alienation. Once a school finds itself with a cohort of pupils voting with their feet against the traditional curriculum on offer, it is easy to justify what is really an expedient on the grounds that it offers these pupils better opportunities. And maybe it does: but it does so by isolating them, by using the curriculum to divide pupils one from another; and it conveniently leaves unanswered awkward questions about a form of curriculum which might be developed to hold the attention of all pupils. It is particularly important to note that the CGLI courses dealt with none of the issues regarding curriculum *structure* in the comprehensive school: the innovation they brought in train was to do only with choice of *content* and appropriate *method*. Schools tackling the issue of the whole curriculum 11–16, on the other hand, were bound to confront innovation in respect of all three of these elements.

The same limitation applies to TVEI: as a bolt-on programme for a selected group of pupils post-14, it cannot address basic problems of curriculum structure 11–16. Compared with the CGLI courses, it had only one of the three advantages I have listed: the rhetoric of vocationalism and employability. It lacked both an assessment package and a clear curriculum framework. But it could take advantage of the pioneering vocational work done by CGLI, and offer an additional attraction: a great deal of money.

A current perspective

It is clear both from the manner of its launch[14] and the scale of its funding[15] that TVEI represents a major attempt by central government to change the nature of schooling 14–16 in a significant way. The word 'initiative' in its title is not to be overlooked: the government's *New Training Initiative* (1981) declared that 'The government is seeking to ensure that the school curriculum develops the personal skills and qualities as well as the knowledge needed for working life' – an uncompromising avowal that 'working life' is to determine both the knowledge and the 'personal skills' addressed by the school curriculum. The TVEI is evidently part of this industry-led view of the purpose of schooling[16] and its aims and criteria make this perfectly clear. One is reminded that in the US, President Reagan's 'Star Wars' programme is officially the 'Strategic Defence Initiative'. In the vocabulary of modern government, an 'initiative' appears to mean a unilateral decision taken without asking anyone who might object.

The language used to present the ideas of TVEI – by the MSC and by schools – repays study. Perhaps the word which recurs most often is 'skill'. It comes under scrutiny in other places in this book: Ruth Jonathan (Chapter 6) examines its importance to the rhetoric of the YTS 'core skills' element and the flimsy basis on which it rests; Richard Smith (Chapter 4) points out that in teaching, too much emphasis on skills is 'effectively a denial' of personality and character; and Jerry Wellington (Chapter 3) not only undermines the curious notion of 'transferable skills', but argues also that education based on skills will not further technical and technological ends. Here, therefore, all I need do is endorse the point made by Hart[17] and quoted by Wellington: that 'talk about skills is simply a kind of incantation, by which one creates the illusion that one is actually saying something about education'. The importance of skills in TVEI jargon is well displayed in this extract from an article by the deputy head of a Welsh TVEI school[18]:

> Under the modular system ... pupils have, to date, 18 modules from which to choose. The only one which is compulsory for all pupils is Interview Techniques/Interpersonal Skills. When we formulated the modular idea we had in mind a skill-based rather than content-based curriculum, the underlying theme being experiential and 'learning by doing'.

Talk of 'transferable skills', 'the negotiated curriculum' and 'experiential learning' has become virtually a trade mark of TVEI exercises, and there is a suggestion that these terms represent wholly new approaches to the tasks of curriculum planning and implementation. But the idea of 'negotiation' – of teacher and pupil deciding together how to develop a curriculum event or transaction – and of 'experiential learning' – of resource-based approaches – was a commonplace of curriculum development in the 1970s in those comprehensive schools committed to core curriculum approaches[19].

The rise of the 'modular curriculum' owes something to TVEI, and rather more to CGLI foundation courses which were constructed – like many FE courses – from distinct components like industrial studies, communication studies, optional activities and so on. it owes someting, too, to the suggestion in the ILEA Hargreaves report[20] that

> a critical change is the restructuring of the two-year courses in the fourth and fifth years into *half-term units*. Instead of setting out on a vague two-year journey towards nebulous and distant goals, pupils should ... embark on a series of six to eight week learning units ... each of which is meaningful in itself ...

There is hardly anything new in the idea of sustaining motivation by breaking experience into smaller units: those National Servicemen who, in the 1950s, crossed each day off the calendar every morning were bringing their nebulous and distant demobilization within reach by the desperate measure of daily modules. Good teachers have always given their programmes an element of longitudinal structure. In higher education, unit structures are common in Open University and CNAA degrees, and I have argued that a modular system, applied to 16–19 education in tertiary colleges, offers one way of replacing A-level and the present mish-mash of segmented lower-level courses with a coherent, genuinely comprehensive system[21].

The important point is that once an accepted technique becomes reified and takes up, in terms like 'the modular curriculum', a life of its own, other ideas and beliefs become associated with it. For that matter, an existing word like 'skill' can be given this treatment and can then be used as a device for conflating quite different ideas in an unhelpful way. Dearden notes how common it has become for politicians and others to do this with words like 'education' and 'training', and calls it 'trading on wider and narrower interpretations of some key term'[22]. We have to ask: what is meant by a module, and for what reason are modules being introduced? What assumptions are implied about the nature of education? At least Hargreaves makes it clear that the ILEA modules have the educational purpose of sustaining pupil interest. It is interesting to note, though, that in another part of the report (p. 30) attention is drawn to a comparison between the 'sense of real purpose and achievement' found in a good primary school, and 'the overall impression ... of fragmentation' experienced by the same pupils when they move to a good secondary school.

There are clearly dangers that modules may cause even more fragmentation. Older students, in colleges and in higher education, have the maturity to cope with this: for 11–16 pupils, unit structures must be underpinned by thematic coherence. Neither is it easy to write effective modules, as an ILEA teacher has pointed out[23]:

> How many of you have written a module? I have. It took three days of sheer slog, consultations with colleagues, trying to interest pupils, and to identify skills for profiles. If you want that kind of development, class teachers should have half timetables.

And these are modules linked to the fairly conventional curriculum strategy of a report which specifically eschews the TVEI and its vocationalism. what are we to make, though, of this next approach?

> By combining fourth and fifth years together, individual pupils can pick various routes through the many modules on offer. As long as certain core areas are covered, individuals can choose different combinations to suit their abilities and interests. This affords a possible way to prepare previously streamed and separated students for a unitary GCSE examination ...[24]

These modules, moreover, form part of 'generalized pre-vocational courses' 14–18, so that:

> Youth training thus moves away from time-serving where apprentices over a given period mastered ... the various aspects of a craft, towards a situation where a person can train in just one aspect of a wider occupational activity.

What we have here is the kind of reductionism identified in the YTS 'core skills' programme by Ruth Jonathan in this volume (Chapter 6); and there are also clear echoes of the skills-based approach to the 'craft' of teaching with all the drawbacks set out in Richard Smith's chapter. Of especial significance is the reference to modules as a way of coping, at age 14, with 'previously streamed and separated students'. It confirms the suspicion that the modular curriculum is little more than an elaborated form of the familiar options scheme. Though superficially offering core experience, it may in reality celebrate elaborate forms of curriculum differentiation. Even where (as in some TVEI schemes) all pupils in years four and five have access to a pool of modules, the technical and vocational bias of the modules prevents a curriculum of real breadth[25].

There are, then, historical reasons for the acceptability in schools of TVEI or at least some aspects of it. Chitty[26] notes that 'from the start there were misgivings', and Bernard Barker's chapter conveys a disquiet which many teachers would share. Yet despite the clear-cut emphasis in the MSC's TVEI rubric on schemes which are non-negotiably 'related to potential employment opportunities', with 'a technical/vocational element throughout', the CGLI courses had established a pre-vocational bridgehead and there was enough ambiguity about the implementation of TVEI in particular schools to give it a basis of support. Thus the Assistant Masters and Mistresses Association – a body not noted for reckless pronouncements – considers that 'TVEI is not a scheme but a concept'[27]. David (now Lord) Young has gone further, and not unfairly, in declaring that 'The response to the Initiative, both in terms of size and quality, was evidence that it had struck a chord within the education system'[8]. It is not too fanciful to suggest that for some schools, TVEI may be on the way to becoming an ideology – a set of beliefs beyond the reach of reason because its support is essentially emotional. For instance, the deputy head of a Bedfordshire TVEI school has written:[29]

> TVEI has energized and transformed our school ... During a difficult period for teachers generally our staff have been offered and taken the opportunity to meet

new challenges ... We have all gained ... We would still be shouting 'Yes' were the chance to come again ... It is difficult in prose ... to present and do justice to the ways in which TVEI has altered our daily experience.

The basis of TVEI support

To discover why the TVEI has acquired the status of a 'concept', and can strike such chords and discords, the basis of its support must be examined more closely. The TVEI appears to draw its strength from two quite different sources, generating the kind of ambivalence that can both attract and repel. On the one hand, there can be little doubt that it appeals to 'industrial trainers', keen to link the 14–16 school curriculum with instrumental ends and industry in particular. By this token one can identify a range of positions. At one extreme, there are those – like Mr Tebbit, co-instigator of the TVEI when Secretary of State for Employment – who seek to make schools wholly subservient to the need of industry. In a speech to industrialists, his injunction to 'Go out into the schools and tell them what you want' was received with the enthusiastic stamping of feet[30].

The MSC, as a part of the Department of Employment, can hardly be blamed for advancing the interests of industry. But to blame schools – as its former chairman has done – for economic ills which are the direct result of industry's own failure to develop new markets suggests a kind of conviction that defies reason[31].

> Lord Young ... told the meeting he did not believe youth unemployment had anything to do with the state of the economy. It had to do with the state of mind of young people leaving school, who lacked motivation and enterprise because their education had been too academic and unrelated to employment ...

This is rather like attributing the Irish potato famine of the last century to the failure of the peasants to vary their diet. The fact that Lord Young is now a member of the Cabinet, however, emphasizes that the government's support for industrial training is matched by a profound dislike of schools and indifference towards the views and efforts of educators.

The supposed need to relate the education of 14–16 year olds to employment is consistent with the 'vocational preparation' favoured by the FEU, a body (now independent of the DES) promoting curriculum development in further education. In 1982 it endorsed the *New Training Initiative* in a 'joint statement by MSC and FEU', and in a subsequent policy document, the FEU found that[32]:

> There is general agreement that the 14–16 curriculum needs to emphasize general education but that it should perhaps begin to look more towards the outside world ... Throughout the 14–19 curriculum, in education and/or training, continuity should exist ...

The note of qualification here reinforces the view, discussed in Clive Seale's chapter, that the FEU seeks, to some extent, to distance itself from the extreme vocationalism of the MSC. Another passage in the same document seems to confirm this:

> There is no coherent government policy on vocational preparation; consequently there are ideological and operational differences between the MSC and DES schemes ...

These differences notwithstanding, the FEU's widely distributed document on one-year post-16 courses, *A Basis For Choice* (1979), has indirectly provided much of the thinking and terminology which has become an accepted part of the TVEI. Under the heading 'Transferability', we read that 'Courses need to ensure the options can be kept open for students by the learning of generally applicable skills'; as well as defining general aims, 'we felt it desirable to describe *specific objectives* ... demonstrably relevant to the young person's future roles'; there is 'a checklist of those *experiences* from which we think students should have had the opportunity to learn'; and, to take account of 'process or student skills (with respect to communication, group-work, vocational tasks, and so on)' and the need for measurable 'levels of competence related to many of the performance-related objectives', it will be necessary to assess the course by means of 'a form of profile reporting which incorporates some grading'. The key words 'skills', 'process', 'experience' and 'profile' constitute the common TVEI currency.

So despite these differences of emphasis, no one should doubt that the MSC and the FEU form the hard cutting edge of vocationalism. It seems extraordinary that educationists have not paid more attention to the FEU: Paul Grosch's chapter (8) helps to make up for this neglect. Of note is the FEU publication *Progressing to College: a 14–16 Core* (1985). This intrusion by a further education body into the 11–16 statutory curriculum is a clear case of the FEU exceeding its brief, and it is therefore doubly disturbing that this document has been given some form of endorsement by the School Curriculum Development Committee[33]. The FEU's excuse for its 14–16 core prescription is that further education needs 'to make realistic assumptions with respect to pre-entry achievement of students'. This might be met by a study of what schools are seeking to do, but instead turns into a list of fifteen 'core aims', with titles like 'adaptability', 'role transition', 'interpersonal skills' and so on. Thus aim ten, 'learning skills', is concerned 'to develop sufficient competence and confidence in a variety of independent learning skills to maximize individual potential in work and leisure'. It is difficult to know what is meant by this kind of incantation – to use Hart's word: but one is reminded of the computing rule 'garbage in, garbage out'. Writing of this sort, though, is less concerned with meaning through continuous prose, than with evoking the right rhetorics through the use of critical 'buzz-words': in this case, 'competence', 'confidence', 'independent learning', 'skills', 'individual potential', 'work' and 'leisure' all have the right vocationalized, forward-looking resonance. It is, perhaps, just the sort of sentence which might be generated by a computer programmed to do so[34].

This is by no means a fanciful suggestion: already some TVEI schools have developed 'comment banks' – sentences to describe a range of pupil outcomes – and in some cases computers are programmed to write reports on pupils by assembling these separate comments together. The absurdity of adding together marks obtained in different contexts to form an aggregate of achievement has never inhibited schools from doing so, once they get the evaluation bit between their teeth. There is a certain chilling logicality, therefore, in doing the same thing with sentences as well as numbers. For a scheme in Clywd, the sixteen comments available for the computer profile under the heading 'Communication skills, oral', for instance, range from 'He is highly articulate and speaks with clarity' to 'He is rather reluctant to take part in classroom discussion'. In another TVEI school, nine comments are listed under 'Communication – talking and listening abilities' and range from 'Takes a mature and creative part in talking and listening activities ...' to 'Is able to take part in talking and listening activities for very short periods of time'. A typical computer-assembled report from this school contains such paragraphs as: 'Sarah has usually tried hard to produce her best work. Improvement is good. She can nearly always be relied upon to carry out tasks'.

It is hard not to be deeply disturbed by these developments. The irony is that, in the name of 'individual learning', 'personal profiles' and similar assertions, what is actually being used to describe a pupil is no more individual than the 'customized options' you can specify when you want to put your own stamp on a production-line car. For cars, this is risible but acceptable; for pupils it is nothing short of tragic. There is no single human mind pausing to consider the entirety of 'Sarah's' work as a person in her own right with her own particular belongings, idiosyncrasies, parents, friends: instead, a machine is being used to stick together a series of phrases which were not even written with Sarah in mind, but rather some disembodied role-playing subject who will undergo certain predetermined experiences, and for whom therefore certain predetermined output states can be specified. The result is, in any event, scarcely English: the tone is flat, the phrases trite and such expressions as 'Impróvement is good' totally gauche. But the technology can, and will, eliminate these solecisms: what is alarming is the idea of putting together separate, generalized comments and daring to pretend that the result is a 'personal' report on a pupil. Behind the rhetoric of the profilers lie moral questions which have so far been given scant attention.

The danger here has already been identified in this volume, by Richard Smith (Chapter 4): for profiling is intimately linked with skills, and 'our skills do not say much about who we are'. A person whose capacities have been reduced to profiled skills is a non-person, for 'we are persons of one sort or another' to the extent that reference is made to 'our dispositions, our wantings and valuings'. Some advocates of profiling, however, might argue that the profile is a tool which can offer not only skill assessments but this other kind of information as well. The danger, if this course is steered, has been admirably analysed by A. Hargreaves[35]:

> The personal record component ... has an extraordinary capacity to restrict young people's individuality, to discipline and control them through the power of an all-pervasive and intrusive pattern of personal assessment.

Hargreaves, while recognizing the potential of profiles to motivate and individualize, sees also their power to become instruments of selection and of control, and suggests that they represent 'a more generalized trend towards the development and implementation of increasingly sophisticated techniques of social surveillance'. This is not the place to carry further a discussion of profiling, but it is important to note that, in Dale's view [36], 'there is a broad ideology in which (the TVEI criteria) are rooted', and that 'the medium through which this broad ideology is often made especially evident in TVEI schools is the development of profiling'. Dale argues that, if we are to catch 'the central thrust of TVEI ideology', we must look at its connection with the 'new FE' pedagogy, which:

> stresses the extrinsic rather than the intrinsic value and importance of education. It is based on the teaching of courses with specific skill and/or knowledge targets ... In terms of pedagogy, too, the emphasis is on the instrumental value of education for students. This places the students at the centre of their own learning and sees them negotiating their own curriculum ...

What is of great interest here is the way in which phrases like 'negotiating their own curriculum' and 'learning how to learn' – which one might suppose are to do with an *intrinsic*, person-centred view of education, turn out in the distorting lens of TVEI ideology to be about the very reverse – about education as an *extrinsic* good, justified in terms of skills and profilable properties and achievements. Here then, in the concept of 'the profile' is not only a vital aspect of TVEI but also a crucially important engine for creating the ambiguity within TVEI, and which allows it to draw support from such diverse interests.

This discussion arose from considering the use of computers, and attempts to introduce IT within and around TVEI schemes are a central part of TVEI. It appeals to those who see high tech as a good in itself. It also gains adherents from a scheme sponsored by the Royal Society of Arts under the heading 'Education for Capability'. Periodically advertisements appear in the press under this heading, stating that 'the imbalance ... described by the two words "education" and "training" ... is harmful to individuals, to industry and to society'. It argues for personal capability in 'the formulation and solution of problems ... in fact, constructive and creative activity of all sorts', and that 'there exists in its own right a culture which is concerned with doing, making and organizing'. As a result, 'education should spend more time in teaching people skills and preparing them for life outside the education system', and such a 're-balancing' would enable the country to 'benefit significantly in economic terms'. There follows a long list of signatories, ranging from leading industrialists, air marshals and Members of Parliament to polytechnic principals and retired civil servants. The distinctive, and ultimately unhelpful, aspects of this approach are the emphasis on skills; the blurring of the distinction between education and training; and the notion that 'doing, making and organizing' constitute a separate culture from 'the idea of the "educated man"'. What is surprising is not that this line of reasoning should appeal to captains of industry, but that it should be accepted so uncritically by a number of educational figures.

The scheme is inspired by the analysis of Britain's decline offered by such writers as Martin Wiener [37] and Corelli Barnett: that our economic weakness is due to an anti-industrial culture with its roots in education. Barnett asserts that 'Education for capability alone can keep Britain an advanced technological society and save her from being a Portugal, perhaps even an Egypt, of tomorrow'[38]. The thesis, as Michael Golby suggests in his contribution to this book, has been accepted much too uncritically. The schools of Japan and West Germany show none of the attributes of 'Education for Capability', yet both countries are economic success stories. Compared with the fiscal, social, political and economic factors which bear on Britain's industrial performance, bringing more computers into schools is very small beer – a cosmetic touch that deflects attention from the real issues. As for the central Wiener-Barnett doctrine, its interpretation of nineteenth-century English technical education and our industrial performance is, at the least, speculative. In an important study, Nicholas[39] concludes – from consideration of the economic and historical evidence – that:

> There is no clear-cut evidence that the greater resources costs and the foregone investment alternatives under state-financed technical education would have been offset by the advantages of having more trained engineers.

This argument is far from academic: it is directly apposite to current circumstances and the unchallenged way in which TVEI gains support because it is a scheme to make schools more technical. For Nicholas points out that 'In economics there is no free lunch; more technical education could only come at the expense of other socially desirable investments'. The real cost of TVEI has yet to be reckoned.

Another organization which should be mentioned as forming – or tending to form – part of the constituency of support for TVEI is the 'Centre for the Study of Comprehensive Schools' – (CSCS), based in offices at the University of York. The CSCS[40]:

> was established in 1980 to develop the standards of Comprehensive Schools by the study and dissemination of good practice, by developing new initiatives and improving cooperation between Secondary Education, Industry, Commerce, Business and Higher and Further Education.

Schools and LEAs subscribe to the centre, which keeps a register of examples of 'good practice', and which is directed by a seconded secondary head on an annual basis. The centre relies, in part at least, on funds from industry and runs conferences and workshops on such themes as 'Commerce and education', and 'School–industry links'. Funds made available, for instance, by British Petroleum have financed twenty-nine grants to 'small-scale curriculum development projects' in schools, under the headings of 'community links, industrial links, in-service training, micro-technology, profiling, skills, and special needs'. In 1984, the centre's director identified 'regional networks, consultancy and industrial partnership' as directions for growth. The centre's report of the 1984 joint workshop with BP declared that:

> Schools and industry should be mutually interdependent and work in partnership ... CSCS and BP recognize that schools and industry face common concerns ... These five contemporary issues of management in schools correspond closely to issues in industry:
> Management of declining resources ...
> Management of a changing market ...
> Management of staff development ...
> Management of conflicting viewpoints ...
> Management of technological change ...

It would, of course, be absurd to suggest that schools have nothing to learn from other organizations, of which industry is one kind; or that schools should isolate themselves from their community, of which industry forms one part. But it is another matter to identify the shared interests of schools and industry so closely that the fundamental moral difference between an organization which exists to help the young make considered choices about how to live, and one which exists to make a profit for its shareholders, may seem of secondary importance. The conflation of the two is not unfashionable: Sir Keith Joseph has himself observed that 'Schools should preach the moral virtue of free enterprise and the pursuit of profit'[41]. But it seems important that an organization dedicated to improving 'the standards of comprehensive schools', yet dependent on financial support from industry, should show some readiness to examine the issue. The centre's identification with TVEI is evident from the 1984 director's report:

> Any current view from the Centre must include the fact that this September sees a large expansion in the number of schools and local authorities involved in the TVEI schemes ... It is equally true that many more schools in many more LEAs are busily concerned with such matters as assessment and profiling, experiential learning, curriculum negotiating, management of learning, problem-solving, industrial links and modular programmes ... All these schools need to make a success of these ventures ...

One source of support, then, for TVEI is the technological imperative and industrialism as an instrumental end of schooling. In sharp contrast to this, and arising from educational institutions rather than from industry, the TVEI finds favour with individuals of a broadly 'progressivist' turn of mind. For them, vocationalism is less an end than a means by which desirable reforms in classroom practice may be brought about. Some teachers, of course, will resent criticism of the TVEI because it brings in money, or because it seems to be a way of helping pupils find jobs (albeit at the expense of their contemporaries, since neither the TVEI nor the MSC is able to create new jobs). But the more emotional support for TVEI – possibly the factor which makes it seem 'not a scheme but a concept' – taps that vein of 'child-centredness' which fitfully breaks through English school practice, and which – allied to clear-sighted understanding of educational purpose – can contribute greatly to the quality of teaching and learning . Profiles and records of achievement are TVEI devices that draw support from this source. But if these invaluable methods are seen as themselves constitutive of educational ends – as, for example, in the Goldsmith's College 'Interdisciplinary Enquiry' (IDE) approach of the late 1960s – then important questions arise about the nature of these ends.

What cannot be doubted, though, is the unwavering personal commitment such approaches can inspire, once the conditions for nourishing them emerge. In the 1960s, they conformed with optimism about youth and the growth of a youth culture. In the 1980s, they owe much to the evident inadequacy of an academic curriculum as a basis for comprehensive schooling. As the HMI secondary survey confirmed[42], this grammar-school model has been extended across the whole ability range, not least because it finds favour with parents and politicians alike. The defects of this subject-based, examination-led model were overlooked all the while school leavers managed to find jobs. It was still possible for teachers to validate it by giving education an instrumental purpose – it served the extrinsic good of passing examinations. But in the indigent 1980s a fresh, but equally instrumental, motivation appears to be the easy answer. This – like the CGLI courses which prefigured it – is just what the TVEI appears to offer. Here are abundant funds for courses with practical emphasis, along with an exciting new vocabulary to justify them. The government, it seems, is endorsing activities which directly challenge the effete, liberal humanism of the grammar school. In come workshops, computers and residential courses: out go chalk and talk, passive pupils and pedagogues. There is more than a whiff, too, of a new togetherness, of youth movements in general and the ethics of Baden-Powell in particular. Specific competencies, 'skills for living' are defined, 'learning by doing' is encouraged, and there is a wholesome emphasis on personal development and the community. An 11–16 programme based on criterion-referenced tests and personal profiles might well be termed the 'Brownie-badge' curriculum. The latent influence on English education of romantic ideas of chivalry, noted by Frank Musgrove[43], should be seen as a part of this nexus.

It would be desirable, at this point, to support this conjecture by reference to official justification of TVEI in educational terms. I am unaware of any such, but it is interesting to consider a document *Implementing the 14–18 Curriculum: New Approaches*, circulated by the Schools Council in 1983, which does not make specific reference to the TVEI but which clearly shares its assumptions and language, and which has been associated with local intiatives directed towards a more vocational curriculum 14–16[44]. The 'main curriculum ideas' it promotes include:

> experience-based learning; personal and social development; negotiated curriculum; profiling; graded assessment; learning from the workplace; basic skills of literacy and numeracy; community involvement; using residential experience ...

The document advocates 'a style of curriculum which is appropriate right across the ability and age range'. It asserts that:

> General vocational courses are more attractive to young people precisely because they build on the motivation of getting a job and becoming independent ... Even when jobs are hard to come by ... they too are concerned about living in a real world, doing, making and being active. It is this motivation which needs to be harnessed.

As Ruth Jonathan remarks in her study of the Youth Training Scheme 'core skills' programme, ' "relevance" and "usefulness" are very dangerous criteria for learning programmes to adopt'. Equally dangerous, too, are statements such as:

> The background theory ... characterizes an approach where experience comes first and theory then follows, so that *experience determines what is to be studied* rather than study determining experience' (italics added).

If this means anything, it seems to advance a kind of 'happenstance curriculum' in which learning is contingent on something interesting turning up. One's worst fears are confirmed by the examples given of actual 'curriculum responses': in one school, 'at the Gold level of the Home Skills section', the pupil is required to carry out such tasks as 'make and wire a lamp' or ' construct a fence'. An implicit behaviourism in this skills–based approach is evident from the injunction that 'The objectives need always to be specified in terms of what the student will be able to do as a consequence of the instruction'. All in all, the bold claims made in this document seem to rest on a slender basis of reasoning.

A personal defence of TVEI has been offered by Richard Pring, a philosopher of education, who sees the scheme:

> as a catalyst that, within a system which for too long has been captivated by a narrowing and inadequate notion of 'liberal education', has stimulated a vigorous and ... imaginative reappraisal of the curriculum and of the educational purposes which it should serve[45].

Assuredly, Pring is right to identify a faulty interpretation of liberal education as the root cause of defects in the secondary curriculum. But what is the nature of the 'reappraisal', the 'educational purposes', which TVEI is applying to the problem? And how likely is it that the 'catalytic effect' of TVEI in solving it will be sustained? The point about a catalyst is that it is essential to the reaction it promotes. Once the catalyst of TVEI funding is withdrawn, the logic of the metaphor is that its effects will peter out. I shall consider this issue of the replicability and sustaining power of TVEI in a moment. For now, we need to know more about the interpretation of liberal education celebrated by TVEI.

One would expect some kind of reasoning to be offered which examines what might be meant by liberal education, what meanings it offers to pupils, what moral principles it embodies. But Pring's account is not like this at all: it consists simply of a list of social and economic factors prominent at the present time:

> Postponed entry into employment, prospects of unemployment, ... the increasing technological base of industry ... all these should enter into that continuing educational debate about aims and values.

He concludes by stating that 'TVEI, *whatever the social function it might eventually serve*, has forced us to reconceptualize processes through which we educate young people' (my emphasis). The means, in other words, justifies the end: we need not worry too much about the social functions of TVEI, as long as it makes us respond to the 'increasing technological base of industry' and all the other transient, empirical factors which appear to constitute the sole 'educational purposes' of TVEI. One would have thought that an undertaking as fundamental as the reconceptualization of liberal education would call for some *a priori* reasoning about the nature of education and the good of man. But it appears that the good of man is constituted in a kind of *effectiveness*: as long as we introduce new learning processes which reflect current preoccupations, all will be well. It is difficult to give much weight to this argument.

Some reservations

There is, of course, nothing at all new about any of the approaches that have been described. Most obviously, the MSC's commitment to make schools more like industry harks back to the utilitarian business ethic which began to influence schooling in North America in the early years of this century, and of which Callahan's study concluded[46]:

> The tragedy itself was fourfold: that educational questions were subordinated to business considerations; that administrators were produced who were not, in any sense, true educators; that a scientific label was put on some very unscientific and dubious methods and practices; and that an anti-intellectual climate, already prevalent, was strengthened.

The concern of the FEU to identify skills and break them down into finite bits which then, paradoxically, add up to some form of transferable capacity has its antecedents in the work of Bobbitt and his imitators, who sought to put industrialism on a securer educational footing in the US by applying what they saw as scientific methods of rational analysis to school experience. Thus Bobbit declared that[47]:

> Activity analysis is the beginning of all curriculum-making. Find the activities which men perform, or those which they should perform: and train for those.

It is strange that the fashions of fifty or sixty years ago should be found so irresistible to planners whose starting point is the challenge of new technology and the need for radical new solutions.

As for the progressivist belief in a kind of born-again secondary-modern-school, activity-based cure for curriculum problems, of the kind represented by the Schools Council document, we have no need to look beyond these shores. It is strongly reminiscent of the doctrine advanced by Sir Percy Nunn in the 1930s and 1940s, who considered that[48]:

> School teaching would be immensely more efficient if teachers could learn to exploit the intellectual energy released so abundantly in play ... The child's impulses to experiment with life should be taken as our guide in teaching him ... We have seen that the boy scout training succeeds on its intellectual side precisely because it follows this policy; what is needed is in effect an extension of the same policy throughout the curriculum ...

Although the amalgam of supportive positions loosely identified with the TVEI might be termed progressivist, it is important to note that the progressive movement in education often associated with Dewey has nothing in common with this strange mixture of industrial training and experience-led learning which the TVEI aspires to. Dewey himself was quite explicit in rejecting what he saw as[9]:

> (S)kill or technical method at the expense of meaning ... It is not the business of education to foster this tendency ... The educative process is its own end ... To predetermine some future occupation ... is to reduce the adequacy for a future right employment ... Such training ... will be at the expense of those qualities of alert observation and coherent and ingenious planning which make an occupation intellectually rewarding.

As a result, however, of the very confusion Dewey abhors, it is possible for the MSC to claim that 'The changes in the curriculum as a result of TVEI go beyond any narrow definition of technical and vocational education'[50].

Yet any such changes are unlikely to affect the curriculum for the ablest pupils. Any hopes that the TVEI is seen by the government as a means of abolishing the subject-based grammar-school style of curriculum have been dashed by its recent decisions. The intention seems to be to foster different forms of curriculum – each broad enought to warrant the vague description of 'general education' – for different pupil streams. The preservation of the grammar-school stream for the most able accords with Sir Keith Joseph's decision to introduce 'distinction' and 'merit' categories in the new GCSE examination at 16-plus for pupils performing at a high level in seven or so subjects. Not only will this encourage schools to form elite sets or streams: it will make it virtually impossible for an able pupil to take the TVEI programme and at the same time secure a distinction or merit category.[51] This is totally in line wiht the view of David Young at the time the TVEI was launched[52]:

> But on further questioning Mr Young said the scheme was not intended for pupils who were taking good O and A levels. 'They are not going to join the scheme. My concern is for those who are bright and able and haven't been attracted by academic subjects ...

Subsequently this line of argument was softened and the official TVEI literature stresses its formal appeal to pupils of all abilities. But in the context of other political decisions – for example, the introduction of the new AS level at 18-plus will further buttress the A-level routes for the ablest pupils – there seems little doubt that the bright pupil who opts for TVEI will be denied access to the prizes which await the traditional academic student. It is not without significance that no independent school has shown an interest in adopting the TVEI, neither has the government indicated its readiness to make cash available to these schools. Yet the justification of the Assisted Places Scheme is to enable bright pupils from the maintained sector to benefit from an allegedly superior education. And since the TVEI is proclaimed to be such, it seems surprising that its benefits are denied to them.

The reality of government policy was, in fact, revealed by Lord Young upon his appointment, in the autumn 1985 Cabinet reshuffle, as Secretary of State for Employment[53]:

> My idea is that, at the end of the decade, there is a world in which 15 per cent of our young go into higher education ... roughly the same proportion as now. Another 30 to 35 per cent will stay on doing the TVEI, along with other courses, ending up with a mixture of vocational and academic qualifications and skills. The remainder, about half, will go on to two-year YTS.

Nothing could be a plainer statement of tripartism than this, with its restriction of access to higher education, its Victorian separation of the bottom half for menial tasks, and TVEI as a programme for the twenty-first century equivalent of artisans and tradesmen. The bright vision of the TVEI turns out to be a rerun of an old – and very bad – movie. The two operational devices for securing this are now apparent. One is the continual funding of TVEI, as Davies notes[54]:

> As, by 1985, TVEI moved from its ostensibly pilot-scheme stage into virtually all LEAs, the chances of its developing along more selective and elitist lines certainly increased substantially. 'Tripartism' lived again, though no offical announcement or damaging political debate about its revival had either occurred or been necessary.

The second device is the CTCs, announced as a post-election Conservative initiative which will run in parallel with selection 'at age 11 or 12' into different schools or streams[55]. The ground for these was prepared by TVEI not only by the segmentation of pupils inherent in all vocational programmes, and which the CTCs can now institutionalize; it is now clear that the contractual basis of TVEI – of, in effect, hiring schools through LEAs to carry out specific kinds of programmes – has directly paved the way for the CTCs, which will be run by trusts of local business people and other worthies, funded directly by central government under contract and independent of LEAs. Some of us argued, from the start, that TVEI was a trojan horse: but the full extent of its achievement in undermining the 1944 settlement and replacing it with a new instrumentalism is only now becoming evident.

But hindsight can be misleading, and everything about TVEI – the haste with which it was cobbled together, the flights of rhetorical fancy it has promoted – suggests that it was born not of quiet conspiracy but of 'shoot-from-the-hip' dogma, well in the forefront of 'new-Right' thinking ever since the first 1969 Black Paper and forming an unholy alliance with the centralism of DES officials and the 'act first, ask questions afterwards' pragmatism of the MSC. It is a serious constitutional weakness in Britain that such costly and damaging innovation can be launched with negligible consultation. For it is notably easy to whip up support for vacationalism, and much harder – as Norton Grubb, the American researcher into the phenomenon, has noted – to counter it[56]:

> There is almost no constituency to resist vocationalism ... The short-run appeal of vocationalism is irresistible but the long-run consequences may be unfortunate ... The power of vocationalism manifests capitalism's ability to bend institutions to its end, but to do so in a way that is collectively irrational, in a way that makes these institutions less useful in the long run.

It might be helpful to draw an analogy from another field of public service. In the 1960s, high-rise blocks as a solution to the housing problem were given almost universal acclaim. There were architects and planners to give them professional respectability; there was the modernistic appeal of using 'the white heat of technology', and – most important of all – there were liberal grants of government money to silence the doubters. Yet the technology was inadequate, professional opinion proved to be fickle, and the underlying argument – that the existing stock of inner-city housing was incapable of improvement on the scale required – turned out to be false, when it was eventually submitted to proper scrutiny. But the whole formulation blended myth and technological magic so irresistibly that it commanded the political intervention of central government. Twenty years on, exactly the reverse is true: any present-day politician who sought to defend the tower blocks would be digging his ministerial grave.[57]

It is not too fanciful to see parallels here with the TVEI, which rests ultimately (as does the YTS, for that matter) on the totally unproven proposition that transferable high-level skills exist and can be made a satisfactory basis for general education, while preparing students for an unpredictable world. But the rational basis of the TVEI is no more evident than was that of high-rise housing: the power of new fashions and formulas derives not from reason, but from their appeal to basic fears and desires, and the need to latch on to certainties in a world dominated by ambiguity.

Evaluating TVEI

Reference has been made to some of the evaluation studies of TVEI. Fourth-year pupils entering the first cohort in 1983 moved into the sixth form or college in September 1985; second cohort pupils transferred in the autumn of 1986. Very little information has been made available about this transition, but the evaluation bulletin of November 1984 of the 14–19 curriculum development unit at St Martin's College, Lancaster had identified the importance of this stage:

> The danger is that TVEI may in some authorities evolve as a 2 + 2 year project rather than a coherent four year progression. Nothing would be more inimical to its principles than to build on to a stimulating two year programme in school a stultifying traditional FE vocational package ...

This is not quite the case: even more inimical would be the defection of TVEI pupils out of the 14–18 course entirely, with no further education of any kind. Yet it is clear that to a large extent this is exactly what has happened. The published MSC figures do not, unfortunately, distinguish between students staying with the TVEI scheme and those leaving it but choosing other FE courses. Even so,

> The number who have decided to stay on ... fluctuates wildly from LEA to LEA and even from school to school ... In Birmingham 65 per cent stayed on, while in neighbouring Sandwell the figure is only 26 per cent ... There is no national picture to be drawn from the figures[58].

This will, of course, be a feature of TVEI generally: the scheme is not the sum of its parts, but a pot-pourri of separate efforts. Few, if any, general conclusions are likely to emerge. Some of the individual accounts will be of interest as case studies, but evaluating the work of the evaluators will be particularly vital, since the formative evaluation favoured by TVEI inevitably has the effect of making the evaluators to some extent part of the scheme; indeed, some TVEI evaluators have made no secret of their support for the initiative.

Measures, therefore, which permit some comparison with public norms are useful and the transition of 16-year-old pupils presents such an opportunity. The figures for the first cohort of the Exeter scheme – one of those in the first TVEI round, and exceptionally well funded – repay study. A report to Devon Education Committee[59] finds, first, that 'the overall GCE/CSE results of the Exeter high schools in 1984 and 1985 are virtually identical'. So the expenditure on the 268 TVEI pupils who sat these examinations in 1985 of at least ten times as much per head as on their classmates resulted in no improvement in performance. This is surprising, since the experience of those schools undertaking coherent curriculum improvement is, generally, that improved examination results are an incidental benefit. They are not the main aim of the exercise, but there is usually some knock-on advantage, even if attributable solely to the Hawthorne effect. And usually such innovations proceed with little extra funding; yet the Exeter TVEI had the advantage of MSC expenditure of £3.9m over five years, leading to new equipment, extra teachers, and teaching groups of twelve or less. And interim evaluation reports talked of increased pupil motivation and new teaching strategies not only among the TVEI pupils but across the non-TVEI curriculum as well. The explanation may lie in the point already made: TVEI, even with abounding resources and teacher commitment, only addresses the superficialities of content and method. It does not articulate them with fundamental issues of curriculum purpose and structure, and therefore its effects – whatever agreeable impressions of pupil motivation may be given to visitors and evaluators – are evanescent and insubstantial.

Second, only one-third of the cohort elected to continue with the 14–18 TVEI course on leaving the 12–16 high schools and transferring to Exeter tertiary college. (Moreover, most of these were girls, showing that TVEI has in this case had no effect on sex bias at 16–plus transfer to full-time education). A further 9 per cent went on to further education at the college but withdrew from the TVEI scheme. Even if we add these to the total, the aggregate participation rate of 43.5 per cent is not impressive for such a heavily funded scheme. On this evidence, claims that TVEI will lead to fundamental changes in attitudes to technical and vocational education look far-fetched, and the notion of the '14–18 curriculum' seems to have little meaning for students, whatever fancies it may have inspired among politicians and others.

Another third of the original cohort have no job, yet have abandoned post-16 education to join YTS training schemes. In his 1984 speech to the Royal Society of Arts, Lord Young declared that 'TVEI is essentially concerned with educating people, about broaden the curriculum to give them new subjects'. The YTS scheme is nothing like this: it is about using the workplae to train for specific jobs. It is inconceivable to suppose that forsaking TVEI for YTS amounts to anything less than a resounding vote against TVEI.

Of the 20 per cent who found jobs at 16-plus, the majority are in the service industries. There is a similar bias in the options of those staying in FE (as part of TVEI, or otherwise). Not one of those students chose, for example, the BTEC at National Level in computing, despite the heavy emphasis on computing and keyboard skills in the 14–16 Exeter TVEI programme. Unsurprisingly, this is entirely in line with American experience of pre-16 vocationalism: it shows 'an inability to address the structural conditions of the labour markets for youth'[60].

A third finding concerned another effect noted in the US – that vocationalism creates 'a dual schooling system' and 'sorts students' so as to form 'a caste system in which social class and curriculum (are) related'. At first, the impression was given that the initial Exeter cohort conformed to national TVEI criteria, and fully represented the whole range of ability. Thus a commentator on TVEI could write 'Devon has recruited 24 per cent of its first intake from the top ability range'[61]. Certainly there has been no suggestion that the cohort was secondary-modern rather than comprehensive in character.

In explaining the 16-plus figures, however, the official report admits that although 'there was a breadth of ability in the cohort', it was 'not randomly distributed'. Very few pupils, it declares, 'were likely to gain very high academic qualifications at 16-plus'. All this confirms the suspicion – as indeed, Lord Young now admits is the case – that TVEI will appeal to the middle and lower ranges of ability and is expected to do so. Since it confronts none of the central questions and assumptions about secondary education, it can hardly do otherwise, whatever resources are poured into it.

Implications for the future

When all the apologists and evangelists for TVEI have had their say, there are three or four basic issues which have to be faced.

First, the TVEI is the result of a central act of government, introduced without consultation and operated by a largely non-accountable body directed not by education but by employment. This raises questions about the way state education should be run in a democracy, about the propriety of centralized control, and the extent to which the concerns of industry should govern educational programmes.

The growth of central government control over education in the last six years has attracted comment[62]. The 1985 White Paper, for example, while increasing the sum of money available to LEAs for in-service education, requires that prior approval for each project be obtained from the DES. And not only must the new GCSE grades in each subject correspond to nationally agreed, DES approved content criteria; HMI are producing a series of statements setting out detailed aims and objectives in each subject[63]. The UK will shortly become the only developed country with a nationally controlled curriculum and a nationally controlled examination system at 16-plus to back it up. Apart from the disturbing political implications of a centrally determined school system, we must ask whether the nature of education is such that teachers can be regarded merely as the means by which centrally defined curricula are implemented, rather than ends in themselves[64].

The TVEI brings these issues to a sharp focus, partly because of the way in which it is administered and funded, and partly because it is expressly directed towards 'education in which the students are concerned to acquire generic or specific skills with a view to employment'[65], and not towards the development of pupils as sutonomous moral agents. The following passage from *Soviet Weekly* seems disagreeably familiar[66]:

> Schools in the Soviet Union are to have a new course on 'rudiments of production and choice of profession' ... The decision was made by the

Communist Party of the Soviet Union central committee and the Soviet government last week, as part of a resolution on improving work training, education and professional orientation of schoolchildren and organizing their socially useful productive work.

Second, it is easy to forget, amid the talk of 'negotiated curriculum' and 'experiential learning', that the TVEI exists to make the curriculum – for some, if not for all – more techincal and more vocational. The justification for this cannot be taken as self-evident. If the 'technical' part of the curriculum refers to the techno-aesthetic area of creative activities and design, then it is the case that many schools have, over the last five years or so, made provision for all pupils to engage in these activities 11–16, and have generally done so by considering the educational benefit conferred by such experiences. The main difficulty schools encounter is not in setting up such schemes, but in finding the money for the materials needed to run them. The TVEI does nothing to help them. If, on the other hand, 'technical' work is to be related to vocational interests, this raises again the question of whether skills-based curricula have any educational value.

The main reason offered for technical and vocational programmes is that they will equip students for jobs and benefit the economy. But it is significant that in Japan, the most successful capilist economy, 'Technology teaching is primitive ... There are no computers in classrooms'[67]. Moreover, the MSC has itself acknowledged that the Japanese are making 'no serious attempt at "vocationalizing" school education ... The emphasis in education is towards even greater generalization, rather than specialization'[68]. Post-16 education continues to be broad, but with a vocational emphasis. In effect, the Japanese do not enter the labour market much before the age of twenty. This approach to education and training is in stark contrast with the bifurcated West German system – an academic route for the ablest, and a technical route for the others – which seems to correspond with MSC thinking. The TVEI is evidently a key part of this hidden agenda. Yet there must be doubts about the suitability of this essentially nineteenth-century model at a time of rapid change, and about the willingness of British industry to accept the huge training costs it implies[69]. So one is inexorably led to question the TVEI not only on educational grounds, but on its value in strictly economic terms.

The *third* point has already been broached – the inherent divisiveness of the TVEI within the school system – but should perhaps be taken a little further in the light of this wider perspective. For observers who have hitherto kept an open mind on the MSC's involvement are now expressing doubts about the direction events are taking. Thus the editor of *The Times Educational Supplement* has commented, given the MSC's evident inclination towards a West German model[70]:

> What is clear is that if these recommendations are not followed by a more far-reaching reform of secondary education, aimed at keeping a much larger proportion of the age-group within the educational network ... then the recreation of elementary education is the logical expectation.

In similar vein, John Tomlinson – a co-signatory of the 'Education for Capability' manifesto – writes[71]:

> The present contradictions in the secondary curricuum require either a full-blooded acceptance of the logic of comprehensive education and the major development of post-secondary education and vocational training which should follow it (as in North America and Scandinavia) or a reversion to more highly differentiated secondary curricula, to elitist higher education, and a straified system of post-secondary technical and vocational education.

The crucial role of TVEI in vectoring the secondary system towards the latter, differentiated option has been recognized by Morris Kaufman who, as chief training adviser to an industrial training board, played a leading part in the production of a curriculum document expressly committed to promoting 'the range of skills, abilities and knowledge required to sustain and expand the productive power and prosperity of the nation'[72]. It is all the more remarkable, therefore, that Kaufman should now write of the TVEI[73]:

> What worries me is that it could well lead to a reversal of trends of the last few decades with a strengthening of the streams in schools ... The strengthening of the vocational element is more and more being seen in the narrow sense of job preparation ...

Given this, and Lord Young's own admissions about the tripartite role of TVEI, it seems extraordinary that the Labour Party has been reluctant to condemn it outright and supports it in some LEAs (such as Devon). The clue to its vacillations lies perhpas in the fact that, as Jackson[74] remarks, 'The MSC is the brainchild of the TUC ... Its creation is seen by the TUC establishment as a great historical achievement to be preserved at virtually any cost'. The problem for the Labour Party is that it needs trade union support, via the TUC: and the TUC, shorn of its beer-and-sandwiches-at-No. 10 closeness to central government, must cling to the MSC despite its manifestly undemocratic way of doing things, and its use by the Thatcher administration as a tool for government policy, as the sole remaining TUC link with the levers of power. For the Conservatives, the MSC provides unalloyed staisfaction: it is not merely the agent of employers, but a wonderfully unencumbered way of vocationalizing the maintained sector of schooling.

So for both major parties the MSC has much to offer. For the SDP, the High-tech aura of TVEI evidently has an appeal. Thus its spokesman Mrs Shirley Williams (a former Secretary of State for Education), while recognizing 'the least defensible and most damanging of all the divisions in our segregated education system, the academic–vocational divide', goes on to espouse 'the present government's commendable Technical and Vocational Education Initiative (TVEI). These courses should be available to all pupils aged 14 and above, including those on academic courses'[75].

This brings me to my *fourth* point: while Mrs Williams rightly notes that sixth form and tertiary colleges 'offer a solution' to the division between academic and vocational courses, she fails to see that 14–18 programmes like

TVEI prevent these developments 16–19. Not the least of TVEI's unfortunate effects is to sponsor talk of the 14–18 curriculum, thus muddying the waters and preventing the two pressing priorities from gaining attention: a common curriculum 11–16 and a coherent, comprehensive 16–19 tertiary system. The break at 16 makes historical, social and psychological sense, as the State of Victoria, Australia, has recognized[76]:

> The development of new structures at the post-compulsory level is now desirable in Victoria on curricular grounds ... The bringing together of larger numbers of students would enable ... students ... to sample or pursue alternative routes into major knowledge areas ... Secondary schools cover an age range from 11 to 19. There are difficulties in providing in institutions covering this age span the kinds of institutional and learning arrangements favoured by and appropriate to provisional and actual adults ... Equity considerations also add weight to the desirability of moving towards the creation of new educational structures.

It is of further significance that these proposals acknowledge that vocationalism is not the answer[77]:

> There is no reason why an education which is 'liberal' in the sense that it feeds informed reflection on the human condition and on how people live their lives should be abstracted from that condition and those realities or from the productive activities of the society

Equivalent vision is lacking in the UK, where the Labour Party 'Charter for pupils and parents' (April 1985) offers a characteristic fudging of the issue:

> We see the break at 16 as a half way marker within a coherent curriculum for 14 to 18 year olds. The curriculum which is offered to young people from 16 to 18 ... must be built on to the curriculum of the last two years of secondary education.

The need for clarity about the purpose of schooling leads to the *sixth* point: at root, TVEI is to do with an instrumental view of the business. Despite the ambiguities of its jargon, it is a hard-headed attempt to make compulsory education respond to industry's needs, at the expense of personal development. For the appeal of vocationalism, as Dale concedes[78], is that of a 'slogan system' with:

> an apparent surface appeal for a wide range of different constituencies who are each able to invest it with the capacity to ... fit in with their own interest ... TVEI incorporates the ambiguities inherent in the notion of vocational education ...

If TVEI had been introduced by an independent body like the CGLI, and funded from charitable institutions, one could hope that these ambiguities could be resolved in a liberal fashion; that the power of such devices as profiles and negotiation could become a virtue, and not a liability. But given its direct connection, through the MSC, with a government committed to radical right-wing dogma, one would have to be remarkably purblind not to see TVEI as a very serious, if not fatal, threat to a tradition of liberal education that has survived two world wars and the narrowness of the grammar-school curriculum, but may not yet survive the market-economy technocrats of the 1980s. There is a very real risk that, in the name of economic recovery, forms of schooling will be introduced which not only suppress personal growth but intrusively monitor and constrain it. In this regard, the close link between TVEI and computers takes on a sinister aspect.

My *final* point returns to the earlier issue of how much effect the TVEI, as an initiative designed to bring about profound change, is likely to have. As a 'catalyst', will it significantly alter school practice? The American experience, again, is useful here. It suggests that central interventions aimed at bringing about change in schools via regional bodies are unlikely to achieve much. The results of President Johnson's 'great society' programme of the 1960s were subject to careful scrutiny, and there is wide agreement that they are disappointing. Thus Fullan and Pomfret have written[79]:

> Less than a decade ago, commentary and research on planned school change revolved almost exclusively around specifying the properties of the innovation, assessing outcomes, and to a lesser extent, planning changes and getting people to try them.

This description of American styles of change in the mid-1960s seems very close to the style adopted for the TVEI in Britain in the mid-1980s. Fullan and Pomfret note that as a result of this approach, 'so many educational changes fail to become established'.

Should we conclude, then, that since the mechanism adopted to deliver the TVEI appears to be so inept, it can have no long-term effect, and therefore constitutes no threat? That at the end of the day, when all the millions of pounds have been spent, there will be little to show for it but hundreds of obsolete computers gathering dust in school cupboards?

Assuredly, studies of educational change repeatedly confirm that 'fidelity' – the reproduction in schools of the intentions formulated in central bureau – is virtually unattainable. The best that can be hoped for is 'mutual adaptation' – some compromise outcome as a result of school intervention, and which will generally be unpredictable. In the case of the TVEI, however, it has been argued here that it is not so much a new programme as a rekindling of old ideas in a new guise. Moreover, it is taking place in a political context which seems itself to hark back to tripartism and old solutions to new problems. Its intended effect is to vocationalize the curriculum for all pupils: if it succeeds in doing this, it will have failed to address the real problems of a core curriculum in an advanced industrial society. What is much more likely is that it will vocationalize at least part of the curriculum for some pupils, which might easily lead to alienation and social division if unemployment continues to grow.

Most seriously, the TVEI rhetoric fails to engage with the issues that must be confronted if the concept of the common school is to animate an appropriate curriculum. The TVEI replaces one instrumental model with another: instead of the grammar–school emphasis on knowledge for its own sake, it substitutes skills for their own sake. Inevitably, the expenditure of so much money and effort will bring about some good developments, and these must be welcomed. But once the funding is withdrawn and the Hawthorne effect wears off, the lack of clear educational purpose in the TVEI approach will show.

It is also a project rich in ironies. It offers a brightly burnished image of new technology and new jobs, but in reality has its roots in ideas which have been tried and found wanting. And in any event, for the million pupils who left school and looked for jobs in 1985, only five thousand jobs were available in information technology.

It is ironic, too, that so much money should be made available for curriculum change through the TVEI by an administration which repeatedly asserts that change can be achieved without extra money; and that, if the TVEI fails to promote change, it will only confirm that throwing money at a problem will solve nothing. Then there is the fact that, behind the grandiloquent language of TVEI, the reality of classroom experience is often either unremarkable or trivial[80]. Under the TVEI banner, pupils may be pursuing just the kind of non–cognitive, 'progressive' activities which were anathematized, in the 1969 Black Paper on Education, by right–wing politicians who now form part of the government[81].

Ultimately, though, the TVEI is a sad affair: partly because its funding could have been put to such better use, but also because, when the promised land fails to appear, the schools will be blamed for missing yet another irresistible opportunity. But TVEI will have left its mark on secondary education, and changed the politics of education. Schools will become much more subservient to national policies, and more inclined to view education as a utilitarian enterprise with extrinsic goals. Yet the real curriculum problems of mass education in a democracy will still be there, waiting to be tackled but now less tractable than they ever were.

Appendix: Aims and criteria of the TVEI

(These are taken from *TVEI Review* (1984), published by the MSC. I have italicized those statements which directly indicate the technical and vocational nature of the initiative.)

Aims
(a) In conjunction with LEAs to explore and test ways of organizing and managing the education of 14–18 year old young people across the ability range so that:

    1 more of them are attracted to seek the qualifications/skills which will be *of direct value to them at work* and more of them achieve these qualifications and skills;

2 they are better equipped to enter *the world of employment* which will await them;

3 they acquire a more direct appreciation of the practical application of the qualifications for which they are working;

4 they become accustomed to using their *skills and knowledge to solve the real-world problems they will meet at work*;

5 more emphasis is placed on developing initiative, motivation and enterprise as well as problem-solving skills and other aspects of personal development;

6 the construction of the bridge from education to work is begun earlier by giving these young people the opportunity to have direct contact and *training/planned work experience* with a numbr of local employers *in the relevant specialisms*;

7 there is close collaboration between local education authorities and industry/commrce/public services etc so that *the curriculum has industry's confidence*.

(b) To undertake (a) in such a way that:

1 the detailed aims can be achieved quickly and cost-effectively;

2 the educational lessons learned can be readily applied in other localities and to other groups among the 14–18 years olds;

3 the educational structures/schemes established to further the aims of the initiative should be consistent with progressive developments in *skill and vocational training* outside the school environment, existing *vocational education* for under 16 year-old people, and higher education;

4 emphasis is placed on careful monitoring and evaluation;

5 individual projects are managed at local level;

6 the overall conduct, assessment and development of the initiative can be assessed and monitored by the MSC and the TVEI Unit it has established for this purpose.

Criteria

The pilot projects selected will represent a variety of approaches to the provision of full-time general, *technical and vocational* studies which are adapted to the varying abilities and interests of young people aged 14–18. 'Vocational education' is to be interpreted as education in which the students are concerned to acquire *generic or specific skills with a view to employment*. Projects should cater for students across the ability range, having regard to the need for project courses to lead to nationally recognized qualifications: the balance between what is offered for different ability levels is expected to vary between projects. Consideration should also be given to accommodating some students with special educational needs.

Content of programmes

Each project should comprise one or more sets of full-time progrmmes with the following characteristics;

1 Equal opportunities should be available to young people of both sexes and they should normally be educated together on courses within each project. Care should be taken to avoid sex stereotyping;

2 They should provide four-year curricula, with progression from year to year, *designed to prepare the student for particular aspects of employment* and for adult life in a society liable to rapid change;

3 They should have clear and specific objectives, including the objectives of encouraging initiative, problem-solving abilities, and other aspects of personal development;

4 The balance between the general, technical and vocational elements of programmes should vary according to students' individual needs and the stage of the course, but throughout the programme there should be both a general and a *technical/vocational element*:

5 The technical and vocational elements shoud be *broadly related to potential employment opportunities* within and outside the geographical area for the young people concerned;

6 There should be appropriate *planned work experience* as an integral part of the programmes, from the age of 15 onwards, bearing in mind the provisions of the Education (Work Experience) Act 1973;

7 Courses offered should be capable of being linked effectively with *subsequent training/educational opportunities*;

8 Arrangements should be made for regular assessment and for students and tutors to discuss students' performance/progress. Each student, and his or her parents, should also receive a periodic written assesment, and have an opportunity to discuss this assessment with the relevant project teachers. Good career and educational counselling will be essential.

(The following sections in the TVEI document deal with 'Qualifications to be attained', 'Institutional arrangements', 'Resources', and 'Local support arrangements'. These have not been reproduced here.)

Notes and references

1 For an amusing yet sharp analysis of the MSC's rapid if unrewarding growth, see Coffield, F. (1984), 'Is there work after the MSC?', *New Society*, 26 January.
2 Dale, R. (1986). 'Examining the gift-horse's teeth: a tentative analysis of TVEI', in Walker, S. and Barton, L. (eds) *Youth, Unemployment and Schooling,* Milton Keynes, Open University Press. The interest of Dale's account lies in his involvement in a TVEI evaluation project.
3 McCulloch, G. (1986). 'Policy, politics and education; the TVEI', in *Journal of Education Policy*, vol. 1 no. 1, 35–52.
4 Valuable accounts are given in Reid, W. A. and Filby, J. (1982), *The Sixth: An Essay in Democracy and Education*, Falmer; and in Reid, W.A. 'Curriculum change and the evolution of educational constituencies: the English sixth form in the nineteenth century' in Goodson, I. (ed.), *Social Histories of the Secondary Curriculum*, Falmer.
5 The quotations are taken from Minute EO/86/315, dated 9 September 1986, of the Further Education Sub-Committee of Devon Education Committee.
6 See, for example, Holt, M. (1982), 'The great education robbery', *The Times Educational Supplement*, 3 December; and Baker, B. (1985), 'Is TVEI compatible with comprehensive principles?', *Comprehensive Education*, 48, January.

7 Frith, D. (1983). 'Caught between opposing forces', *The Times Educational Supplement*, 21 January.

8 Jones A. (1983). 'Door need not close when Young comes in', *The Times Educational Supplement*, 7 January.

9 Both the School of Education, University of Exeter, and St Martin's College, Lancaster, are evaluating local TVEI projects and have published interim reports.

10 BBC television, on the other hand, has transmitted three programmes which take a critical look at TVEI. In January 1983, *Panorama* presented 'Good enough for your child'; in January 1984, the Continuing Education Department presented 'Education: for what?'; and in February 1985, *Open Space* devoted its progrmme 'Class encounters of a secondary kind' to TVEI.

11 The quotation comes from an undated (but c. 1979) CGLI leaflet 'Foundation for a Career'. It describes a Foundation Course as 'a coherent course of grouped and interrelated components'. The leaflet is striking for its direct, clear exposition and freedom from the jargon of later, post-FEU writing.

12 The 1963 Newsom Report *Half Our Future* addressed the needs of pupils 13–16 'of average or less than average ability'. It recommended 'a choice of programme, including a range of courses broadly related to occupational interests' (p. xvi). When I went to an Oxfordshire 11–18 comprehensive as deputy head in 1966, I found 'Newsom courses' for the 'Newsom children' an option on the fourth year timetable. Topics like 'Communication' and 'Design for Living' occupied double- and treble-period slots, and were often team-taught by teachers on a cross-curricular basis. Girls attended a child-care course to which mothers brought their babies for what would now be called 'experiential learning'. It is worth adding that Newsom also recommended an 'internal leaving certificate, combining an internal assessment with a general school record' (p. xvii).

13 From R.H. Tawney's *Secondary Education for All* (1922), quoted in Max Morris's excellent article 'Vocational preparation and the wisdom of the tawney owl', *Education* 3.5.85, p. 397.

14 Newspaper accounts at the time indicated that the TVEI was the result of an after-dinner conversation between Mr. Tebbit, Mr. Young and Mrs. Thatcher, and that Sir Keith Joseph was informed later.

15 It is not clear whether the money for TVEI is part of normal budget expenditure, and therefore diverted from existing allocations, or whether it derives in part at least, via the MSC, from EEC training budgets and must be spent on programmes that are essentially vocational in nature.

16 For a penetrating study of this issue, see Jonathan, R. (1983). 'The manpower service model of education', *Cambridge Journal of Education*, autumn.

17 Hart, W.A. (1978) 'Against skills', *Oxford Review of Education*, vol. 4, no. 2, p. 206.

18 Williams, J. (1984). 'Abergele – trail blazers in TVEI', *The Careers and Guidance Teacher*, spring.

19 See, for example, Holt, M. (1978), *The Common Curriculum: Its Structure and Style in the Comprehensive School*. London, Routledge & Kegan Paul.

20 *Improving Secondary Schools*, (1984), (Hargreaves report), London, ILEA, p. 74.

21 Holt, M. (1980). *The Tertiary Sector*. London, Hodder and Stoughton, pp. 113–130.

22 Dearden, R. (1984). 'Education and training', *Westminster Studies in Education,* vol. 7, p. 58.

23 Veronica Kotziamani, deputy head of Hurlingham and Chelsea School, quoted in *The Times Educational Supplement*, 29.11.85, p. 15.

24 Ainley, P. (1985). 'The modules are coming', *The Times Educational Supplement*, 6 December.

25 See, for example, *TVEI Bulletin No. 12* (1984), St Martin's College Lancaster 14–19 Curriculum Development Unit, November, p. 35 ff.

26 Chitty, C. (1986). 'TVEI: the MSC's trojan horse', in Benn, C. and Fairley, J. (eds.), *Challenging the MSC*, London, Pluto Press.

27 AMMA (undated, but c. 1985). *Report to Members,* no. 15.

28 In 'chairman's foreword' to *TVEI Review 1984*, MSC.

29 Jackson, D. (1984). 'TVEI – the school's experience', *Contributions* No. 7, winter, CSCS.

30 Report of speech to the Institute of Directors (1985), *Daily Telegraph*, 19 March.

31 As reported in *Education*, 1.2.85.

32 FEU (1982). *Progressing from Vocational Preparation*.
33 See *SCDC Link*, Autumn 1985, pp. 14–15.
34 The evocation of rhetorics to create constituencies for support is discussed in Holt, M. (1987), *Judgment, Planning and Educational Change*, London. Harper & Row.
35 Hargreaves, A. (1986). 'Record breakers' in Broadfoot, P. (ed.), *Profiles and Records of Achievement*, Hodder.
36 See note 2.
37 Wiener, M. (1981). *English Culture and the Decline of the Industrial Spirit, 1850–1980*. Cambridge, University Press.
38 Barnett, C. (1979). 'Technology, education and industrial and economic strength', *Journal of the RSA*, February, 127.
39 Nicholas, S.J. (1985). 'Technical education and the decline of Britain, 1870–1914', in Inkster, I. (ed.), *The Steam Intellect Societies*, Nottingham. University Department of Adult Education.
40 CSCS (1984). *Contributions*, no. 7, winter.
41 In a speech to the Institute of Directors, March 1982.
42 DES (1979). *Aspects of Secondary Education*, London. HMSO.
43 Musgrove, F. (1979). 'Curriculum, culture and ideology', in Taylor, P. (ed.), *New Directions in Curriculum Studies*, Falmer.
44 Brockington, D., White, R. and Pring, R. (1983). *Implementing the 14–18 Curriculum: New Approaches*. London, Schools Council, for the Bristol Social Education Project.
45 Pring, R. (1985). 'In Defence of TVEI', *Forum*, autumn, pp. 14–17.
46 Callahan, R.E. (1962). *Education and the Cult of Efficiency*. University of Chicago Press, p. 246.
47 Bobbitt, F. (1962). quoted in Bode, B.H. (1927), *Modern Educational Theories*, New York, Macmillan.
48 Nunn, Sir P. (1945). *Education: Its Data and First Principles*, Arnold, p. 96. I am grateful to Michael Golby for pointing out this connection to me.
49 Dewey, J. (1966). *Democracy and Education*. Macmillan, p. 308.
50 *TVEI Review 1984*, MSC.
51 The argument is set out in Duffy, M. (1985), 'A tempting taste of cordon bleu', *The Times Educational Supplement*, 8 March.
52 As reported in *Education*, 24.12.82.
53 'Young plans two-prong jobs battle', *The Times*, 4 September 1985, p. 1.
54 Davies, B. (1986). *Threatening Youth*. Milton Keynes, Open University Press.
55 The need for early selection into appropriate forms of schooling, and for a national curriculum, was made clear in an interview with Mr. Kenneth Baker in an ITV *Weekend World* programme in December 1986.
56 Grubb, W. N. (1984). 'The bandwagon once more: vocational preparation for high-tech occupations', *Harvard Educational Review*, November, p. 451.
57 This argument is elaborated in Holt, M. (1984), 'The high-rise curriculum', *The Times Educational Supplement*, 12 October. It is interesting to note that the then Secretary of State for Education, Sir Keith Joseph, was responsible – as Minister of Housing in 1958 – for launching the policy of high-rise building.
58 'TVEI scheme', *Education*, 14 February 1986, p. 141.
59 Devon Education Committee: Report EO/86/123, March 1986 'TVEI: Management committee minutes and destinations and work experience'.
60 Grubb, W.N. and Lazerson, M. (1981). 'Vocational solutions to youth problems: the persistent frustrations of the American experience', in *Educational Analysis* vol. 3 no. 2, pp. 91–103. The following quotation is also from this paper.
61 Robinson, T. (1984). 'Sea change', *The Times Educational Supplement*, 6 July, p. 19.
62 See, for example, Lawton, D. (1985), *The Grip Tightens*, Bedford Way Papers.
63 DES (1984). *English from 5 to 16*, HMSO.
64 For an exposition of the argument that people should be treated as ends and not means, see MacIntyre, A. (1981), *After Virtue*, Duckworth.
65 Statement of TVEI criteria – see Appendix.
66 *Soviet Weekly*, 12.5.84.
67 Stevens, A. (1982). 'Lessons Japan can teach the West', *Observer*, 19 December.

68 MSC with NEDC (1984). *Competence and Competition.*
69 See David, Tudor (1985), 'Germany Calling', *Education* 1 February, also Merritt, G. (1982), *World Out of Work.* london, Collins.
70 The extract comes from the editorial in *The Times Educational Supplement* of 31.8.84. As for the MSC penchant for Britain adopting a West German model of schooling, it was clear from the December 1986 ITV interview with the education secretary that this is now government policy too. The interview was preceded by a glowing account of the tripartite secondary system common in West German Lander.
71 Tomlinson, J. (1985). 'Stalled on the road to recovery?', *The Times Educational Supplement*, 22 February.
72 Rubber and Plastics Processing Industry Training Board (1982), *The Way Forward.*
73 Kaufman, M. (1985). 'YTS and TVEI: hopes or threats?', *Comprehensive Education*, 48, January.
74 Jackson, M. (1986). 'A seat at the table?', in Benn, C. and Fairley, J. (eds.), *Challenging the MSC*, London. Pluto Press.
75 Williams, S. (1986). 'Schools: the lessons still for learning', *The Times*, 25 March.
76 Victoria Ministry of Education (1984). *'Ministerial Review of Post-Compulsory Schooling.*
77 For a fuller discussion of 16–19 education in the UK and new interpretations of liberal education, see Reid, W.A. and Holt, M. (1986), 'Structure and ideology in upper secondary education', in Hartnett, A. and Naish, M. (eds.), *Education and Society Today*, Falmer Press.
78 See note 2.
79 Fullan, M. and Pomfret, A. (1977). 'Research on curriculum and instructional implementation', *Review of Educational Research*, winter.
80 Examples of futile TVEI activities are given by Benn, C. (1984), 'NTVEI: Time to speak up', *Careers and Guidance Teacher*, spring.
81 One of the leading Black Paper authors, Rhodes Boyson, was, until recently, a Minister of State in the Department of Education and Science.

CHAPTER 6

The Youth Training Scheme and core skills:
an educational analysis

Ruth Jonathan

In the budget speech of March 1985, the Chancellor of the Exchequer announced the expansion of the YTS into a two-year programme, as a measure to combat unemployment by improving the education and training of young people. The expansion of the scheme will clearly improve the unemployment figures, by removing up to half a million young people from the unemployment register for a further year. Whether the scheme or its expansion will reduce unemployment in other ways depends upon the validity of two assumptions: the claim that unemployment in the young results from inadequate education and training, and the related claim that the provisions of the YTS represent a programme of worthwhile education and training for young people.

There has been much discussion of the first of these claims, casting serious doubt on the suggestion that attention to the supply side only of the labour market will have significant economic effects in the short or medium term. Whether or not education and training provision will have beneficial social and economic effects in the long term, in combination with other measures, depends of course on the quality of the provision offered, together with further discussion about what counts as beneficial, and to whom. Thus even as an economic measure the value of the YTS depends in the long term on evaluation of the content of its learning programme.

However, it is one of the distinguishing features of a free society that sections of the population cannot be centrally drafted into particular economic activities for the presumed good of the economic collective. We must suppose then that the YTS is not to be seen as a purely bureaucratic measure, designed simply to improve collective economic efficiency, but rather as an initiative for the improvement of education and training which is hoped to have, as well as beneficial consequences for its clients in terms of cognitive gains and improved life chances, some wider economic effects which would in turn be to their advantage as well as that of others. Clearly, individual and collective dimensions of benefit cannot be neatly separated, whether in economic or (less obviously) in educational terms, but neither should they be conflated, for many of the relations between individual and collective benefit are contingent upon alterable social circumstance. When the modification of social circumstance is itself one of the aims of public policy, the prime focus is appropriately placed on benefit to individuals, with benefit to the wider society as indirect consequence. Thus as an education and training measure, the YTS is to be evaluated primarily in terms of its benefits to trainees, for it is in any case only through these that social and economic improvements in which they could share might accrue to the wider society.

Moreover, in evaluating a programme of education and training from the public policy point of view, we are required to understand trainee benefit in terms of cognitive gains and increased life chances related to them which might be achieved by the cohort of trainees. For incidental advantages of a purely positional sort gained by particular individuals make no contribution to the increased collective welfare sought through improved education and training. Thus, for particular individuals, benefits to trainees in terms of increased employability in the immediate future may well relate, not to the content of the scheme or its worth, but to employers' perceptions of that content and worth. When too many young people are chasing too few jobs, it may well be prudent from the young person's viewpoint to undergo any form of preparation which is seen as giving a competitive edge in the job market. Similarly, it may well be useful for employers to select young recruits from an otherwise undifferentiated pool of candidates by using any yardstick which seems to suggest motivation and persistence. But though such reasoning may be rational for individuals in crisis conditions, it is no basis for policies intended to have long-term beneficial effects. Unless the learning content of the programme of education and training offered has inherent value in addition to its usefulness as a screening device, it will provide neither individual nor collective long-term gains. Though some individuals rather than others may secure existing jobs, as a result partly of attendance, they will neither secure more demanding work than they otherwise would have done, nor perform what they do secure more effectively. Though existing jobs may be more readily allocated to motivated individuals, there will not be those cognitive gains in the pool of labour on which is posited the more skilled, versatile and capable labour force which would facilitate quantitative increase and qualitative change in economic activity.

Thus on all counts, fundamental questions to be asked of the YTS relate to the quality of the learning experiences it offers to the trainee. It is on that matter that this paper will focus, rather than on questions of those social effects (on wage expectations, on the hierarchy of economic rewards, on the power of trade unions) which depend not on the content of the scheme, but on the manner and circumstances in which it is developed. This is not to suggest that educational questions can be neatly separated from social and political questions, or that only the former should be addressed in examining the scheme: an analysis of the content of the YTS learning programme will show that its education and training content is highly charged with a range of political and social commitments. It is simply to insist that the rewards and status of trainees, though important, are modifiable secondary questions, which have up to now distracted attention from a more fundamental issue: what is the value of this one/two year programme of education and training as a learning experience for its young clients?

It should be noted on this point that when we are talking of a programme put together at great speed for nearly half a million clients, which subsumes pre-existing training provision as well as extending it to a mass clientele for radically altered purposes, it is clear that the individual experiences of trainees will be very diverse. A small proportion of selected trainees will find themselves being trained for a particular occupational role, as under the apprenticeship system, with a prospective employer, and another relatively minor group will be following FE courses with considerable carry-over of content and method from earlier provision, though now under the umbrella of the YTS. Since these arrangements predate the scheme and are not typical of the experience of the mass of its clients, these are not the experiences of individuals by which it is to be judged. Just as the worth of the scheme tends to be judged by its clients in terms of the incidental effects of their participation, so it merits and demerits are often weighed by providers and managers in relation to what they are able to offer, incidentally, under its umbrella. Whilst both of these are important considerations, the worth of any particular scheme of education and training relative to other actual or possible schemes must relate to the central distinguishing features of the scheme under consideration. Intended consequences should not blind us to important side effects, but attention to side effects alone precludes relative evaluation of alternative policies where side effects are common.

The hallmark of the YTS, which is claimed by its designers to be its central element, is the Core Skills programme – a collection of 103 'skills' which are generic and transferable, can be learned and assessed in quite diverse contexts, and which as well as equipping young people for an unspecified range of occupational roles, also make good prior failures of education and socialization. We are told that 'it is the core areas ... that provide the content of YTS'[1]; that they are 'an essential element of the YTS (which) could lead to the setting up of a work-based alternative to O-levels and CSE as a route into further education and employment'; and that they could provide 'a common framework for accrediting performance in vocational and pre-vocational education and training'[2]. If the Core Skills comprise the content of the scheme, if it is this central part of the programme which permits its extension to half a million youngsters, and which furthermore legitimates its claim to be a programme of education as well as training, this is the element which must be examined in order to evaluate the scheme as a learning programme. If, moreover, transferable Core Skills are claimed to have a significant part to play in the reform of secondary schooling, an analysis of that central element in the YTS will be of interest to educators in general.

This paper, then, will attempt to examine the content of the YTS learning programme by focusing on the Core Skills which provide its central element. It will become clear that this is a far from straightforward task, since the system of training embraced by the scheme is not only pluralist in practice, with differences in aims and philosophies both within and between groups of teachers and policy makers; this pluralism is encouraged by the ambiguity of policies formulated to secure maximum support across a range of interest groups who have not traditionally been in concert. The crucial question to be asked about the Core Skills programme is whether this is indeed the meat common to a range of incidentally varying sandwiches, or whether it is an opaque packaging device which simultaneously permits variety and inhibits quality control.

The examination will fall into four parts. Section 2 will look at the background of ideas and circumstances which gave rise to this radically changed approach to training. Section 3 will examine the development of the programme's rationale whic followed the publication of the New Training Initiative. Section 4 will examine the final recommended content of the programme in the light of this rationale, paying attention to its hidden as well as its overt curriculum. These three sections together are designed to provide an evaluation of the learning programme, but first a preliminary section is required to establish the criteria according to which this evaluation should be conducted.

Evaluation criteria for this 'programme of education and training'

The YTS presents us with an interesting problem: it purports to be a programme of education and training – should it be evaluated according to criteria appropriate to training, or according to the more complex criteria normally applied to education? Traditionally, there has been a sharp dichotomy in Britain between educaion and training, both in theory and in practice.

In practice, the divide between education and training has become considerably blurred during the past decade. Accelerating demands that education should become more relevant and useful, to individuals and to society – with relevance and use being understood in economic terms – are currently the prime force for curriculum change. The introduction of TVEI in Britain as a whole, and in Scotland the Standard Grade in Social and Vocational Skills and the modularization of the curriculum post-16, are evidence of a growing vocational impetus in schooling. The YTS, on the other hand, imports educational aims to a mass post-school training programme just as those other inititiatives import training objectives to schooling. The acceptability of this blurring of the divide *in practice* between education and training depends upon claims about the existence of certain skills and their transferability. The skills in question are not the narrow mechanical skills of the operative or fitter, they include life skills, social skills, reasoning skills, survival skills, problem-solving skills etc. etc. Since these, it it claimed, once learned, can be readily transferred to a vast range of contexts and since, collectively, they comprise the cognitive, social and emotional equipment needed by tomorrow's adults, skill training is no longer the limited addition to education that it was once thought to be. It is presented as an adequate alternative or even a desirable substitute.

Moreover, the aims of a *generic* training programme such as the YTS represents go far beyond the specific vocational training purposes of the apprenticeship schemes and Industrial Training Board programmes which preceded it. For the skills it seeks to promote are not particular technical facilities, but a range of general developmental attributes, dispositions and capacities. This is not 'training' as hitherto understood in vocational preparation, for only in the military context has training overtly encompassed attitudes and dispositions. Although troops are drilled not just so that they will march and reload efficiently, but also so that they will obey orders, respect rank and respond predictably, plumbers are trained simply to solder pipes, so that the pipes will not leak. It might here be objected that any learning has a dispositional carry-over, or that even the most task-related training contains or implies an aspect of professional socialization. Nonetheless, though consequences are ultimately what matter, these are likely to be more far-reaching if they are deliberately promoted as well as incidentally produced. Outside the military context the aims of training have hitherto been specific and limited in scope, with the development of personal attributes, dispositions and capacities thought to be the province of education and socialization. Where these broader personal developments are the aim of learning programmes, broader questions of justification arise concerning the aims, method and content of those programmes.

It is thus not surprising that the YTS is billed as a programme of education as well as training, since its aims go beyond those of traditional vocational preparation. For the scheme does not offer (as might be supposed) traditional training plus added educational features: it embodies a concept of training which is itself so radically revised that it no longer exhibits the three distinguishing features which formerly helped to characterize vocational training, and which legitimated the divide between education and training which has existed in theory as well as in practice. Although there are no doubt historical and sociological reasons for an overemphasis in Britain on that divide, there were in the past three sound reasons for that professional demarcation line, which allowed theorists to apply different evaluating criteria to the two activities.

Firstly, where training is task-specific, the ends of the activity are not matters of dispute, and what is the most effective means of securing that end is an empirical matter. Secondly, this type of training is generally separated from and subsequent to the process of general education, assumed to have already proceeded to a satisfactory minimum level. Thirdly, training programmes have been thought to require less stringent moral justification than the processes of compulsory education, since their clientele are volunteers and no longer children. None of these traditional features of training are applicable to the learning programmes of the YTS, as will be briefly indicated. If that case can be made, then the sort of evaluation appropriate to the scheme will be an educational analysis.

Why then does generic training require the more complex and stringent criteria of justification which have long been thought appropriate to educational programmes? If training is task-specific, it can be judged simply on whether it achieves its objective. If an adult is taught to drive, or a child to tie his shoelaces, we merely ask if the end has been achieved efficiently and subject to the normal moral constraints. These, of course, are more stringent when trainees are children or non-volunteers. But generic training, such as the YTS claims to offer, is not specific to tasks, and its objectives cannot therefore be defined in terms of specific tasks. It might be supposed that they can be defined in terms of a *range* of tasks, but the more this range is extended, the more any definition of prerequisite competencies undergoes a change of focus, from skills to be mastered to capacities necessary for mastery. When maximum adaptability is the watchword, as in the YTS, then learning objectives are rather defined in terms of changes sought in the dispositions of the trainee. The Core Skills of the YTS aim to develop the trainee in cognitive, social and personal terms, remedying prior failures of education and socialization. It is therefore not enough to ask whether such a scheme achieves its objectives: the objectives themselves need careful examination.

How stringent our evaluation of means and ends needs to be depends upon the moral status of the trainee. It is generally accepted that we have a greater moral responsibility towards those who are in our power, than towards those who by reason of maturity or circumstance are in a position to reject or refuse the treatment they are offered. Since entrants to training programmes are adult volunteers and school pupils are under-age conscripts, we require distinctive moral justification of schooling programmes in terms of their long-term benefit to the learner. We justify compulsory education on the twin grounds that those being taught have insufficient knowledge and understanding to decide for themselves how they can best develop henceforward, and that the learning experiences offered them are such as to enhance their development of rational autonomy. Since entrants to training programmes are adult volunteers, these stricutres traditionally have not applied to them.

It is of course true that children are obliged by law to undergo a process of education, and it is true that no one is compelled to join the YTS (I am not concerned here with proposed extensions of the scheme, since policy statements vary on that matter[3]). However, to leave the matter there is rather like insisting that we are all free to dine at the Ritz, as there is no law or rule which would bar any one of us from admission. At the age of sixteen the choice for over half of our young people is between courses at school or in FE, paid employment (obtained by 21 per cent of the age group in 1983[4] and by roughly similar proportion subsequently), unemployment with or without supplementary benefit, or the YTS. The first option often demands academic prerequisites these young people lack, the second is clearly not open to that majority of sixteen-year-old leavers who have failed in recent years to find employment within six months of entering the labour market, and the third option has been declared undesirable and subject to review by the governments[5]. The prospective trainee might well echo Charlie Brown: 'Life is full of choices but you never get any'. I would therefore argue that most trainees, by force of circumstance, can scarcely be considered volunteers. If that is a fair point then its implications for evaluation criteria are substantive but negative. Where learning programmes are devised for non-volunteers they must be compatible with further development of the learner's rational autonomy: they must not stunt critical faculties, narrow horizons, lower expectations or diminish moral discrimination.

If, in addition to not being a volunteer, learners are also at such a low level of cognitive and emotional development that others have the right to make developmental decisions for them on the grounds of their incapacity (as we do with children), then along with those rights of decision go corresponding duties of a more positive kind. In such circumstances, teachers are normally thought to have positive duties to develop critical faculties, to broaden horizons, to inform expectations and to develop moral discrimination in the learner. I would be happy to argue simply for the negative criteria enumerated in the preceding paragraph, but the designers of the generic training programme for the YTS seem to be working on assumptions about the capacities of trainees which would logically bring the second, more stringent, set of criteria into play. If, on examination, the Core Skills turn out to be very rudimentary, then either they are redundant, or a scheme in which they are central should be subject to the strictest evaluation of an ethical sort.

Thus, whatever additional criteria are relevant on economic and political grounds, the content of the scheme and the status of its clients point to the necessity of evaluating the YTS firstly according to educational criteria. If these points of principle are not sufficiently compelling, there are further pragmatic considerations which imply that an educational evaluation of the scheme is urgently required. Whatever the force of the arguements above, it would be simplistic to view the YTS as a training measure quite separate from policies and practice in education, and thus to be evaluated by training policy makers according to their own criteria; the scheme is part of the educational context, for four main reasons.

Firstly, if the designers of the scheme have, as they claim, identified developmental needs in trainees which society endorses and which the schools have failed to meet, then either the education system is failing large numbers of young people, or schools and society are at cross purposes concerning the aims of education. Either case requires a response from educators, whether in modifying methods and broadening aims or in presenting the case for aims and methods worthy of retention.

Secondly, the YTS (and particularly its generic training element) is likely to have a significant backwash effect on the secondary school curriculum for the less academic pupil, not only through direct import into the period of compulsory education via the measures of TVEI, but also indirectly. The assessment profiles of the YTS have been frequently referred to by the MSC and the IMS as an alternative to O-levels. Indeed the Director of the MSC announced in September 1984 that;

> The package extends backwards into schools to catch that group numbering 20 per cent or more of the age cohort who are given nothing by the formal 16-plus examinations and, despite nine yars of formal schooling, so very little by way of basic cognitive skills.[6]

At the time of writing it is hoped to introduce a new YTS Certificate in April 1986, covering the four key areas of the scheme[7].

Thirdly, the rationale for generic training and the eventual Core Skills programme is not something dreamt up by the MSC simply to provide an educational legitimation for a national scheme of youth training. The momentum for the rapid implementation of the proposals of advisory bodies such as IMS could scarcely have been secured by a huge input of funds alone. In the development of the YTS, as in the general blurring of the distinction between education and training, political expediency coincides happily with certain popular (though misguided) trends in educational thinking. Many of these (such as the claim that what you learn does not matter, it is *how* you learn that is *all* important; that we should teach what is relevant and useful, and that those judgments are straightforward; that the economic needs of the group should determine the learning experiences of the individual; that equipping the young 'for life' means equipping them to fit into and 'cope with' circumstance, not to evaluate and possibly modify it, etc etc) are taken careful account of in the specifications of learning programmes in the YTS. With some exceptions (such as the Social and Vocational Skills course for 14–15 year olds in Scotland, some elements of the Scottish Action Plan for 16–18 provision and various elements of TVEI), the emphasis in schools on 'skills' ('life-skills', 'social-skills', 'survival-skills', 'coping-skills') is still at the level of exhortation and exploration: the YTS Core Skills programme offers an opportunity to evaluate the 'skills' movement when it is translated from rhetoric to reality.

The fourth reason for scrutiny of the scheme on educational criteria is that curriculum change, direct or indirect, is not simply a matter of whether the innovation in question is acceptable in itself. Time and resources are finite, and to include A in a curriculum is to exclude B. In FE Core Skills threaten Liberal Studies courses, in secondary schools TVEI pre-empts the development of courses for its clients which are not subject to the approval of an extra-educational quango. We therefore need to be satisfied not simply that these programmes are unobjectionable, but that they are equally or more worthwhile than alternatives which could be offered to the client groups concerned, whether these are conscripts by statute or by circumstance.

I would therefore argue that the YTS, because it is a formal learning programme designed to influence the development of a captive audience, and because furthermore it is indissolubly linked with past and future educational practice, should be subjected to scrutiny in educational terms. There are other bases for scrutiny, but these fall outside the focus of this paper.

Educational and social change and the Youth Training Scheme

In order to understand the development of the Core Skills programme and its centrality to the YTS rationale, reference must be made to the background of interlinked economic, social and educational circumstances which gave rise to it. Although, for political reasons, *something* has to be done about the alarming rise in youth unemployment, precisely what should be done depends upon a set of diagnoses of past economic failure, present educational ills and future social trends. Before we can evaluate the treatment, we should examine the diagnoses and the symptoms on which it is claimed to be based. From the late 1970s to the present there has been a growing tendency to redefine the problem of youth unemployment as a probem of inappropriate or inadequate education and training for young people. What trends in thinking have lent plausibility to that redefinition?

When explanations are sought for past economic failure, comparisons between the UK and its major trading partners are inevitable. Although of course the political, social, economic and educational arrangements of any given society are indissolubly linked in complex ways, attention in this instance has been focused heavily on *educational* differences between the UK and its trading partners, singling out a causal factor which was both politically acceptable and potentially remediable. And indeed there is ample evidence that youngsters in the UK find themselves in the labour market earlier, in greater numbers, and with less preparation than in comparable industrialized countries[8].

The diagnostic focus on educational shortcomings was the more persuasive at a time when cracks in the educational consensus were widening. Growing awareness that comprehensive reorganization had still left a secondary school system geared principally to the needs of the more able and offering little to motivate the many who leave school uncertificated, gave ample scope for orchestration of public demands for more say in the aims and content of education. Over the past decade, the 'Great Debate' was followed by the accountability movement, curriculum review, proposals for examination reform, the introduction of market forces via the Parents' Charter, increased

central interest in curriculum content and assessment, central attention to
teacher quality and training, and the introduction of the Technical and
Vocational Education Initiative. Though the grounds for dissatisfaction with
present educational policies and practice varied widely within and between
groups of interested parties (parents, teachers, employers, pupils, politicians),
the general breakdown of consensus created a climate in which firm diagnoses
and hard-headed remedies appear particularly attractive. The more so, of
course, when those remedies accord or appear to accord with current fashions
in education thought.

This latter point is also relevant to the diagnosis of future social trends. The
restructuring of the economic base is more easily presented as a manageable
problem of education and training when many educators themselves stress
knowledge obsolescence and the primacy of discrete procedural skills, and
when 'continuing education', 'recurrent education' and 'lifelong education' are
presented as inevitable and desirable developments. Against this background,
youth unemployment becomes, not a result of economic recession, but a
concomitant of inadequate education and training, now seen as a significant
cause of recession. The case for a large-scale programme of nationally
organized youth training becomes persuasive on educational, economic, social
and political grounds, the more so as it allows a range of lobbies in education,
training and employment to secure support for independently favoured
measures.[9] Thus the Youth Opportunities Programme was swiftly replaced by
the more extensive YTS, and in September 1984 the Director of the MSC
envisaged 'an end to youth unemployment when no one would enter the
labour market until the age of 18.'[10] Although at the time of writing the YTS is
still technically a voluntary scheme, this prognostication was brought one step
nearer to realization by the expansion of the scheme into a two-year
programme, announced in the Budget Speech of March 1985. The new
two-year programme is planned to be in place in April 1986, consisting of
foundation training for the first year (cf the present programme of the YTS),
followed by more specific vocational training in the second year, to the extent
to which the availability of places with employers or in training workshops
makes that possible.

Criticism of the YTS has initially focused on both the purposes of policy
makers and the effect on trainees in political and economic terms. Objections
have been raised to a measure which disguises the true level of unemployment
and also depresses the wage expectations of trainees and hence of related
disadvantaged social groups. Notwithstanding the force of these objections,
they divert attention from the central point which concerns the quality of the
learning programme offered. They are too easily answered – at cross
purposes – by the opposing faction which urges us to welcome a policy that
promises to provide initially a year and subsequently two years of structured
learning and attainable qualifications for that large segment of school leavers
whose alternatives are aimlessness or at best unskilled labour. That *some*
programme of education and training, open to all 16-year-old school leavers,

would in principle be desirable (provided its claimed harmful side effects were mitigated) is hard to deny. But endorsement of any particular programme must depend upon an evaluation of its content.

As noted earlier, this cannot be, with the YTS, a straightforward evaluation of the efficiency of means to prespecified ends, since the key innovation of the scheme is that this is not training with a particular occupational task in view. In this respect the New Training Initiative of 1981[11] represents a turning pont in training policy from employer-based training for specific jobs, and the boosting of key occupational skills through Industrial Training Boards (partially financed by pay-roll levies on employers), to the provision of a period of planned education, training and work experience for all under 18 and not at school.[12] The £1,000 million per year YTS is intended to initiate a universal foundation training for 16-year-old leavers which would provide a broader and more generic type of vocational orientation than hitherto with, if circumstances permit, more specific training in the second year of the proposed two-year scheme. Indeed the avowed rationale of the scheme[13] echoes liberal demands for a vocational preparation characterized by generic rather than specific skills, flexibility and choice of training, and attention to the social and personal as well as the technical development of trainees[14].

At the policy level this shift from specific to broadly-based training is justified primarily in economic and social terms[15]. Though it is also noted that a broad base is educationally sounder for the trainee, actual and envisaged economic circumstance is stressed as requiring the change. A decline in unskilled work, the increased pace of technological development and consequent structural changes in the industrial base, are seen as necessitating a more competent, broadly trained and adaptable work force. The MSC's Corporate Plan for 1985-9 reiterates this point:

> ... the need will be for people with dual or cross trade experience and it is likely that job prospects will be best for people with transferable skills they can use in several industries. Britain's international competitiveness will depend to some extent on the rate at which those new skills are acquired[16].

A cynic might add that since one cannot train for particular jobs when there are few of these available to graduates of the training, the strategy likely to cause least frustration is to train for 'jobs in general' – a strategy which appears to coincide happily with liberal demands that learning should open doors rather than close them. Again, we should ask not whether this apparently virtuous change of policy was born out of necessity, but where its presumed virtue for the trainee is supposed to lie. And the answer to that is of course in the identification and development of the Core of the programme.

Basic to the shift in training emphasis is the assumption that it is possible to identify Core Skills which would be transferable across a broad range of related occupations and which could be taught and assessed during a one- or two-year period of education and training, in order both to remedy deficiencies in the previous education and socialization of trainees and to enhance their future employability. Whilst government stresses the economic benefits of training, the designers of the YTS initially stressed its social and educational benefits, in contradistinction to YOP which is widely acknowledged to have served primarily to remove youngsters temporarily from the unemployment register[17]. Thus transferable skills are seen as the key to three separate sorts of problems: economic, social and educational. In education, the identification and promotion of such skills promises to solve the perennial problem of worthwhile content and also the pedagogical problem of motivation for 'non-academic' pupils[18]. Socially, the fostering of these claimed skills legitimates the occupation, off the labour market, of hundreds of thousands of young people who would not willingly remain in education, and for whom there are few jobs waiting for which they could be specifically trained in the traditional sense. Economically, the decline in unskilled work, the increased pace of technological development and the consequent restructuring of the industrial base, are seen as requiring a more adaptable work force. Clearly, it is precisely in virtue of the Core – the very element claimed to be of educational value to the trainee – that the extension and expansion of training post-16, and the introduction of an allied 'vocationally enhanced curriculum' for the 14–18 age group in schools, is legitimated. It is therefore this element of the YTS which requires educational evaluation.

Core Skills: The design rationale

The large claims made for the Core Skills programme cannot be assessed by looking at the programme itself and its guides and manuals, for in those presentations the rationale for the scheme is nowhere to be found, except in the vaguest rhetorical terms. However, there *is* a detailed rationale, and it is crucial to understanding how these transferable skills have been identified and why they are to be learned and assesed in the manner eventually prescribed. I shall be concerned here to offer a critique of the design rationale of the Core Skills programme, before discussing subsequent revisions of design, for these are entirely pragmatic and obscure its underlying rationale. I shall not explore shortcomings in the implementation of the scheme[19].

The IMS was commissioned by MSC in 1981 to prepare a report on *Foundation Training Issues* which would underpin implementation of the New Training Initiative[20]. It noted that to avoid the unevenness of YOP provision, a more precise specification of learning objectives was required, and further noted that:

> Possible growth points and innovations come under five headings: additional basic skills; world of non-employment; broadly related skills; personal effectiveness skills; and ability to transfer and ownership of skills. The first three are extensions of the YOP achievement[21].

The last two are thus the areas of innovation. The innovations are justified by the changing economic and social conditions noted earlier, so that 'To strengthen young people's adaptability, versatility and employability, it will be necessary to formulate learning objectives at a higher level.' The writers of the report note, however, that 'there is, as yet, no common understanding of what they are or how they can be learnt, although some YOP schemes are moving in this direction'[22]. (sic) This mixture of disarming candour about ignorance of the destination, and blithe confidence concerning how to get there, was to characterize the Core Skills development programme. Thus, less than eighteen months before the launch of the Core, this report asserts that even with level-one skills (for World of Work and World of Non-Employment) there is 'insufficient collective wisdom for syllabus writing'; and that, worse still, for levels two and three (Personal Effectiveness and Transferability) 'we are on much thinner ice'[23]. The report's authors state that they are not at all sure that there is teachable content here at all:

> There is no clear understanding yet whether they are learning objectives which 'govern' other learning and for which it is impossible to devise content organization and methods, or whether they are learning methods, i.e. policy instruments for use in implementing learning objectives[24].

These doubts notwithstanding, the same body then set about investigating relationships between these dubious entities. Their report, published within the year[25], was designed not only to identify learning objectives, but to suggest assessment procedures and to 'consider the relationship between the learning objectives within a framework consisting of specific and broadly related work skills, the world of non-employment, personal effectiveness, and the ownership of skills'[26]. Achieving the impossible in this way was facilitated by the fact that 'The remit asks that this project be concerned with *outcomes*, not with the processes by which they are to be achieved'[27]. In layman's language it is thus a question of stipulating what changes the YTS should seek to bring about in the understanding, capacities, attitudes and responses of young people, and of devising assessment procedures for the changes desired, without giving thought to how these might be brought about. The report states openly that the criteria behind this stipulation of desirable change in competences, attitude and behaviour are that they should be non-controversial and consistent with envisaged shortcomings in provision. The report thus announces that since:

> Opinion among educational and voluntary organizations is divided. We have tried therefore to produce proposals that would meet with general acceptance, would benefit the economy as well as the individual trainee, and could accommodate the unavoidable stresses involved in setting up a voluntary, multi-agency Scheme with limited resources for 460,000 young people[28].

The first point to need comment here is that in the design of a programme whose rhetoric constantly reiterates the primacy of process over content in learning, no consideration of process plays any part in the establishment of desirable learning outcomes. Programmes of learning normally take account of three differing types of criteria: psychological considerations relating to the cognitive and emotional capacities of the learner, epistemological considerations relating to the logic and structure of what is to be learned, and ethical constraints on both process and content. Matters of public acceptance and practical implementation are the cart that these horses have to pull. In the development of the Core Skills programme it is not that the cart has been put before the horse: all the horses concerned have been ceremonially shot dead at the outset.

Given the criteria remaining for recommendations – general acceptability and consistency with an uncontrollable diversity of provision – their principal characteristic is inevitable, namely specification of outcomes at a high level of generality, allowing for radical ambiguity in interpretation. And indeed this is the case. There are plenty of things that we are all in favour of: personal development, responsible behaviour, clear thinking, freedom, fresh air and fun. These are also the very things about whose nature we argue most. There are plenty of things that are so self-evidently desirable that we all agree with promoting them, whilst disagreeing radically about what they are and how that should be done. We are all in favour of a broader, rather than a narrow, preparation for working life; we would all support the promotion of skills which prepare for many activities rather than one; we all prefer adaptability rather than lack of it or social adjustment rather than its converse, and we would all endorse systematic rather than haphazard learning. At the level of broad specification, the outcomes proposed for trainees are likely to secure general assent. What then are these broad specifications?

Types of competence recommended

These are divided broadly between competences required in employment and those required in 'the world outside employment'. There is no space here to explore the assumption that an individual's economic activity is the most significant feature of his life, nor the even more questionable assumption (revealed when employment competences are discussed under the heading of 'The Benefits to Employers and Young People'[29]) that the interests of capital and labour necessarily coincide in a free-market economy. To be competent in the world of employment seems *prima facie* of benefit to the individual, and this is therefore the aspect of a programme of education and training traditionally thought of as least problematic. However, things are less straightforward when employment competences are to be generic, rather than task or occupation specific, for it still has to be decided what competences are relevant to the future employment situation of trainees. With generic training we do not know what this employment will consist in, so that relevance in this case may be to the assumed capacities of the trainee or his envisaged social role, rather than to the prespecifiable demands of a particular job.

Demands for the liberalization of training have long suggested that young people should be prepared for a broad range of occupations, in order to keep options open as long as possible. If broad ranges of occupation could be identified and prepared for generically, the problem of relevance seems avoidable, for in that case relevance would once again be simply instrumental, though broader. This is the approach adopted by the YTS designers in establishing what competences are relevant to the world of employment as it will be experienced by graduates of the scheme.

If employment competences are to be generic, occupations must be aggregated into groups, unless we are talking of competences thought desirable in all types of employment. Any competences so generally applicable, whether personal attributes and social skills or the basic skills of numeracy and literacy, would also seem to be prerequisites for full adult autonomy in an advanced society. They thus could not comprise the innovative element in a generic training programme, since they should constitute the minimum (though not always achieved) objectives of a programme of general education. By 'generic' is thus intended 'widely applicable' rather than 'universally applicable'.

Accordingly, the IMS established eleven Occupational Training Families (OTFs)[30], each with an identified 'Key Purpose' (KP). For example: OTF 2 Agriculture, Horticulture, Forestry and Fisheries – KP Nurturing and gathering living things; OTF 8 Food Preparation and Service – KP Transforming and handling edible matter; OTF 11 Transport Services – KP Moving goods and people. According to the IMS, competences relevant to training within any OTF can be broken down into two sorts; those which directly reflect the key purpose of related activities within the group, and those common to all. Additionally, there are Transfer Learning Objectives (TLOs) 'concerned with the ability to find out rather than to do'[31], so that the trainee can later extend his acquired competence.

For the wider world outside employment, the report summary can be quoted directly:

> Six roles were identified. Two essential roles were *Personal Survival* and *Exercising Citizenship*. The four optional roles were Contributing to the Community; Self-Employment; Continuing education; Pursuit of Leisure Activities[32].

At this level of generality, who could fail to endorse these goals, which seem to accord well with liberal requirements for the sort of vocational preparation which is of lasting benefit to the trainee? This has been thought to require the identification of 'broad ranges of vocational competence as the basis of courses of study which underpin a variety of crafts and within a broad occupational field'[33] and further to constitute 'a genuine educational experience in that it inculcates knowledge, skills and attitudes which lift the worker's perspective beyond the demands which the job itself imposes'.[34] Closer scrutiny, however, may qualify that endorsement.

Competences for the world of employment

Through it seems desirable in principle to group various occupations, the value in practice of doing so depends upon the criteria used to establish a group. Such criteria will of course also determine what competences are common to the group. The best way to see what effective criteria have been used in this case is to look at the occupations comprising OTFs. OTF 2 (Agriculture, Forestry and Horticulture) lists 34 occupations including beekeeper, florist, market gardener, fisherman and market porter. OTF 4 (Installation, Maintenance and Repair Occupations) lists 27, including cobbler, electrician, garage mechanic and window cleaner. OTF 8 (Food Preparation and Service Occupations) lists 22 including baker, kitchen porter and vending machine operator. OTF 1 (Transport Services Occupations) lists 25, including air traffic control assistant, milkman, refuse collector, lift attendant and ship's agent.

One of two interpretations can be placed on these rather suprising groupings. If criteria relate primarily to the notional 'key purpose' of a general field of employment activity, irrespective of the competence differences of both level and type which obtain within that field, then there is clearly no basis for common competence and consequent skill transfer between occupations within the family which would adequately prepare for any, let alone all, of the named occupations. OTFs established on this basis would defeat the purpose for which they were set up. The second possible interpretation is that whilst the key purpose generates a list of occupations, the competence envisaged is not for the trades, crafts and skills listed, but for low-level tasks in their general area. It certainly appears that whatever occupational competences are required in common by both a florist and a fisherman, or an electrician and a window-cleaner, or an air-traffic control assistant and a lift attendant, they must be at a very low level of skill content. Since it is possible to train somebody to be either an electrician or a window cleaner as well as an electrician. But if that the same person to be a window cleaner as well as an electrician. But if that person is trained *generally* for either rather than *specifically* for both, he or she ends up competent in neither role, though the shortfall in necessary competence will vary with the skill demands of each role. Where the level of skill demand is highly variable within an OTF (as in OTF 1 from air traffic control to lift attendant) or where the types of skills are very diverse (as in OTF 4 between cobbler and garage mechanic), any commonality between competences required will be in the area of rudimentary prerequisites, which as they stand can only prepare for unskilled work in the general area of these trades and tasks rather than for the trades and tasks themselves.

These groupings are supposed to benefit both employers and trainees. From the employer's point of view, there is clear benefit, in terms of employee transferability, in the grouping of jobs. That the OTFs are not discrete suggests that they are indeed a convenience for the grouping of trainees, rather than a coherent grouping of occupations, for the benefit of trainees. Indeed, benefit to the trainee depends upon which of the above interpretations of groupings criteria is justified. To trainees and their parents it matters a great deal whether traineeship in OTF 11 will prepare learners for a career in transport or whether it promises to teach them part of what they need to know to be a lift attendant. Or again, will traineeship in OTF 8 prepare a youngster for a career in catering or does it offer some of the competence needed to fill a vending machine? For any educational evaluation of the scheme we need to know whether the OTFs, by broadening the skill base, keep options open and horizons broad for the trainee, or whether, by offering only training in and habituation to rudimentary performances, they do precisely the reverse. To suggest this is not to subscribe to any conspiracy theory, merely to assert that unless the *genus* on which generic training is founded is coherent in terms of both type and level of skill, such training will necessarily be a blend of compensatory socialization and preparation for unskilled labour.

Detailed *Work Learning Guides* were produced for each OTF, breaking down the prerequisites for relevant competences: a study of these guides leaves little doubt that here this is indeed the case. Thus for OTF 8 (Food Preparation and Service) the learning objectives are either devoid of content, since context is unspecified, (e.g. 'perform own role to standrd of timeliness and hygiene') or, if specific, devoid of skill ('dress correctly', 'maintain clean and tidy work station', 'avoid safety hazards', 'use appropriate language and behaviour', 'create attractive environment'). These typify learning objectives related to the 'key purpose' of this OTF. As for the second sort of competence arrived at, that which is transferable to other ranges of occupation, the overall competence of 'contributing to the efficient running of the organization' breaks down into 'adapt working hours to customer needs', 'stand in for others', 'perform others' jobs', 'carry out allocated group tasks on time' and 'keep utensils clean'. No doubt all these so-called competences would contribute to the efficient running of the organization, but what do they contribute to the vocational preparation of the trainee, other than to fit him, by modifying his attitudes, behaviour and expectations, for the role of flexible operative? The reality of the vocational element of the skill programme is thus diametrically opposed to its rhetoric. When the broad specification of goals is translated into detailed (and assessable) learning objectives, we have moved away from liberal demands for generic training to the illiberal social reproduction of a pliant underclass.

The point ot be emphasized here is that once training becomes generic in the sense implied by OTFs, based on skills claimed to be transferable across activities which vary enormously in the type and level of demand they make on practitioners, the identification of relevant learning objectives ceases to be a straightforward empirical matter, since they can no longer be related instrumentally to a particular training outcome. Relevance is now related to the assumed characteristics of trainees and the social roles envisaged for them, rather than to a particular task for which they have themselves chosen to be trained. Judgments of relevance thus entail social and political evaluations concerning the appropriate future activities of trainees. Superficially, transferable skills look like an escape from the murky waters of ethical jusification, in that they apparently keep options open for youngsters. In reality, they require close ethical scrutiny, since they necessarily define the parameters in which those options will be exercised.

It might be supposed that this would be remedied by the incorporation in the programme of Transfer Learning Objectives, since the 'ability to find out rather than to do' seems to echo current educational emphasis on 'learning how to learn' as an answer to the claimed obsolescence of knowledge. Current emphasis on process in education arises in reaction to the bad old stereotype of rote learning and in over-reaction to a new awareness that knowledge is open to development and revision. Insight that the learning process is itself important is replaced by the false claim that it is all-important: learning skills are no longer seen as a means of applying and extending knowledge, they are offered as a replacement for it.

A recent Bow Paper on 'lifelong learning' typically describes as a skill 'The ability to frame an intelligent question and to recognize a sensible answer'[35], apparently unaware of what is involved in doing so. What sorts of questions are intelligent and what answers are sensible depends upon context: knowledge and understanding of context is required to make these judgments. The YTS claims to prepare the trainee for changes of employment context by means of increased competence in learning skills. Thus, we are told, the aim is to enable the trainee, in a new context, to answer two questions '*What* do I need to be able to find out about the thing with which I am unfamiliar?' and '*What* do I need to ask myself about where and *how* to find out?'[36]. Imagine someone stranded by the roadside with a car breakdown, or puzzled about why a recipe has failed to produce the expected result. If they can answer either of these key questions, it is surely not that they now know how to develop the knowledge and understanding needed, but that they have it already. As Humphrey Lyttelton remarked 'If I knew where jazz was going, I'd be there already!'. If the value of 'learning skills' is that they facilitate the acquisition of new knowledge, their success depends in part on an attitude of confident inquiry, but much more importantly on the possession of a considerable fund of existing relevant knowledge.

However, once again, when the TLOs are translated from vague goals into explicit learning objectives (LOs) are it becomes clear that the ability to develop and acquire worthwhile knowledge is not what is at issue. From the TLO 'Behave in order to create and maintain satisfactory work relationships' the LO is derived 'Find out how to behave in order to create and maintain satisfactory work relationships'[37]. The list of items headed 'What you need to know' includes 'What style of language the other person would like you to use', 'at what time the other person would like to communicate with you', and 'What rules or requirements the organization has about how to behave' etc etc[38]. Under 'How to find out' various suggestions about whom to imitate and whom to obey are listed. It may well be useful to know what others expect of one, and to be able to adapt, chameleon-like, to different situations. But transferable learning skills are promoted in education precisely on the grounds that they incrase initiative, non-dependence on authorities, and a reflective, critical attitude. The TLOs of the YTS, on the other hand, are designed to foster malleability and conformity. Thus this innovation in the vocational element of the YTS again reinforces its anti-educational characteristics.

If the 'vocationally enhanced curricula' proposed for secondary schools exhibit similar features, as the Director of MSC has promised,[39] then the educational climate will have turned full circle in two centuries. In 1806 Colquhoun wrote 'Let it not be conceived for a moment that it is the object of the author to recommend a system of education for the poor which shall pass the bounds of their condition in society'[40]. In 1981 the Bow Paper quoted above announced 'You don't need O-levels to be a road-mender .... Too high a qualification is really a disqualification for a contented, competent employee'[41]. When Colquhoun was writing, it was unremarkable to presume that any education charitably provided for the poor in society should primarily serve the interests of the providers. For the past decade the presumption that education provided by the state should serve the interests of the state, viewed primarily as an economic collective, has been quietly growing in strength. I have argued elsewhere that even in social and economic terms this policy trend is misguided[42], but those are by no means the primary criteria which should be used to evaluate YTS as a scheme of education and training. The benefit *to the trainee* of the vocational element in the content of YTS is hard to discern unless we assume:

1 that up to half a million school leavers each year are potentially capable of only the lowest-level tasks;
2 that such tasks will exist at an adequate level of reward;
3 that it is in the individual's interest to be socialized into his/her inevitable role in a hierarchical social and employment structure.

All the above relates of course only to intended benefit and core content, and it will again be objected that the redeeming features of the scheme are to be found in its unintended effects and contingent consequences. For some, it is true, this vocational programme may stimulate interest in and determination to acquire the specific training which the Core does not offer. And for some the circumstances of their work placement may offer worthwhile learning experiences which make the rationale for the Core irrelevant. But again I would maintain that it is a poor justification of any learning programme to support it either on the grounds that it does not work or that it does not matter.

Competences for 'the world outside employment'

The scheme's designers give four reasons why 'any proposals for the learning content of YTS should include consideration of the world outside employment'.[43] Firstly, for this group, unemployment will be an inevitable feature of life: 'YTS would not be helping young people to prepare for the reality of adult life if it did not attempt to help them to cope competently outside the world of employment'.[44] Secondly, this being the case, if 'employment competences' are not used outside the context of a job, they will atrophy during the trainee's inevitable periods of unemployment. Thirdly, it is argued that those who 'come to terms with unemployment' and 'develop alternative activities' are more likely to find eventual re-employment. It is suggested that an 'employment ethic' should be replaced by a 'work ethic'[45]. Fourthly, the YTS will lack credibility, it is argued, if it prepares largely for employment in an age of mass unemployment.

Thus the next important point to be noted about this scheme of education and training is that it is not to consist, as one might expect, of a training element to prepare for working life and an educational element to prepare for personal, social and cultural development in adulthood. Rather, the training element seeks to fit the individual for his place in a pool of adaptable unskilled labour, and the so-called educational element aims to adapt him for his place in the economically (and, often, politically) marginalized pool of the unemployed. The 'World Outside Employment' looks, on closer inspection of consultative documents, like the world of unemployment. In a scheme of education and training one would expect the content of the educational element, at least, to be determined by the capacities and interests of the trainee, in order to broaden his choice of potential social role. In the rationale for the YTS this element also is determined by envisaged constraints of the labour market, claimed to be inevitable, which are beyond trainees' control and to which it is therefore in their interest to adapt. The economic lot which policy makers envisage for these young people is the central consideration in *both* the training and the 'education' elements of the scheme.

It would be hard to find a clearer demonstration of the fact that 'relevance' and 'usefulness' are very dangerous criteria for learning programmes to adopt, since both of those concepts are context and purpose dependent. We need therefore to examine what context is being prepared for and whose purposes are being served, before we endorse any programme of learning characterized by its 'relevance' and 'usefulness'.

Once again, at the level of broad specification, no one could object to the six roles in the world outside employment in which the scheme's designers aimed at trainee competence. These are: Personal Survival, Exercising Citizenship, Contributing to the Community, Self-Employment, Continuing Education, and the Pursuit of Leisure, the first two being essential, the others optional. If, as claimed, young people are to be given the competences involved in 'deciding what goals are personally important to pursue' and in 'beginning to direct their own lives', [46] this seems highly educationally desirable. Leaving aside the point that they are to pursue these goals and live these lives in circumstancs which are taken as given, and which may be higly unfavourable to the individuals concerned, a study of the *Work Learning Guides*[47] gives no clue as to how these laudable aims might be achieved through the programmes proposed.

As with the occupational competences examined earlier, the learning objectives and their prerequisites listed are either devoid of content or devoid of skill, though in this case the former type predominate. In order to achieve Personal Survival, the trainee should be able to 'Maintain physical and mental health'[48]. On the physical side he should be able to 'obtain heating' and 'obtain housing' – no further prerequisites being listed for these abilities. On the mental side he should be able to 'undertake a range of activities each day', 'create and maintain satisfying relationships with others' (divided significantly into family, friends and 'authority figures'). Satisfying relationships will be maintained by the ability to 'make assessments about own and others' influence on situations that seem realistic to other people'. It is clear that what counts as a reasonable assessment of situations or appropriate behaviour in them, is again not for the trainee to decide; he is to defer to the judgments and standards of others on these matters. The trainee is scarcely 'beginning to direct his own life': he is being trained to take responsibility for coping with adverse circumstances which he has not chosen, and also for conforming to expectations which he is not expected to question.

The other essential area of personal development is outlined in the *Exercising Citizenship Learning Guide*[49] which aims to enable the trainee to 'obtain rights and fulfil responsibilities as a citizen'. Again, nowhere is it considered that an important part of adult citizenship in a free society is understanding, evaluating and possibly seeking to modify the currently accepted rights and responsibilities of citizens in the society to which one belongs. Moreover, in a society where citizens, however equal they may be before the law, are certainly not equal in social circumstances, different clusters of rights and responsibilities will appear relevant and appropriate to different types of citizen. This *Learning Guide* leaves no doubt as to what type of citizenship trainees are to be prepared to exercise. The overall aim is broken down, unexceptionably, into 'contribute to society' and 'obtain social, financial and legal benefits to which entitled as a citizen'. Now, every member of a social group is expected both to contribute and to benefit; but what the type and manner of these transactions are to be for a given individual is revealing.

The contribution to society envisaged for these young people consists in, 'Help other people in the everyday life of the community' and 'Exercise right to vote in elections'. The obtaining of rights is clearly not to be a matter of seeking parity of equality or freedom with more privileged citizens, but simply of obtaining welfare relief entitlements by rule-following and subservient behaviour. Thus to exercise their rights these young people need just three prerequisite competences: 'Apply to the right body/person at the correct time'; 'Apply by means seen as appropriate by body/person'; and 'Create a favourable impression'.

I do not question that one of the skills of citizenship is to be able to operate within the social system obtaining; but there are two major objections to the

YTS interpretation of citizenship training which require that the label 'education for citizenship' be withheld from the programme. Trainees are firstly required, not to understand and evaluate the social structure and its institutions, but to fit into it and secondly, they are offered only the competence to fit into it at the lowest level of personal control and power.

It would be tedious to repeat this analysis from high-level aims to specific learning objectives and their contributory competences for each of the six 'Learning Opportunities' which the YTS was originally designed to foster (Basic Skills, World of Work, World outside Employment, Job-Specific and Broadly Related Skills, Personal Effectiveness and Skill Transfer). In each of these areas there is the same slide from fashionable and high-minded but empty phrases ('YTS aims to ensure that young people take responsibility for their own learning'[50]) to the recommended fostering and testing of low-level skills and dependent attitudes (find out how to behave by imitating and asking others). The competences envisaged for trainees in each of these six areas are either:

1 meaningless without specification of some content and context (perform own role to appropriate standard).
2 meaningless altogether (use senses correctly);
3 of dubious value to the trainee (behave ethically by finding out what counts as ethical behaviour in an unfamiliar situation);
4 at a very low level of skill (count items singly or in batches).

We are told that 'It is the core areas, as part of the learning opportunities, that provide the content of YTS'[51], yet the initial problem which IMS noted – that there may be no teachable content here after all – is unresolved. It is avoided in practice by declaring that:

The core areas are a tool for developing and organizing the training programme. They msut be incorporated into the planned work experience. They are not 'subjects' to be taught in the off-the-job element. They must be integrated into all aspects of learning throughout the 12 months training programme[52].

Thus, the remit given to the designers of the YTS was to identify transferable skills, which could be acquired and assessed in a diverse range of contexts, and which would meet with general public endorsement. Lest anyone suggest that at the end of the YTS development exercise, the Emperor still does not appear to have any clothes, we are warned pre-emptively that these are special, invisible clothes. Moreover, being invisible, they are all the more serviceable, for they are suited to all shapes and sizes, fitting for all occasions, usable in all climates, and not subject to changes in fashion.

The design revised: the Core Skills Programme

Without an examination of the bulky IMS reports which detail the development of the YTS recommendations, the final glossy presentation of the Core Skills programme to managing agents, sponsors and trainers would be quite baffling. For the elaborate rationale for the YTS, the detailed design which underpins its claim to be a programme of education as well as training, is a complex set of posited generic occupational competences and of personal and social attributes which are not to be explicitly taught at all, since they are 'embedded in tasks' and 'inferred from task performance'.

The Core Skills Programme was accordingly announced in May 1984. In a press notice, Dr G. Tolley, head of the MSC Quality Branch (sic) unveiled 'an essential element of the YTS (which) could lead to the setting up of a work-based alternative to O-levels and CSE as a route into further education and employment'[53]. A model for schooling is also explicitly envisaged since we are told that 'It could also provide a common framework for accrediting performance in vocational and pre-vocational education and training'[53]. The equivocations and hesitations of the IMS feasibility studies have now disappeared – as indeed have many of the more liberal notions of bodies such as the Youth Task Group – and a tidy programme of skills which are claimed to underlie the successful performance of almost all tasks at work and many practical activities outside the workplace. The skills are now grouped into four core areas of number, communication, problem solving and practical, which itself represents a paring down of the scheme's scope, emphasizing remediation of prior failures of education and socialization.

The Practitioner Guide to the YTS Core[54] and the *Core Skills Manual*[55] were published a month later in June 1984, together with a *Guide to the Revised Scheme Design and Content*.[56] The Revised Guide reiterates 'the emphasis on the "transfer" of skills to new situations and personal effectiveness', although under the heading 'What are the benefits?', the trainee is no longer separately mentioned:

> the overall aim of the YTS will be to produce a better motivated and more adaptable workforce, capable of developing skills to meet changing employment needs. This will have the effect of reducing training costs as well as minimizing wastage and should prove in the long term to be of benefit to employers and to the economy as a whole[56].

Four simplified outcomes are now specified: trainees should achieve:

'1 competence in a job and/or a range of occupational skills;
2 competence in a range of transferable core skills;
3 ability to transfer skills and knowledge to new situations;
4 personal effectiveness.[56]'

These indeed have been endorsed as the four key outcomes for the proposed two-year scheme. The last three of these look consistent with educational criteria, and indeed it is envisaged that the trainee should become consciously aware of the Core Skills they possess, should learn to analyse those required in new situations and should be able to find out how to acquire them. In developing personal effectiveness trainees whould be encouraged to 'use their initiative, think for themselves, find out things for themselves, solve problems and plan, handle interpersonal relationships, accept responsibility and become independent.[56']

Although, then, the aims of the programme make no reference to the trainees' benefit except in so far as it is in their interest to be adapted to whatever employment they are offered, the content of the programme (within a more limited range) sounds as if it would accord with educational demands that young people's autonomy be encouraged and respected and their rational development fostered. The methods of learning advocated also seem to echo up-to-date educational thinking, since stress is to be on 'experiential learning, learning through doing, an emphasis on skills and tasks rather than knowledge or theory (i.e. taking an *active part* in the learning)'[56].

Again, however, the latent ambiguity in all these fine phrases is exposed by the list of Core Skills to be promoted and by the context in which the trainee is to acquire them. Since learning is to be through doing, and these skills are prerequisites to the performance of tasks, the trainee will acquire them in the context of a task. The tasks most frequently used as illustrative examples in the *Practitioner Guide* are 'filling a supermarket shelf' and 'sorting incoming mail'. A surprising number of Core Skills are implicit in both of these activities, from 'plan the order of activities' (9.1), through 'decide which category something belongs to' (10.2), 'estimate quantity of observed items or materials' (3.2), to 'count items singly or in batches' (1.1). However, since it is clear that all of these skills are involved in getting oneself up and out of the house in the morning, it is hard to see what *new* skills the trainee is acquiring. This is not 'learning through doing'; it is simply 'doing', and not doing anything very stimulating at that.

The important point here is that when emphasis is to be on skills common to tasks, this is necessarily the case, since the learning potential of a new situation lies in its distinguishing features. It would be objected to this that there are two aspects to a new situation: the changed context and the procedural skills a person brings to it – conscious awareness of the facility in these skills serving to minimize contextual variation. This indeed is the assumption behind demands for the promotion of 'problem-solving abilities' and 'thinking skills' in education, and it exhibits all the same difficulties.

One of the reasons for the downgrading of content in education is the observation that after years of studying 'subjects', pupils are frequently unable to solve real problems or to think critically, It is therefore easy to suppose that content is unimportant and that the skills of problem-solving and critical thinking should be approached directly. However, although a knowledge of content – badly taught – is not enough to promote these skills, they can be neither acquired nor exercised without it. For there is no such thing as 'problem solving' or 'thinking': there is only solving this particular problem, or thinking about this particular matter. Not only is a great deal of relevant understanding required to solve a problem: this understanding is required to recognize that there is a problem in the first place. Moreover, this understanding is not simply a matter of appropriate information, for different *procedures* are necessary for the solving of different types of problems and for effective thinking in different areas of life. An education with adequate depth and breadth of content is essential to these valued 'skills' precisely because technical problems, social problems, social problems, aesthetic problems and moral problems differ from each other in both content and procedures.

There is thus no shortcut to the acquisition of basic (or core) skills, if by basic we mean *fundamental*. Human thought and activity are richly varied and there is no Holy Grail of skills or competences which can substitute for broad knowledge, understanding and experience. If, however, by basic we mean *rudimentary*, then there are certainly common prerequisite competences for most tasks which reflect the mental and physical capacities of ordinary human development. What is needed for 'successful performance' in a given context in addition to these common human capacities is an understanding of that context. Where a context is complex the understanding required will be considerable, and the ordinary capacities will be taken for granted. Where a context is trivial, little understanding will be required, and there will be little task content beyond the exercise of rudimentary capacities. This does not show that in the new context trainees are learning by doing – it rather shows that there is nothing here for them to learn.

Four representative Core Skills will illustrate this[57]. *Skill no 1.1* 'Count items singly or in batches' requires the ability to count (which we can suppose a trainee to have) and sufficient familiarity with the situation to know what counts as an item or a batch. *Skill no 10.2* 'decide which category something belongs to' is both more rudimentary and more context-dependent. Fishermen and florists both do this, because in addition to an ordinary human brain they have, respectively, a knowledge of fish and a knowledge of flowers. *Skill no 13.3* 'manipulate objects and materials' is yet more rudimentary and hence more context-dependent. Abstracted from context it does not even require a human brain – ants and sparrows do this too. What makes this activity *skilful* is an understanding of the nature and purpose of context: the florist might display it arranging flowers to best effect, and the fisherman setting his trawl, but no amount of flower arranging will promote skill in fishing. *Skill no 9.8* 'diagnose a fault' is as vacuous as 'problem-solving', since to diagnose a fault, say, in the engine of a car I need to know something about cars – a lot of fault-diagnosing – skill, developed in finding out why my cakes do not rise, will not get me very far.

It would be objected that I am wilfully misunderstanding the nature and purpose of skill transfer here: I may need additional information, but past success in diagnosing faults will give me an attitude of confidence and a procedural head start. Even this more modest claim is false. Unless confidence is based on an awareness of the limits of my knowledge and the extent of my ignorance, it will only mislead. I need a real understanding of what differentiates the unfamiliar from the familiar context before I can decide what sort of additional information I now need. I may either need to understand a different set of technical principles, or, worse still, I may need to bring quite other principles into play – a design fault will involve aesthetic considerations, a breakdown in customer relations will call for social and personal understanding. Even if we consider problems which are purely technical, there are no skills of fault diagnosis which are necessarily transferable. Trial and error, or a process of elimination are the sorts of procedures which might be effective in some situations in the absence of relevant knowledge (as in trying to get a car engine to fire by adjusting the plug gap), but in a different situation such techniques would be disastrous (a dentist searching for the cause of toothache or a hairdresser investigating the cause of her client's thinning hair).

I am not arguing here that people cannot be helped to get better at solving problems or at diagnosing faults: clearly a thorough knowledge of car mechanics, dental disease or hair treatments will enable practitioners in those areas to understand and possibly solve related problems and faults. I am also not suggesting that people cannot be taught to be more effective in solving problems or in diagnosing faults in an enlarged range of relevantly similar situtaions. The careful teaching of appropriate procedures (whether this be the identification of causal chains, the recognition of cyclic systems, or the ability to test assumptions), together with plenty of opportunities to practise them in situations which motivate the learner, will certainly enable him/her to extend acquired knowledge and further develop specific skills. None of that is new, and has characterized good educational practice from the time of Plato[58].

What is novel in the fashionable skills-based approach to learning are the twin suggestions that procedural learning supersedes content learning, and that the transferability of procedural skills is independent of context[59]. What is truly innovative about the YTS approach to skill training is that these assumptions are compounded by the claim that those transferable skills are not to be taught at all, but simply to be picked up by trainees in whatever situation they find themselves. If, while 'sorting incoming mail' or 'stocking a supermarket shelf' trainees show that they can readdress mail to a relocated department, or remove misplaced sausages from the jam shelves, it is no help to them, or to future employers, to assess them favourably on the skill of 'diagnosing a fault'. And it is highly misleading to claim that they are learning to diagnose faults, or are being taught to solve problems in general.

This brief examination (which has avoided both the most rudimentary of the Core Skills e.g. 'Find out information by speaking to other people' and the most vacuous e.g. 'decide between alternative courses of action') should demonstrate that not only is there nothing here for trainers to teach – as the MSC admits – there is nothing for trainees to learn, at least in the cognitive sense. However, there is plenty for them to learn about attitude. In accordance with the rationale of the YTS developed in the IMS reports examined in section 3, trainees are learning the habits and attitudes appropriate to individuals who will join the pool of the marginally employed. They are being habituated to routine tasks – checking, sorting, cleaning, loading, running errands. They are expected to accept the hierarchy of the workplace, and their position in it, to be cooperative and obedient, to 'show willing', to 'be prepared to do more than the minimum', to 'find out what is expected' etc etc.

Of course, none of these dispositions as they stand is objectionable: rational autonomy is all very well, but few organizations would run efficiently if everyone exercised it all of the time. It is clearly important for adults to understand the purposes and structure of the institutions in which they have a role, and a scheme of education and training might well be expected to promote understanding of that aspect of adult life. A YTS Core Project *Starting Work* claims to teach this understanding. But it does so, typically, by means of a booklet in which trainees fill in the names of the people who give them instructions, the instructions, and the names of 'your boss' 'his/her boss' and 'his/her boss' in ascending hierarchical order. The transfer learning here is limited to 'Find out who is in charge of you when you are doing a particular job'. Far from promoting an understanding of the structure and purpose of an institution, this type of learning is anti-educational, leading trainees to believe that what happens to be the case socially must be accepted without question. What is offered to these young people is indeed mere information rather than knowledge and understanding, and information selected in such a way that possibilities for the development of understanding are foreclosed. Similarly, the social and personal development involved in these Core Projects consists in trainees finding out what authority figures want and in learning to act accordingly. To persuade young people, as do these *Work Learning Guides*, that ethical behaviour consists in doing whatever one's immediate superior believes to be acceptable, is not just to fail to promote moral autonomy: it is to subvert it.

Thus, though there is little in YTS to develop the minds of those hundreds of thousands of sixteen-year olds who, for want of a real alternative, find themselves on the programme, there is a great deal to mould them for their envisaged social role. Though they are to 'use their initiative, think for themselves, find out things for themselves, solve problems and plan, handle interpresonal relationships, accept responsibility and become independent'[56], they are to do this in a prescribed manner and in a particular context. Indeed, here as elsewhere, it is context which puts flesh on the bones of empty phrases. In effect, trainees are rather to adopt instructions, find out who is in charge, discharge their allotted tasks efficiently, comply with expectations, and internalize the supervisor.

Though there is nothing to teach in the Core, and little to learn which could claim value in either educational or training terms, there is much to assess. Trainees are to be assessed on their supervisors' judgment of whether they show competence in the Core Skills in going about their allotted tasks. Schemes provided by managing agents (voluntary organizations, colleges, LEAs, large firms, small employers in shops and workshops) are to be judged by the same supervisors' judgments of trainee attributes and competence. There are two potential kinds of benefit to a person undergoing a course of education and training: the inherent value of the course he follows, in terms of his own personal development, and its exchange value in enabling him to use his qualifications as economic or social bargaining counters. I have suggested that the inherent value of this programme to the trainee is dubious to say the least. Though the certification offered by the scheme is spoken of by its designers as 'an alternative to O-levels', it is hard to see what could be the exchange value of a certificate of competence with the inevitable characteristics of the YTS.

Where competences are meaningless without specification of content and context, there will be no comparability between levels of competence exhibited in a bewildering and uncontrollable variety of contexts. Where competences are altogether meaningless, they are open to the wildest variation in judgment. Where competences are so low-level that it is assumed trainees will be able to achieve them without teaching, then by definition graduates of the scheme are either being judged on competences they started out with, or on trivial gains in competence. Finally, given the characteristics either of vacuity or of redundancy which characterize the basis of the assessment, and given the fact that in making these nebulous assessments, the judges of the trainees are also judging the quality of their own schemes, then neither objectivity nor precision in judgment seem likely. Since these are the two characteristics on which the exchange value of a criterion referenced assessment is based, then it would appear that for the trainee the exchange value of the YTS is as dubious as its inherent value.

Once again, this is not to say that a YTS training will not give a competitive edge in a severely restricted job market to some trainees. Employers may regard graduates of the scheme, generally, as likely to be more motivated than those who rejected it, just as they will be likely, specifically, to take what recruits they require from those who have responded well to placement with them under the YTS umbrella. But as has been argued above, to note this merely indicates the desirability of *some* training programme from the individual's point of view: it neither endorses this particular programme from that point of view, nor does it answer the expectations of benefit from the cohort of young people as a whole, nor from the wider society. Any such endorsement of a particular programme should be dependent upon favourable evaluation of its distinctive characteristics.

Conclusion

This paper has concentrated accordingly on the Core Skills programme, following its development from the first announcement of NTI to the Revised Scheme at the end of the first year of implementation. Plans to date for the new two-year scheme leave Core Skills in their central position, albeit endorsing the desirability of some more specific vocational training in the second year, in so far as circumstances permit this development. Since the Core Skills are claimed to be 'the Heart of YTS', the locus of benefit to the trainee, and the rationale for conflating education and training, it is this element of the scheme which requires scrutiny.

There are several basic questions to be asked in judging the value of learning something – let us call it X:

1 What is X?
2 Is it teachable?
3 Do the learners know it already?
4 Of what value will it be to them?
5 Of what value will their learning X be to others?
6 Is the balance between (4) and (5) morally acceptable if the learners are not volunteers?

Only if satisfactory replies can be offered to those questions is it worth pursuing further questions of how X can best be taught or learned.

I have tried in this analysis to suggest answers to those basic questions in respect of the content of the YTS. If we let X here stand for the Core Skills around which the Youth Training Scheme is built, the answers seem to be as follows:

1 X may be anything or nothing, depending on context.
2 X is here not even claimed to be teachable, but rather learnable in any undemanding context through exercise.
3 But X can be exercised without teaching only if the context is so undemanding that the learner knows X already.
4 The value of X is claimed to lie in its transferability, but since that part of X which is transferable (a rudimentary capacity) is already known, and that part which is context-dependent (the element of skill) must be taught in context, X itself has no value without teaching.
5 The attitudinal learning promoted may have considerable value to others, given acceptance of certain moral premises about what social arrangements are desirable. These premises, far from representing social consensus, are at the heart of public moral and political debate.
6 Even if such disputes were settled in favour of the premises adopted by the designers of the Core Skills programme, the balance between (4) and (5) would not be morally acceptable unless trainees were genuine volunteers, neither penalized for rejecting the programme nor lacking viable alternatives to it, and unless they were already in possession of the normal human capacities which the Core Skills describe when abstracted from context. Thus as the central element of the YTS, X – the programme of Core Skills – is either redundant or it is morally unacceptable.

I referred earlier to the normal criteria for educational evaluation – soundness on epistemological, psychological and ethical grounds — and it is my contention that the Core Skills programme fails on all counts. This critique should not be construed as a defence of our arrangements for education and training before the advent of NTI. There is clearly a need for reform in the secondary sector, most urgently for those pupils who leave at sixteen, but also for those who are sufficiently motivated to suspend their disbelief in the value of what is offered to them. There is also a need for a programme which prepares young people to bridge the transition from school to adult life, which builds confidence, enhances skills and provides an understanding of our social and economic institutions. Such a programme is needed and should be welcomed, but the Youth Training Scheme, built as it is around the concept of Core Skills, is not such a programme.

Notes and References

1 *The Youth Training Scheme Minimum Criteria*, 1984–5, produced by Community Schemes Uint of NCVO, 1984, p. 10.
2 MSC Press Notice 72/84, *Skills Training at the Heart of YTS*, MSC pres office, May 1984.
3 The 1981 White Paper, *A New Training Initiative: a Programme for Action*, (Cmnd 8455), suggests that YTS should eventually cater for all 16-year-old school leavers, as do many MSC policy statements. However the 1984 White Paper, *Training for Jobs*, (Cmnd 9135), in March 1985, still leaves it technically voluntary.
4 Statistics for destinations for 16-year-old school leavers from *DES report by HMI on the Youth Training Scheme 1983–4*, DES 1984, p. 4.
5 This review is again shelved at the time of writing, but it is not unreasonable to suppose that it may well reopen when the two-year scheme is in place.
6 *Training News*, no. 10, September 1984, p. 2 (Newsletter of Advisory Committee, Education and Training, Scottish Local Government Employers).
7 i.e.   1 Competence is a job and/or range of skills.
        2 Competence is a range of core skills.
        3 Ability to transfer skills and knowledge to new situations.
        4 Personal effectiveness.
    See Cmnd 9482, April 1985. 'Education and training for young people', HMSO; and Interim paper issued by MSC Working Group on Funding and Administration, 1985, 'Posible framework for development of the youth training scheme', paras 8 and 12.
8 *Competence and Competition* (1985). London, National Economic Development Office.
9 For the exponential growth in initial training, see Ryan P. 'The new training initiative after two years', *Lloyd's Bank Review*, April 1984, p. 33.
10 Quoted in *Training News*, no. 10, *op. cit.* p. 2.
11 White Paper, *A New Training Initiative: a Programme for Action*, Cmnd 8455, December 1981; see also Manpower Services Commission *A New Training Initiative: a Consultative Document,* (May 1981), and *A New Training initiative: an Agenda for Action*, (December 1981).
12 See also White Paper, *Training for Jobs*, Cmnd 9135, (January 1984).
13 See Manpower Services Commission, *Youth Task Report*, (April 1982).
14 e.g. Entwistle H. (1970). *Education Work and Leisure*. Routledge & Kegan Paul.
15 Institute of Manpower Studies, report no. 39 *Foundation Training Issues*, C. Hayes, A. Izatt, J. Morrisson, H. Smith, C. Townsend, February 1982.
16 Manpower Services Commission, *Corporate Plan for 1985–9*, MSC, 1985, para. 3.
17 The above report (14) largely accepted the board condemnation of YOP expressed in an unpublished working paper of OECD, 1981.
18 It has been noted that when training becomes generic much of its motivating force appears to be lost, c.f. HMI report on first year of YTS.

19 For such a critique, see *the Youth Training Scheme in Further Education 1983–4: an HMI Survey,* DES report, 1984. Ryan (1984) *op. cit.* Raffe D. (1984), 'Small expectations: the first year of the Youth Training Scheme', paper presented at *Young Person's Labour Market Conference,* University of Warwick, 1–2 November 1984. Dutton P. (1982), 'The new training initiative: what are its chances?'. *Discussion Paper, 18,* Institute for Employment Research, University of Warwick, 1982. *Times Educational Supplement,* 22 October and 24 December 1982; 25 March, 4 April, 13 May, 22 July 1983; t January 1984.

20 IMS report, no. 39, *op. cit.* 1982.

21 *ibid,* p. 4.

22 *ibid,* p. 3.

23 *ibid,* pp. 46 & 47.

24 *ibid,* p. 47.

25 IMS Report no. 68, 1983, *Training for Skill Ownership,* C. Hayes, N. Fonda, M. Pope, R. Stuart, K. Townsend.

26 *ibid,* p. 9.

27 *ibid,* p. 9.

28 *ibid,* p. 9.

29 *ibid,* p. 27.

30 *ibid,* p. 50 for full list.

31 *ibid,* p. 14.

32 *ibid,* p. 5.

33 Entwistle H. (1970), *op. cit.,* p. 89.

34 *ibid,* p. 56.

35 Virgo P. 'Learning for Change, Training, Retraining and Lifelong Education for Multi-Career Lives', *Bow Paper,* 1981, p. 2.

36 IMS Report no. 68, p. 14.

37 *ibid,* p. 228.

38 *ibid,* p. 228.

39 *Training News,* no. 10, *op. cit.,* p. 2.

40 Colquhoun *Treatise on Indigence,* 1806.

41 Virgo, 1981, *op. cit.* p. 9.

42 Jonathan R. 'The Manpower Service Model of Education' in *Cambridge Journal of Education,* vol. 13, no. 2, 1983; and Jonathan R. 'Education and the "Needs of Industry"', in Hartnett A. and Naish N. (eds.), *Education and Society Today,* Falmer Press, 1986.

43 IMS report no. 68, *op. cit.,* 1983, introduction.

44 *ibid,* summary 4.2.

45 *ibid,* summary 4.5.

46 *ibid,* summary 4.19, 4.20.

47 IMS Report 1968, *op. cit.,* 1983, Annex C, pp. 161–175.

48 *ibid,* Annex F, p. 246.

49 *ibid,* Annex F, p. 247.

50 YTS information booklet for Managing Agencies *ESF Youth Training Scheme Core Project*

51 *The Youth Training Scheme Minimum Criteria 1984–5,* produced by Community Schemes Unit NCVO, 1984, p. 10.

52 *ibid,* p. 10.

53 MSC Press Notice 72/84 *Skills Training at the Heart of YTS,* MSC press office, May 1984.

54 *Manpower Services Commission Round Robin No. 8/84 – Core Skills in YTS, Quality Branch, MSC, 15 June 1984.*

55 *Core Skills in YTS, Part 1: Youth Training Scheme Manual,* Quality Branch, MSC, June 1984.

56 *Guide to the Revised Scheme Design and Content,* YTS, 84(a), MSC, Quality Branch, 1984.

57 The full list of 103 Core Skills is to be found in the *Core Skills Manual* (55 above).

58 c.f. the development of the slave-boy's geometrical skills in 'Meno'. Plato, *Protagoras and Meno,* trans. W.K.G. Guthrie, Penguin, 1956.

59 For a critique of this approach, see McPeck J. *Critical Thinking and Education,* Martin Robertson, 1981.

CHAPTER 7

Policy makers and the Youth Training Scheme:
concepts of education and training

Clive Seale

The Youth Training Scheme is a fascinating example of central government cutting through the usual channels of control over education in order to promote the new vocationalism. Impatient with the mediation of government policies by local education authorities, the government used the MSC under David (now Lord) Young as a means of more direct control over the educational system. A combination of circumstances made this possible. Primarily, rising unemployment created a new need during the 1970s to find something for young people to do. In the late 1970s the emerging consensus between political parties was that some form of national training system was desirable. Growing recognition of the dissatisfaction which many young people felt about traditional academic education was accompanied by a need perceived by politicians in both the Labour and Conservative parties to gear the educational system closer to the requirements of the economy. these various factors combined in 1982 to produce plans for a new Training Initiative (MSC 1982b) which included the YTS.

My purpose here is to explore the impact which this massive new scheme has had on Further Education colleges. In particular I will show how the debate about curricular philosophies for YTS reflects a struggle between proponents of the liberal educational approach that achieved widespread recognition in the late 1960s and 1970s, and the emerging new vocationalism of the 1980s. How this struggle was played out between policy makers for the YTS curriculum will be described, and how actual practice in FE Colleges reflected the policy debate in the first year of YTS will be assessed. For this latter assessment, the results of a major national survey of FE provision for YTS will be drawn upon.

To begin with it is relevant to discuss the political context of YTS from which the curricular debate emerged.

The politics of youth training: some recent history

In 1974 the MSC was set up, a quasi-governmental agency agency intended to take on some of the responsibilties of the DoE. Apart from taking over the running of labour exchanges (renamed Job Centres) the MSC, through its Training Services Division, took on responsibility for organizing government provision of training opportunities for young people and adults. In 1976 the MSC, in response to government concern about the growing level of youth unemployment, added the Work Experience Programme (WEP) to its list of special training measures. Over 15,000 places were provided under WEP during the following financial year. In addition to this 15,000 places were offered to young people under the Training Opportunities (TOPs) programme, which had previously catered solely for adults. All these courses were later to be combined under the general title of the Youth Opportunities Programme (YOP) which, between 1978 and 1982, provided training and work experience for progressively larger numbers of entrants (150,250 entrants in 1978–9; 440,000 in 1981–2. (Statistics from MSC Annual Reviews).

In their various forms YOP courses provided young people with work experience and vocational preparation designed to make them more attractive as potential employees, so that young people's relative disadvantages compared with older job applicants might be ameliorated. However, as numbers of YOP entrants grew in proportion to rising levels of unemployment the programme came under criticism from some politicians and unions as being one of cheap labour with inadequate facilities for training. In particular, the MSC was criticized for failing to inspect programmes adequately; indeed a large backlog of monitoring and inspection visits had been allowed to build up. At the same time by 1980 it had become obvious that unemployment was unlikely to fall in the near future.

It is important to emphasize that the perception of a need for a national training scheme was not the prerogative of the Conservative Party alone. The Labour Party and the TUC saw the provisions of training facilities for young people as essential. Statements from Labour Party politicians show that they too have contributed to the new vocationalism that emerged more fully during the 1980s under the Conservatives. For example, Fred Mulley, Secretary of State for Education in 1976 stated:

> The essential feature of (YOP) courses must be relevance: relevance to all the demands and opportunities of the adult world which the young worker is entering, and relevance above all to his working situation.

and Shirley Williams in 1978 as Education Secretary went further;

> Schools should not allow themselves to fall into the trap of thinking that there is a clear and natural antithesis between general and vocational education, and that

the acquisition of pure knowledge is of necessity of higher educational value than the learning of applied skills.

Much was made by the MSC of the consensus between politicians, unions and other interested parties such as the CBI and youth workers' representatives that lay behind the 1982 document that proposed the Youth Training Scheme (MSC 1982b). It is true that at a certain level consensus existed. But underlying this apparent agreement about the need for a scheme were differences in approach which divided not only party politicians but curriculum policy makers and future providers of YTS.

Conservative Party representatives have made their views about youth training clear on a number of occasions. In 1978 a Conservative Party study group argued for the importance of 'developing among young people a respect for moral values' in any social education component of training (*Guardian* 1978). A Department of Employment memo in 1983 confirmed that it was the government's aim to exclude material concerning the 'organization and functioning of society' from the YTS curriculum (*The Times Educational Supplement*, 16.9.83). The Labour Party, on the other hand, emphasized a 'critical awareness of society through economic and political literacy (*Labour Weekly* 1982) as an important aim for the social education component of training. Labour has also argued for the inclusion of cultural and recreational activities in the YTS curriculum and opposed the Conservative attempt to include military training as a part of YTS. Labour, in opposition, has also been critical of what it sees as the indulgent approach of the government towards employers. The Labour Party would have placed a statutory obligation on employers to participate in YTS, rather than relying on a voluntary response as did the Conservatives (THES 1981). Behind Labour's policy was the fear that employers would use young people as cheap labour, failing to provide adequate training facilities.

The developments in youth training policy that led to plans for YTS largely conformed to what employer's organizations and industrial training bodies wished to see. The CBI took action to support the MSC's recruiting drive for employers to offer work placements for the scheme. Economic arguments for the need for training have carried particular weight with employers' organizations. Thus the CBI in 1982 pointed out that YTS:

> would help to provide participating employers with a young workforce with some competence and practical experience in a wide range of related jobs or skills and help to provide the country as a whole with a more versatile, adaptable, motivated and productive workforce to assist us to compete successfully in world markets.

The more short-term arguments for the economic benefits of YTS to employers were pointed out by David Young in 1982:

> YTS ... is attractive financially to employers. You now have the opportunity to take on young men and women, train them and let them work for you almost entirely at our expense, and then decide whether or not to employ them.

The CBI's position on the curriculum of YTS allows little room for liberal education principles. Employers have long-standing complaints about the education provided by schools. Thus research done for the Holland Report (which proposed YOP) found employers to be dissatisfied with schools, wanting more to be taught about 'the meaning of earning a living' (MSC 1978). The CBI in 1980 were arguing that preparation for work should include studies of the :

> role, nature and importance of industry and commerce in the nation's economic and social life ... to promote a general understanding of the means by which the nation's way of life and standard of living is sustained which we regard as vitally important for staff and students alike throughout the educational system as a whole.

The implied criticism of the current provision is clear from the inclusion of 'staff and students alike'. Proposals outlined by the MSC for the New Training Iniative were criticized by the CBI for dealing with the purposes of training in:

> A confusing variety of ways, as an activity of general benefit to the community, as a possible helpful alternative to unemployment and, in the more usual sense, as a preparation for a job or change of occupation (CBI 1981).

It is precisely around the competing definitions of the purposes of YTS identified in the above quotation that much of the debate about the YTS curriculum has been aligned. The movement from YOP to YTS may be seen as an attempt by the government and the MSC to move towards the CBI's preferred definition: that YTS should be a national training scheme which promote economic recovery, a break with the image of YOP which was that of a short-term measure to provide social support for the unemployed.

The DES under the Conservatives has avoided any direct involvement with the running of YTS. This standing aside by the DES to allow the Department of Employment to exercise direct control through the MSC has enabled the government to circumvent the Local Education Authorities' control over educational provision. The appointment of David Young in 1981 to replace Richard O'Brien (who had been critical of government proposals) as chairman of the MSC has been criticized (e.g.: Cunningham 1984, Wellens 1984) on the ground that the MSC then lost any vestige of independence from the government that it might have had. This is not entirely true; Young was critical of proposals in the 1981 White Paper (Great Britain 1981) to reduce trainees' allowances and to make the scheme, in effect, compulsory by withdrawing social security benefit from those not taking part. But it is true to say that the MSC has been an important agency in promoting the new vocationalism, and that its rise in power represents the complaisant acceptance of their exclusion from the decision-making process.

As Maclure (1982) has stated, the growth of MSC provision for youth training outside the aegis of the DES has been 'a matter of almost paranoid anxiety for the educational world'. In the light of the barrage of criticism of the educational system mounted by MSC representatives this is hardly surprising.

A speech given by Holland in 1982 at the annual meeting of Regional Advisory Councils for Further Education is an example of such criticism. Holland claimed that FE colleges had tended to treat young people on YOP schemes as inferior and second-rate. Social and Life Skills (a subject which expanded rapidly in FE provision for YOP) were often 'an alibi for those who have no real idea of what to do or what the market requires.' As a result, YTS would not be the responsibility of the education system: YTS:

> must be work-based and therefore employer-based, not classroom-based ... the role of the education service must be a support role, the role, at best, of a partner not of a focus around which all else must or should, revolve.

It was to this end that MSC proposed organizing the majority of YTS courses around Managing Agencies (Mode A funding), whereby employers would set up such agencies to run a YTS programme, buying an off-the-job training package from an educational or training agency – be it a private agency or an FE college. Funding under Mode B2, whereby colleges were responsible for organizing programmes, would form only a small minority of YTS programmes. In this way, the MSC sought to ensure that learning would be based in the work place, where work priorities would determine what was learned.

Teachers and their representatives had mixed reactions to the YTS proposals. Schools were worried about falling sixth form rolls; colleges were concerned about the decline in apprenticeship work. Thus there were powerful economic reasons for teachers' unions to press for involvement in YTS provision. On the ideological level, however, there were severe doubts expressed about the new curricular philosophy that YTS appeared to represent. As well as this there was resentment that the MSC was getting money that would otherwise have been channelled into education via the DES and local authorities.

As far as actual participation in YTS was concerned, the economic reasons for teachers to become involved largely outweighed ideological objections. Early hopes by school representatives that schools would get a proportion of the work (e.g.: Schools Council 1982) were dashed when it became clear that the MSC was only interested in FE colleges. It now appears that the CPVE has been offered to the schools so as to provide them with a programme that may tempt a small minority of young people away from YTS.

NATFHE, the FE teachers' union, exhibited an interesting mixture of willingness to gain work for its members and criticism of the YTS approach. In 1982 it was arguing that LEAs should be fully accredited sponsors of YTS schemes (NATFHE 1982a) and warning that YTS provision should not be allowed to jeopardize full-time vocational preparation courses (NATFHE 1982b). With intensifying criticisms of the education sector coming from the MSC, Farley, a NATFHE official covering YTS, argued that:

> If the education service anywhere, either through its own volition, or at the dictate of others, fails to become involved in a substantial way in providing for

young people then a dangerous and major situation will arise. On the one hand there will be young people in full-time education provided for through the education service, and on the other will be those young people in the Government's scheme provided for through the Manpower Services Commission. This divide would ... exacerbate current class divisions, further worsen race relations and widen the gap between the 'haves' and the 'have-nots' (NATFHE 1982c).

While this sort of message was coming from the leadership of the union, and it is worth noting that Farley was later to become an employee of the MSC, individual members at NATFHE conferences and through other outlets voiced their concern about the ideological effect of YTS. As early as 1977 (NATFHE 1977) members were arguing that provision by FE should not be solely devoted to servicing the needs of industry. The effect of Social and Life Skills material in producing conformity to the work ethic has been criticized by NATFHE members in their journal (Pates 1982, Barr and Aspinall 1984). Woolcock (1983) and Moos (1983) provide wide-ranging critiques of the government for using YTS to cover up the realities of unemployment, and advocate that NATFHE adopt a policy of non-cooperation.

Any discussion of curricular philosophies in YTS must take account of the political context of YTS. This includes not only the political parties, but the unions, educationists and employers who have been involved both in making policy and in implementing the scheme. From what has been described above, it will be seen that plans for YTS emerged from the interaction of a number of interest groups during a period of worsening unemployment. While the MSC, with government backing, wielded the most power, the scheme could not go ahead without cooperation from employers' and educationists. On the whole, the government preferred to satisfy employers' wishes in order to gain their cooperation, relying on economic pressures to gain educationists' participation. This has had consequences for the debate about the curriculum of YTS, and this debate can be most usefully explained by examining the relative positions of the FEU, the MSC and the body which the MSC had used to develop its curricular philosophy, the IMS.

The curricular debate

In the early days of YOP most of the effort of the MSC was devoted to organizing the programme and attempting to have its officials visit and monitor the quality of individual YOP programmes. The MSC's resources were stretched so that they fell behind in their monitoring visits. There was little effort to provide a curricular philosophy for YOP, partly because only a minority of YOP students received any off-the-job training. Of those that did, this was usually provided in FE colleges and most frequently consisted of Social and Life Skills or some basic vocational skills such as workshop skills or typing (Bedeman and Courtney 1982, Greaves *et al* 1982).

The MSC's earliest attempt at providing curricular guidelines was in 1977 when it published 'Instructional Guide to Social and Life Skills' (MSC 1977). This document was notable for its narrowness of educational vision, and might be described as an example of crude vocationalism as opposed to the more sophisticated new vocationalism later promoted by the IMS. The author of the booklet appears to have viewed the requirements of workplace discipline as paramount, and the purpose of Social and Life Skills as being to instil such discipline. 'Taking orders' is defined as a 'social skill'; an individual's 'satisfactory private life' is relevant to the Social and Life Skills teacher only in so far as it can 'contribute to a person's work motivation' and the author's distillation of the 'skills' necessary for this private life 'are those of making friends, resisting provocation and making conversation'. The astonishing simplification of the complexities of human experience evident in the document meant that it fell a long way outside the educational discourse to which most teachers are accustomed. The effect of this can only have been to distance practising teachers further from supporting the approach of the MSC.

It is instructive in this light to examine a comparable document produced by educationists working within the FEU: *Developing Social and Life Skills: Strategies for Tutors* (FEU 1980). The approach of these authors falls far more readily within accepted definitions of educational discourse. Firstly, the document is much longer than that of the MSC and it uses longer words and longer sentences (see note 45 in Seale 1984). The authors also support the idea that different approaches to the teaching of Social and Life Skills are worthy of debate, since they propose several different models into which teaching approaches for the subject may be categorized. Preparation for the workplace is seen as one of many possible functions for Social and Life Skills. The authors generally avoid stating their own point of view, but when they do, they suggest that the subject can be an aid to the 'successful transition to adulthood in his or her own terms' on the part of the young person; it may 'most usefully be regarded as an aspect of personal development'.

In the absence of any significant or credible initiatives concerning the curriculum by the MSC, the FEU were able to dominate the field during the period of the YOP programme. In documents such as *A Basis for Choice* (FEU 1979a), *Vocational Preparation* (FEU 1982) and *Supporting YOP* (FEU 1979b) the FEU developed an approach to vocational preparation that was imbued with the principles of progressive liberal education. A key concept for the FEU was that of negotiation. *Vocational Preparation* put forward the idea that the curriculum should be a matter for negotiation between teachers and young people. This would involve young people at the start of a vocational preparation course coming to an agreed learning contract between themselves and their teachers. The contract would have arisen from a thoroughgoing assessment of skills and knowledge already possessed by the individual, coupled with a plan for future acquisition of new skills and knowledge.

The FEU's view of assessment was linked to the concept of negotiation. A profile of the individual would be constructed on the basis of the learning contract and individuals would be assessed according to their progress towards the negotiated objectives on 'their' profile. The process of assessment would be closely linked to guidance and counselling for future directions to be taken by the young person. Indeed, in their enthusiasm for preserving the rights of trainees, FEU on at least one occasion (FEU 1983) argued that trainees on YTS should have responsibility for monitoring their own assessment records.

The fundamental discomfort about assessment experienced by the progressive liberal theorist is evident in some of the FEU discussion. In discussing profiles FEU emphasize that tutors should record competencies in a 'vocabulary that is specific and supportive rather than general and punitive' (FEU 1983) and should achieve this by only recording what trainees can do, not what they can't. This, of course, is logically impossible since if a trainee is marked as having acquired a certain level of proficiency in a particular skill, by definition he has failed to acquire a higher level of proficiency.

As well as this approach, which may be defined as an approach to pedagogy, the FEU sought to preserve a general education component in the definitions of curriculum content which it proposed. In almost every document it produced up to about 1982 the FEU printed a list of 'core skills'. Basically, the core skills list was a formulation of a Social and Life Skills curriculum under a different name. For the most part it consisted of basic numeracy and literacy accompanied by vaguely defined areas such as 'problem solving skills', 'interpresonal communication' and learning about the 'world of work'. A curriculum composed of these elements fits perfectly into the agenda of the General Studies teacher who would, typically, have had experience of teaching Scoial and Life Skills on YOP courses and who might hope to continue this activity under YTS.

Significantly, the MSC has taken less and less notice of FEU ideas as its own efforts to fill the gap in curriculum development, which it left open under YOP, have developed. The MSC, as a newcomer to the educational scene, originally faced a problem in legitimizing its programmes in the eyes of educationists. Its *Instructional Guide to Social and Life Skills* was a notable early failure. As plans for YTS developed and the MSC struggled with the massive task of organizing the scheme and ensuring both employers' and educationists' cooperation, its relationship with the FEU was important. The MSC invited FEU to participate in its plans for YTS, an invitation to which the FEU appears to have responded eagerly, no doubt seeing this as a way of preserving its influence in an area which would otherwise move away from liberal or general educational principles.

This brief period of accord between the two organizations is, no doubt, what lay behind a joint statement issued in 1982 (FEU/MSC 1982) whose purpose was to 'demonstrate the degree of accord that exists between the two organizations' and where it is claimed that 'It is our impression that at national level there is little or no discrepancy between us'. The illusory nature of this accord was revealed less than a year later when the director of the FEU wrote in *Supporting YTS* that:

Complete unanimity with the MSC criteria is not always possible and there is
evidence to indicate that some attenuation of the principles and aspirations of the
Youth Task Group (the body that produced the document proposing the YTS
scheme) is taking place as the full demands of this ambitious scheme are realized.
(FEU 1983)

It appeared to the head of the FEU 'regrettable and unnecessary ... [that] the
place of education in YTS will have to be argued and justified.'

I have presented elsewhere (Seale 1984) an account of how the MSC watered
down FEU ideas about negotiation and assessment in guidelines which they
published at the start of the scheme (MSC 1982c). Of relevance here are the
various initiatives which the MSC sponsored to produce a curricular
philosophy that would break with the liberalism of the FEU at the same time
as avoiding the crudity of MSC's earlier attempts. The organization which
played the most important part in developing the new vocationalism now
espoused by the MSC is the University of Sussex-based IMS led by Hayes,
who previously worked for the MSC (Maclure 1982).

This organization, employing staff who generally have backgrounds in
industrial training, has developed an elaborate rationale for YTS, pivoting on
the concept of transferable skills. Before the term was generally current the
MSC evidently were hoping to identify clusters of skills common to groups of
occupations. The IMS quote the MSC as being concerned with:

> Such clusters or groupings (which) cut across industries. They are founded in the
> common factors of jobs in terms of industrial, occupational and material
> knowledge required for their performance. The fewer the clusters or groups, the
> greater the potential mobility of the individual.
>
> (MSC quoted in IMS 1981, p. 8)

An early attempt that might have established empirically the existence of
such clusters was the London Into Work Development Project (LITW)
sponsored by the MSC and conducted by the IMS (IMS 1982). This aimed to
identify the skills which young people needed in order to do their jobs and to
this end a survey of approximately one thousand young people was
conducted, asking them about the skills involved in their jobs. While this
exercise resulted in a series of reports about which jobs required which skills,
no cluster analysis was ever conducted on the data by the LITW researchers in
order to establish whether any empirical justification could be found for
grouping jobs together in families sharing 'generic' skills.

Thus the exercise that resulted in the IMS grouping the jobs commonly
available to 16-years olds into Occupational Training Families (IMS 1981) did
not draw on empirical evidence about the skill content of the Families. The
OTFs were drawn up by committees who consulted a series of 'experts' such
as careers officers about which jobs they thought were most likely to be
suitably grouped together. The resulting OTFs were not tested against LITW
data in order to establish whether the OTFs really contained common, generic
or 'transferable' skills. Indeed, the authors of the IMS report proposing OTFs
admit that:

Finally our concern with skills and their organization makes us very much aware of the limitations of using job titles when we are really considering skill content. (IMS 1918 p. 13)

However, the IMS has pressed ahead with its idea of Occupational Training Families and the MSC enthusiastically adopted the concept, urging that all YTS proposals should indicate into which OTF the organizers think their scheme would fit.

The IMS subsequently produced *Training for Skill Ownership* (IMS 1983) in which it was stated that a key purpose of job training in YTS schemes would be to ensure that trainees 'own' their skills so that they could be transferred from one situation to another. Experimental projects have been set up by the MSC to explore ways in which transferable skills can be taught, along the lines suggested in *Training for Skill Ownership*. It is clear that the MSC has invested much of its confidence and considerable resource to promote the hastily constructed rationale of the IMS. Essentially, the concept of transferability has been used by the MSC to justify the provision of training courses in a time of high unemployment. To young people facing the prospect of unemployment and to teachers uncertain whether trainees on YTS will get jobs in the area for which they are being trained, the concept of skill transfer has, nevertheless, been used as a justification for learning and teaching vocational skills. As the IMS have stated, skill redeployment is 'probably the most important single criterion by which young people will judge the value of YTS – once they have understood that the scheme cannot guarantee a job' (Hayes *et al* 1983). Accompanied by weighty and complex documentaion and detailed guidelines about methods of teaching for skill transfer, the IMS approach has also achieved greater legitimacy amongst educationists than earlier attempts by the MSC. The adequacy, though, for their task of the concepts of transferable skills and OTFs is discussed in Ruth Jonathan's paper in this volume (Chapter 6).

The FEU, meanwhile, has had less influence on curricular deliberations for YTS. In its document *Supporting YTS* it appeared to be fighting a rearguard action to preserve its influence. In particular it presented a diagram indicating how its notion of core skills could be linked to the IMS idea of OTFs. What FEU seemed to be suggesting was that its core skills might be regarded as generic or transferable between jobs within an OTF, or between OTFs, and as such essential to the fulfilment of IMS ideas. This, however, would remove the IMS even further from any claim that their selection of skills as generic is based on empirical evidence since the FEU core skills list does not even pretend to be constructed on the basis of evidence about skill content. In fact, the FEU have moved away from YTS recently, preferring instead to promote their ideas in the development of CPVE courses, over which they have a far greater say than over YTS.

It is instructive to reflect on the function of the curricular policies which have been described in this section. Presumably those who make the policies do so because they want to influence practice. But, as the investigation reported in the next section suggests, most teachers find that FEU, MSC and IMS documents have as yet little influence on their practice compared to examination syllabuses and what they perceive to be the needs of trainees. Documents, conferences, resource centres, workshops and staff development exercises accompany the production of the curricular policies to dubious practical effect. Perhaps the chief function of the policies – apart from creating an ideology by which change may be legitimated – is to regulate at an ideological level the conflicts between interest groups (such as between teachers and employers) arising from the reorganization of youth training provision. What happens in actual practice may, in the short term at least, have very little to do with the aims of policy makers.

The first year of YTS in Further Education

I shall draw here on a survey of teachers and trainees in FE colleges conducted by me at Garnett College in 1983–4, the first year of YTS. The methods and findings of the survey are more fully reported elsewhere (Seale 1985, 1986a, 1986b). Suffice to say that a postal survey of a representative sample of 163 organizers of YTS courses, 337 teachers and 954 trainees on the same courses provided the data, along with ten case studies of selected YTS courses.

Although only 52 per cent of all YTS courses involved FE colleges (the rest being covered by private training agencies) the introduction of YTS meant a rise in the amount of MSC work done by colleges compared to the position in the preceding years. This is because YTS was a year-long provision where all trainees received off-the-job training, whereas YOP was of variable lengths under six months and only a minority of YOP entrants received training. A survey of 161 colleges conducted by the Association of College Registrars and Administrators (ACRA 1985) found that during the year concerned 'traditional full-time student numbers fell by 4 per cent whilst YTS or equivalent rose by 100 per cent'. This would suggest that YTS work was replacing traditional work done by colleges.

The YTS trainees in my sample had higher qualifications on entry to YTS than did YOP entrants in the year before. This, and the information from ACRA, would suggest that many of the young people on YTS were the sort of people who, in earlier years, would have been on apprenticeships or other, traditional FE courses. We may go along with the following statement of Holland's if we apply it to YOP trainees:

> (They are the sort of young person who) would not have gone anywhere near further education if we had carried on as we have in the past. (Holland 1982)

Clearly this does not apply to all YTS trainees, some of whom were precisely the sort of young person who, in previous years, would have attended at FE.

In fact, the Garnett survey revealed that the MSC had succeeded in integrating many of the YTS courses with traditional patterns of education and training. Thrity-two per cent of the courses counted towards an apprentice-ship and 56 per cent of the courses led to an examination qualification, with CGLI and B/TEC being the chief providers. This widespread use of 'off-the-shelf' packages by FE colleges has been criticized by H.M. Inspectors (DES 1984) as hindering the development of innovatory curricula for YTS. However it clearly furthers the MSC's aim of creating a new image for YTS as being a permanent national training scheme, linked to existing provision rather than a temporary system of social support. Ruth Jonathan, in this volume, offers a valuable critique of IMS policy and the 'core skills' component of the YTS. This survey has suggested that, in its first year, YTS was at least in part a repeat of previous FE courses. This is consistent with my point that, in the main, curricular policies in this area have served to regulate conflicts between interest groups. But as policies are firmed up and YTS takes shape as a two-year skills-based programme (a point much stressed in the 1986 YTS advertising campaign), policies may be reflected more closely in practice.

An important finding of the survey was that YTS was a provision streamed by educational achievement. Broad-based Mode B2 courses, based in colleges and covering about 6 per cent of YTS trainees are good examples of lower stream YTS. Frequently aimed at recruiting from special schools (ESN) such courses were usually a YTS equivalent of the 13-week Work Introduction courses (WIC) that were provided under YOP. They usually aimed to provide remedial education and basic vocational skills in a number of occupational areas. The survey showed that the young people who entered these courses, compared with Mode A trainees who constituted some 76 per cent of YTS trainees, were less well qualified and were more likely to enter the course because they needed the money allowance of help with coping with unemployment. Their teachers, compared to Mode A teachers, who were more likely to be from General Studies departments or be teaching some form of Social and Life Skills, gave low estimate of trainees' chances of getting a job and were more likely to want to help trainees cope with future unemploy-ment. WIC courses rarely led to a qualification and never to an apprenticeship. In interviews during case studies, some teachers suggested that these courses were used as a 'dumping ground' by careers officers where trainees were unable to get into a Mode A course. MSC statistics (MSC 1984a) show that Mode B2 courses, in which WIC courses form the largest group, were more likely than Mode A courses to contain trainees from ethnic minorities.

Trainees on WIC courses conform to the image of young people on YOP ofered by O'Brien: 'many ... do not respond to orthodox education or training' (O'Brien 1978). What the survey demonstrated was that teachers, responding to this situation, used different teaching methods on WIC courses compared to Mode A courses. The FEU model of a student-centred, negotiable approach using learning contracts, profiles and student-centred reviewing sessions was far more likely to obtain on WIC courses than Mode A courses. Thus WIC teachers were more likely than Mode A teachers to argue that they tried to teach for individual learning needs, to plan their teaching to allow for differences in ability between trainees, to use learning contracts and to involve trainees in assessing themselves and in discussing their assessment results. One or two quotations from interviews with teachers suggest how this worked in practice. Mode A teachers emphasized how similar their courses were to previous training work:

> Most people teaching in college are pretty traditional and they don't make exceptions for YTS students (Mode A teacher).

> The vast majority we tend to treat as if they were on an ordinary day-release course. I haven't found it a great deal different really (Mode A teacher).

> (It's) a normal standard college course.. (with) a set syllabus. No choice at all (Mode A teacher).

Whereas WIC teachers spoke of negotiating with trainees:

> Very different, totally different ... A key word is flexibility ... you've got a lot of freedom on this course which is very nice ... Negotiation with the students – we don't negotiate with the students on the other courses (WIC teacher).

> I think (it's) open to negotiation all the time between the individual tutor and the student concerned (WIC teacher).

The MSC policy of changing the image of YTS from a social support scheme for the unemployed to that of a permanent national training scheme has been quite successful. The integration of Mode A YTS courses with traditional apprenticeship and examination structure suggests this. But this policy worked against the aims of the FEU in promoting a student-centred, negotiable approach to learning, since this teaching style is difficult to reconcile with coverage of an examination syllabus. It was only on the lower stream WIC courses, where social support was a more important aim, that the FEU policy actually gained ground. Clearly, the FEU cannot have anticipated the extent of the use of examinations in YTS.

The degree to which the liberal education lobby has been successful in YTS curriculum practice, in so far as FEU has been the representative of this lobby, has then been limited. The survey also enables us to assess the extent to which actual practice in YTS accorded with the views of the dominant policy makers in YTS: the MSC. The concept of work-based learning, whereby experience at the work place was used as a primary motivator to learn, was one that MSC were keen to promote. In accord with the views of the CBI and the governement, much of the MSC policy was devoted to taking responsibility for organizing YTS out of the hands of educationists and putting it into those of employers. Managing Agents, who were usually groups of employers, were set up to organize the 76 per cent of YTS falling under Mode A provision. These Agents were to ensure that good liaison occured between college staff providing off-the-job training and work experience providers giving on-the-job training so that interation between the two should occur.

However, the survey revealed that Managing Agents all too frequently failed in these responsibilities, a finding repeated in other studies of YTS in its first year (Stoney and Scott 1984, FEU 1985). Teachers in written comments on questionnaires had many more criticisms than praise to make of the level of integration on the courses, as well as the level of employer participation in training. While 53 per cent of course organizers reported that some consultation with employers about the course had taken place, this was frequently cursory and superficial. In only a third of the courses had Managing Agents or employer's representatives been involved in planning off-the-job training. Sixty per cent of the teachers surveyed had no contacts at all with employers participating in the schemes and only 20 per cent visited trainees on work experience. Paradoxically, contacts with employers were more frequent on WIC courses than on Mode A courses because here there were no Managing Agents to take away from teachers the responsibility for visiting trainees. An internal MSC evaluation (MSC 1984b) of a small sample of YTS courses recommended that urgent action needed to be taken to improve the quality of employers' contributions, presumably because the evaluators found similar problems to the Garnett survey. The evaluation team, amongst other things, recommend changing the name of 'Work Experience Provider' to 'Work Experience and Training Provider'. This would suggest that the Labour Party's view that employers would fail to respond adequately unless participation was made a statutory rather than a voluntary matter, may have been well founded.

In spite of these shortcomings on the part of employers, however, trainees themselves generally found work experience to be the best part of the scheme. In this respect trainees' views supported the assumption of the MSC that they would reject anything that reminded them too much of school work. The results showed that trainees' reasons for entering YTS tended to focus around gaining experience and training that would lead to a job. Indeed, most agreed that they would never have come on the scheme had a job been available. When asked an open-ended question 'What have you liked most about the scheme?' 50 per cent wrote that it was work experience. Only 3 per cent wrote that it was college. When asked to write about what they thought of work there was a tendency for trainees to find practical training sessions more valuable than Social and Life Skills.

These findings would suggest that the trainees tended to view YTS as the next best thing to a job, and to value anything which, in their eyes, gave them experiences that felt like having a job, or looked as if they were directly relevant to work. On the face of it, what trainees were saying was more supportive of MSC policy to provide work-based learning than of FEU policy to provide general education. This, in the light of Ruth Jonathan's analysis, is perhaps not surprising.

These findings about what young people think of their training are nothing new. Many studies have found the same perspective being adopted by trainees (e.g.: Into Work 1979, Hofkins 1980). In case study interviews teachers would sometimes despair at what appeared to them as trainees' narrow-minded views about what parts of training were relevant to work. These teachers found that trainees tended only to value things that helped them in the immediate future, and did not recognize the value of skills learned for other jobs they might do in the more distant future.

Perhaps it is the difficulty which many teachers experience in persuading trainees of the relevance of the more general aspects of off-the-job training that is behind teachers' acceptance in principle of IMS ideas about teaching for skill transfer. Few questions in the survey related to IMS policy, since it was judged that these ideas had been developed too late for them to be expected to have influenced teachers' practices in the first year of YTS. However, two questions did relate to this issue. Teachers were asked to rate their level of agreement with a statement 'It is important to persuade trainees that the skills they learn on the course can be used in a variety of jobs'. This statement received the highest level of agreement of any of the 30 statements about YTS that teachers were presented with; 89 per cent either strongly or mildly agreed. However when asked to rate their agreement with the statement 'I ensure that trainees practise transferring their skills from one job to another' the corresponding figure for agreement was lower: 51 per cent. This would suggest that while teachers liked the IMS approach in principle, their practice sometimes fell short of fulfilling IMS ideas. It remains to be seen whether the complex practical system outlined in *Training for Skill Ownership* will be put into practice by teachers of YTS in colleges. It is possible that the MSC may achieve more success on the ideological front by promoting IMS ideas than it did with earlier, cruder offerings of curricular policy. This is because IMS ideas address important areas of conflict for teachers; persuading trainees to persist in their courses in the face of poor employment prospects, and persuading them that certain aspects of off-the-job training will be valuable to trainees in future, even though they do not appear immediately relevant.

Conclusions

Plans for YTS arose when a number of otherwise conflicting interest groups, for a brief period, found it in their interests to produce and support such a scheme. The circumstances which gave rise to this episode of apparent consensus included a continuing rise in unemployment levels, dissatisfaction with the operation of YOP, followed by a massive injection of cash backed up by political will on the part of the government. In the plans for YTS, employers saw an opportunity to influence education and training in the way they had been desiring for a number of years; the Labour Party and unions saw it as an opportunity to improve training provision for a previously neglected group. In spite of misgivings about indoctrination on the part of left-wing members, the teachers' union saw the scheme as a way to preserve their members' jobs. This coming together of interests lay behind the production of the Youth Task Group Report (MSC 1982b), the crucial document proposing the scheme.

I have tried to show how the consensus was accompanied by pressures drawing the interest groups apart. This was most evident in the haggling over the actual form and content of the scheme, most particularly in the area of the curriculum where the chief protagonists of the debate were the MSC and the FEU. The results of empirical investigation indicate that both organizations had a measure of success and of failure. On the whole, the MSC view prevailed. Using its powerful position as the organizer and provider of finance for the scheme, the MSC was able to block attempts by colleges to be the local organizers of schemes. However, the results show that MSC's reliance on employers to provide effective arrangements for work-based learning was misplaced since inexperienced Managing Agents in many cases failed to fulfil their responsibilities.

On the ideological front, after a slow start, the MSC has made progress through commissioning the IMS to provide a curricular philosophy of sorts while preserving MSC's reputation as primarily an agency training young people for jobs. MSC has made great practical advances in avoiding the image of YOP as a programme of social support and replacing it with an image of YTS as a permanent national training scheme.

The FEU, however, has had more limited success. Indeed, in many respects the FEU's efforts could be seen as a rearguard action by liberal educationists to preserve their influence within the new vocationalism. The FEU approach was clearly relevant to the non-exam, college-based and lower-stream YTS courses, where social support remained the major aim of teachers, rather than training for jobs. But on Mode A courses FEU was less succesful because of the prevalence of examination syllabuses and training for particular trades.

It is likely that YTS will continue to become integrated with established apprenticeship and examination structures, while adding new structures of its own to occupational areas where training did not exist before YTS. The extension of YTS to a two-year programme is likely to involve employers to an even greater extent than did the one year programme. The proposal that all YTS courses should be under one Mode suggests that the WIC courses of 1983–4 may not continue, and that YTS will move still further away from providing social support for those with special needs. Perhaps these young people will gravitate towards the new CPVE qualification (JBPVE 1984), which promises to fulfil FEU ideas about vocational preparation. If YTS does continue to move in this direction it would seem essential that some investigation into employers' provision for YTS be conducted. This is a neglected area in the evaluations of YTS conducted until now, and if employers are to be given even greater responsibilities for implementing the new vocationalism then their practices should be examined most rigorously by bodies independent of the MSC.

References and bibliography

Association of College Registrars and Administrators. (1985). *YTS Questionnaire*. Unpublished report available from F. Evans, Ebbw Vale College of FE.

Barr, G., Aspinall, P. (1984). 'FE and the YTS: time to pull out', *NATFHE Journal*, October.

Bates, I. (1984). '*Schooling for the Dole: the New Vocationalism*'. Macmillan.

Bedeman, T., Courtney, G. (1982). *One in Three: the Second National Survey of Young People on YOP*. MSC Research & Development series, no. 13.

Confederation of British Industry (1980). *CBI Education and Training Bulletin*. vol. 10, no. 3.

Confederation of British Industry (1981). 'Manpower and training', *CBI Education and Training Bulletin*, vol. 11 no. 3.

Confederation of British Industry (1982). *CBI Education and Training Bulletin*. vol. 12 no. 3.

Cunningham, J. (1984). 'Young Blood', *Guardian*, 6 April.

Department of Education and Science. (1984). *Report by H.M. Inspectors on the Youth Training Scheme in Further, Education 1983–4*, DES.

Further Education Unit (1979a). *A Basis for Choice*. FEU.

Further Education Unit (1979b). *Supporting YOP*. FEU.

Further Education Unit (1980). *Developing Social and Life Skills: Strategies for Tutors*. FEU.

Further Education Unit (1982). *Vocational Preparation*. FEU.

Further Education Unit (1983). *Supporting YTS*. FEU.

Further Education Unit (1985). *Evaluation of the FE role in YTS*. FEU.

Further Education Unit/Manpower Services Commission (1982). *A New Training Initiative: Joint Statement by MSC/FEU. No. 1 General Principles*. FEU/MSC.

Great Britain (1981). *A New Training Initiative: a Programme for Action*. HMSO.

Greaves, K., Gostyn, P., Bonsall, C. (1982). *Off the Job Training on YOP*, MSC Research and Development Series, no. 12.

Guardian, The (1978). 'Tory call for 700m youth training scheme', *Guardian*, 21 June.

Hayes, C., Fonda, N., Noble, C. (1983). 'YTS and training for skill ownership', *Employment Gazette*, August.

Hofkins, D. (1980). 'The fruits of unemployment: YOP at South Tyneside', *NATFHE Journal*, June/July.

Holland, G. (1982). Speech given at Annual Meeting of Regional Advisory Councils for Further Education, 10 September.

Institute of Manpower Studies (1981). *Occupational Training Families*. IMS Report, no. 34.

Institute of Manpower Studies (1982). *Skills Needed for Young Peoples' Jobs*. vols 1–v, IMS.

Institute of Manpower Studies (1983). *Training for Skill Ownership: Learning to Take it With You*. IMS.

Into Work (1979). *In Need of Experience: a Study of the Views of Unemployed Young People on the YOP*. Into Work.

Joint Board for Pre-vocational Education: consultative document. JBPVE.

Labour Weekly (1982). 'Education for all', *Labour Weekly*, 8 January.

Maclure, S. (1982). 'The educational consequences of Mr. Norman Tebit', *Oxford Review of Education,* vol. 8, no. 2.

Manpower Services Commission (1976). *Annual Review 1975–6*. MSC.

Manpower Services Commission (1977). *Instructional Guide to Social and Life Skills*. MSC.

Manpower Services Commission (1978). *Young Peopld and Work*. HMSO.

Manpower Services Commission (1979). *Annual Review 1978–9*. MSC.

Manpower Services Commission (1982a). *Annual Review 1981–2*. MSC.

Manpower Services Commission (1982b). *Youth Task Group Report*. MSC.

Manpower Services Commission (1982c). *Guidelines on Content and Standards in YTS*. MSC.

Manpower Services Commission (1984a). *Ethnic Minorities and the Youth Training Scheme*. MSC.

Manpower Services Commission (1984b). *Evaluation of YTS Content*. MSC.

Moos, M. (1983). 'The Training Myth', in Gleeson, D. *Youth Training and the Search for Work*, Routledge & Kegan Paul.

Mulley, F. (1976). DES press notice, 23 March.

National Association of Teachers in Further and Higher Education (1977). 'Harrogate conference 1977 – decisions and debate' *NATFHE Journal*, June–July.

National Association of Teachers in Further and Higher Education (1982a). *NATFHE Journal*, March.

National Association of Teachers in Further and Higher Education (1982b). *NTI White Paper – NEC Statement Circular*, 24 February.

National Association of Teachers in Further and Higher Education (1982c). press release, NATFHE, ref. PR 17/82.

O'Brien, R. (1978). 'MSC's new programmes for the 16–19 age group, and their implications for Further Education', AGM of Association of Colleges for Further and Higher Education.

Pates, A. (1982). 'Social and life skills: materials – or immaterials?', *NATFHE Journal, March*.

Schools Council (1982). news release to press, 25 February.

Seale, C.F. (1984). 'FEU and MSC: two curricular philosophies and their implications for the Youth Training Scheme', *Voc. Aspect,* vol. 36, no. 93.

Seale, C.F. (1985). 'Young people on the Youth Training Scheme: a survey of the first year', *Educational Review,* vol. 37, no. 3.

Seale, C.F. (1986a). 'The Youth Training Scheme in Further Education: a comparison of employer based and college based, special needs schemes', to be published in *British Educational Research Journal*.

Seale, C.F. (1986b). 'Further Education and the Youth Training Scheme: a survey of the first year', to be published in *Research in Education*.

Stoney, S. Scott. V. (1984). *The Youth Training Scheme and the FE response*. NFER Research in progress, no. 7.

Times Higher Education Supplement (1981). 'Labour reveals training plans for 16–19 year olds', *THES* 7 August.

Wellens, D.J. (1984). 'Review of recent developments', *Industrial and Commercial Training*, vol. 16, o. 6.

Williams, S. (1978). DES press notice, 8 June.

Woolcock, P. (1983). 'The idiot's guide to work', *Guardian*, 10 May.

Young, D. (1982). *The Director*. October.

CHAPTER 8

The new sophists: the work and assumptions of the FEU

Paul Grosch

To a greater or lesser degree education has always suffered from the uncritical prescriptions and practices of pseudo-missionaries out to stamp their own brand of philosophy on the system. From the fifth-century sophists to the modern-day vocationalists, education has often been characterized as a means to competitive personal success for the individual, or as an instrument to achieve competitive economic success for the nation. The rebirth of the Greek sophist movement, in its current guise of vocationalism and pre-vocationalism, represents another attempt to transform education into just such an instrument.

In this chapter I intend to take a look at a relatively new but increasingly influential body on the modern vocational landscape: the FEU. Despite its generally recognized ability to make a significant impact on education, surprisingly little had been written about it. Pring (1981)[1] views the FEU in an extremely favourable light, recommending its method of curriculum innovation to the secondary sector. Seale (1984)[2] compares and contrasts it with the MSC in relation to the YTS. But other than these two brief pieces, most of the literature *about* the FEU is written principally *by* the FEU.

Although a comparatively small body, dwarfed by the two organizational giants – the DES and the MSC – the FEU is beginning to gain a significant foothold in many of the areas which have traditionally lain outside the purview of mainstream vocational education and training. Not only has the FEU made a widely acknowledged impact on the Further Education (FE) sector, for which it was originally devised and created, but its voice is rapidly beginning to be heard in the secondary sector as well. This largely uninvited but direct incursion into the arena of compulsory schooling needs to be laid out for public inspection and consideration.

The FEU's voice is being heard in the secondary sector through two structurally distinct but philosophically and politically similar channels – the TVEI[3] and the CPVE[4]. Through TVEI (an invention of the MSC), the FEU has forged important links with another newly created body which is also beginning to have more than just a ripple effect on the secondary education sector, namely, the SCDC[5]. The FEU in conjunction with the SCDC has recently published *Supporting TVEI* (1985), a companion document, it would seem, to the FEU's singularly successful publication, *Supporting YTS* (1985) now in its third edition. And through the CPVE (an invention of the DES), the FEU has strengthened its links with the DES by agreeing to mount a series of CPVE Staff Development Programmes in and across those of the 104 LEAs that have sought to enter into a loose 'semi-partnership' with the Joint Board for Pre-Vocational Education (JBPVE)[6] by agreeing to offer the recently sanctioned 17–plus qualification in their schools and colleges.

By first examining the FEU and its various workings in a rather general manner, and then by concentrating on its favoured models of curriculum design and development I hope to throw a little light on some of the deeper issues embedded in the particular brand of vocationalism being propounded, peddled and proferred by this increasingly powerful body.

The sophist route: vocationalism and instrumentalism

The Sophists, or 'wise men', were a fifth-century Greek school of philosophy committed to a particular view of education. Protagoras, its main proponent, regarded education purely as a means to practical success in life for the individual. The pursuit of true and irrefragable knowledge was deemed to be a fruitless quest; hence, the only intellectually justifiable alternative to this quest was the direct pursuit of useful knowledge and skills which would enable an individual to make a success of him or herself in the workaday world. Socrates, however, was deeply concerned that such 'schools for success', with their emphasis only on the knowledge and skills necessary to negotiate life in a practical way were basically misconceived. Socrates argued that unless one acutally *knew*, or at least could argue with conviction, the rightness or wrongness of a course of action, unless one was fully aware of the central moral nature of one's decisions and/or actions, then one's so-called 'success' in life could well lead to moral and intellectual ruin, not only for oneself but for everyone else besides.

It is not stretching the bounds of credibility too far to maintain that the recent trends towards modern vocationalism (and their connection with what is supposed to constitute success in adult working life), derive their underlying rationale from the same kind of instrumental view of education that was once held by the Sophists. The newly spawned agencies of vocationalism currently making a purchase on education in general and the curriculum in particular, represent newly revised and rehabilitated forms of these ancient 'schools for success' – modern versions of Sophism. What is wholly significant is the predominantly instrumental view that the new vocationalists tend to have of everything and anything. Everything becomes merely a means to a collection of preordained ends. Not only do knowledge and skills become purely instrumental in the sense that they are 'acquired' only for the use they can be put to in order to achieve or produce something beyond their 'mere' acquisition, but people also become instrumental in the sense that their principal *raison d'etre* is seen to be synonymous with their prospective contribution to the nation's economic success. 'Success' for the individual is then already defined for him. All he has to do is strive to become that which the vocationalists decide he ought to become and then the future, however morally, aesthetically or intellectually bleak, will hold no fear or threat for him. Certain worthwhile activities to which are attached, primarily, internal or intrinsic qualities and values (such as those associated with the arts), gradually become subordinate to certain activities (such as those associated with science and technology) which have massive instrumental value inasmuch as they lead to direct material pay-offs. One has only to scrutinize both national[7] and local[8] curriculum documents in order to discover the growing accent on the notion of vocationalism and the increased emphasis being placed on science and technology, with the concomitant indifference towards the arts and humanities. This is a pattern that is seemingly being repeated throughout all levels of education[9].

Of these freshly-spawned agencies of vocationalism, two in particular stand out as being especially significant: the MSC and the FEU. Although the former is by far the larger, the more politically secure, and the more generously funded organization, it may be argued that the latter, being more subtle in its interventionist tactics, tends to be more successful in achieving its stated objectives. Contained within the rhetoric and perceived image of modern vocationalism there are two identifiable instrumental attitudes, or two forms of instrumentalism (Scrimshaw 1983)[10]: the 'traditional' and the 'adaptive'. The traditional form of instrumentalism, manifested by the MSC, is effectively the unacceptable face of vocationalism. The MSC has little or no refined educational image; its pronouncements on education smack more of the director's boardroom or the manager's office, than of the professor's study or the teacher's classroom. One has only to compare and contrast some of the educational liturgies composed by the MSC with, say, those composed by the now defunct Schools Council in order to witness its relatively impoverished understanding of what, generally speaking, education is conceived to be about. The following example is relevant to the overall argument inasmuch as it was the FEU who commissioned these responses from all the agencies that had attended one of its seminars on 'Progressing from Vocational Preparation'.[11] The language of unblushing instrumentalism characterizing the MSC response contrasts with the tentative and semi-philosophical account offered by the Schools Council.

The support of the examining and validating bodies is essential to the task of ensuring that within a standard-based system every young person is able to acquire a range of competencies and experiences which facilitate the transition into working and adult life and serve as a foundation for subsequent employment or continued training or relevant further education.

(MSC, 1982, from FEU, *Progressing from vocational preparation.*, p. 52)

Indeed the overarching aim of education – expressed in familiar but not redundant terms – remains the development of the whole person. The pace of change that forces constant reappraisal of the objectives and processes of education also demands that we eschew narrow and debilitating interpretations of relevance and preparation. Post–16 education should, inter alia, extend students' appreciation of world, society and community and develop an understanding of work as part of this fabric.

(Schools Council, 1982, ibid., p. 42)

Taking these two responses to the same issue, one can judge for oneself why it is that in the mid 1980s the Schools Council is no longer with us, while the MSC continues to grow inexorably in both fortune and fame. Woolly notions of the 'whole person' cut no ice with governments intent upon calling education to account. The FEU tends to steer a middle course between the approaches of the MSC and the Schools Council and has, in many of its documented responses and publication, modified or at the very least masked the more overt signals of extreme instrumentalism. It may be argued therefore that in doing so it represents the more acceptable face of vocationalism. Using Scrimshaw's terms the FEU signifies a move towards 'adaptive instrumentalism'. For example, witness the style and content of the FEU's original discussion document upon which the seminar was based:

We have in the UK a history of persistent neglect of the majority of our young people once they leave school; a neglect that has been exposed in the light of increasing youth unemployment ... much of the existing YOP provision has been criticized because of its non-educational approach and its ephemeral value. It is essential, in any new system, that we move away from schemes based on youth unemployment towards programmes focused on personal development.

The primary aim of this paper is to emphasize that if vocational preparation is to become a central educational process available to all young people whether or not they are involved in other study or training, then it msut be recognized as such.

(FEU, 1982, *ibid.*, p. 11)

The similarities between this and the Schools Council response are fairly self-evident: the emphasis that needs to be placed on 'education' in any new initiative; the criticism of the 'non-educational' nature of past training schemes, and the focus on 'personal development'. Also, in summarizing its own and others' responses to the seminar, the FEU partly endorses the scepticism expressed by the Schools Council; but there is a sting in the tail.

In deliberately spanning the 14–19 curriculum, the Schools Council is obviously reluctant to unreservedly endorse a skills based approach to the curriculum. As is the FEU; unless we can get a more enlightened definition of *skill* and this we have attempted elsewhere.[12]

(FEU, 1982, *ibid.*, p. 6)

Having first agreed with the Schools Council, the FEU then pledges allegiance to the vocational idea of a curriculum founded principally upon a set of prescribed skills, provided only that it is the set prescribed byt he FEU itself!

But what of the FEU itself? What kind of agency is it? Who created it and why, and where is it now headed?

The FEU takes shape ...

The Further Education Curriculum Review and Development Unit (FEU) was set up in 1977 under Callaghan's Labour Government by the then Secretary of State for Education and Science, Shirley Williams. It remained as a separate department within the DES until 1 January 1983 when it gained independent status as a company limited by guarantee[13]. Its official four-fold remit is as follows:

1 to review and evaluate the range of existing further education curricular programmes and to idenfity overlap, duplication, deficiencies and inconsistences therein;

2 to determine priorities for action to improve the provision of further education and to make recommendations as to how such improvement can be effected;

3 to carry out studies in further education and to support investigations of, and experimentation in and the development of, further education curricula and to contribute to and assist in the evaluation of initiatives in further education;

4 to disseminate and publish information and to assist in the dissemination and publication of information about recommendations for and experiments and developments in further education

(FEU, 1984, *Annual Report*, p. 11)

With reference to funding, the FEU receives an annual grant from the DES. In 1984–5 this amounted to a sum of just under two million pounds. Out of this, approximately one million pounds covers all administration expenditure, which includes a salary bill of half a million, and a printing and publications bill of three hundred thousand. In 1980–1 its Research and Development costs amounted to a mere fifty thousand pounds. This has risen to its present (1984–5) figure of just over seven hundred thousand.

For a wide-angle perspective on the FEU's overall activities, nine basic areas of concern could be identified in 1983–4[14]. These were: vocational preparation; curriculum review; new technology; staff development and education management; adult education and training; experimental colleges; special needs; multicultural education, and the creation and maintenance of its own organizational network: the Regional Curriculum Bases (RCBs). These nine areas have remained fundamentally the same, although there have been some additions and revisions since 1984–5.[15] Consequently, the current areas of concern may be understood to include the following.

1 Vocational preparation

This the FEU sees as a 'priority area' and it 'continues to support the implementation and evaluation of vocational preparation schemes whether employer, college or school-based' (FEU, 1985, *Annual Report 1984–5*, p. 3) This, of course, relates not only to the CPVE, but also to the multiplicity of TVEI schemes in which FE colleges are actively encouraged, by the FEU, to participate.

2 Mainstream vocational education

Here the FEU has concentrated much of its energies on three major initiatives: engineering, business studies and distribution[16].

3 New technology

In this field the FEU's general policy is to encourage the extensive application of Information Technology (IT) to the *whole* curriculum and not just in terms of selected curriculum areas[17].

4 Education and training of adults

Here the FEU is engaged in a two-pronged approach. Firstly, it has linked up with the DES in its Professional, Industrial and Commercial Updating (PICKUP) programme, and currently has over fifty projects already approved with a further hundred Local Collaborative Projects underway. In addition, the FEU is responsible for the general coordination of the PICKUP Regional Development Agencies (RDAs). Secondly, it is involved in the DES REPLAN programme, a programme designed to enhance the opportunities in education for the adult unemployed. To date, thirteen of its proposed projects have gained DES approval[18].

5 Women and FE

The FEU has at least two major projects (Nos 246 and 302)[19] aimed at reappraising the curriculum in order that the 'needs and potential' of women are fully acknowledged.

6 Special learning needs

Since 1980–1 the FEU has conducted, on a fairly consistent basis, some wide-ranging and extremely valuable work in this area. Intent upon integrating students with special needs into mainstream FE, the FEU has maintained close liaison with the National Bureau of Handicapped Students (NBHS)[20].

7 Curriculum development for a multicultural socitey

Here again the FEU has made substantial advances in dealing intelligently and far-sightedly with what many see as a deeply embedded educational problem. Many of the FEU utterances have alienated it from its political masters since the FEU continues to focus on the 'disproportionate unemployment among young black people; (and) the continued manifestations of racism in our society' (FEU, 1984, *Focus on Multicultural Society* no. 3)[21].

8 FE management

With the upsurge of interest in management studies in general and education management in particular, the FEU has endeavoured not only to keep pace with contemporary styles and approaches but to forge ahead with them. As a consequence the FEU set up an Education Management Advisory Committee in 1983 and has three major projects currenly due for publication[22].

9 Marketing FE

In its 1984–5 *Report* the FEU 'recognized that *marketing* has become a major development issue within FE' (p. 10). The FEU has since engaged the services of a professional marketing research organization which it hopes will help to improve, through a series of five institutional evaluations, the overall public image of FE.

10 Curriculum review

A significant aspect of the FEU's remit to review the curriculum in FE is its present involvement in the 'Working Group on the Review of Vocational Qualifications (RVQ)[23]. In addition, the FEU has informally extended its remit by involving itself directly in the secondary curriculum through its joint publication (with the SCDC) of *Supporting TVEI* (1985). Through membership of the Working Group (RVQ), it maintains close contact with the 'Working Party for Pre-Vocational Courses: Pre–16', established by Sir Keith Joseph in April 1985[24]. Finally, the FEU is monitoring the implications of the MSC's increased financial involvement in non-advanced further education (NAFE) which was written into the 1984 White Paper: *Training for Jobs*.

11 Curriculum innovation and delivery

In one sense this represents a catch-all heading for much of the work carried out by the FEU and it would be beyond the scope of this chapter to chart all the direct and indirect influences the FEU has exerted on the myriad curricular innovations within both secondary and further education. Its most recent activity however, apart from the pre-vocational work already mentioned, can be classified under the following subheadings: interactive video[25]; flexible learning[26]; and numeracy skills[27]. Nonetheless, the FEU's fundamental thrust in curriculum innovation stil remains within the mushrooming field of assessment. And its two publication *Profiles* (1982) and *Profiles in Action* (1984) have figured as principal texts in the current debate about 'alternative' modes of assessment.

12 Experimental colleges

This is a noteworthy area of FEU activity as the Department of Trade and Industry (DTI) has expresed a close interest in the FEU's network of eleven

'Experimental Colleges'. Each of these eleven has gone through a three-phase programme involving:

> (a) the conducting of individual curriculum projects and expeiments:
> (b) the carrying out of curriculum innovation across a range of FE themes;
> (c) the agreement to act as a test-bed for specific FEU designated curriculum projects.[28]

13 Staff development

This, coupled with 'Curriculum Innovation and Delivery', 'Pre-Vocational Education' and 'Mainstream Vocational Education' constitutes one of the foremost features of FEU work. I shall argue that although in one respect it has proved to be the mainstay of FEU success, it also represents the most potentially disturbing aspect of FEU activity. It has conducted much of its staff development work through its ten Regional Curriculum Bases (RCBs), particularly in respect of its incursion into the pre-vocational field[29].

14 FEU/LEA links

In conjunction with its policies on staff development and its careful nurturing of the RCB arrangement, the FEU's embryonic role within the structure of the LEA system is highly significant. It is possible to interpret this proposed wide-ranging and influential, but as yet informal, education management network as constituting the best means of deliberately securing FEU or FEU-type curriculum objectives within both the secondary and further education sectors. A senior professional and social network stretching across the 104 LEAs, and plugged into the ten RCBs would be of incalculable value to the FEU in its continued fight for financial survival and political support against a grudging DES and a notably hegemonic MSC. Also, in order to strengthen its sphere of influence the FEU has actively sought to make some lasting connections with the Association of County Councils (ACC) and the Association of Metropolitan Authorities (AMA)[30].

These fourteen areas of concern[31] play a major part in creating a multi-faceted and all-pervasive image of and for the FEU. And it is not difficult to begin to perceive what kind of complex political manoeuvrings the FEU is obliged to engage in to secure its objectives in each of these areas. Firstly, within education's vertical sturcture the FEU is, very obviously, placed firmly within the FE sector whilst simultaneously thrusting its tentacles down into the secondary sector and pushing them up into the regions of higher education. Secondly, within a horizontal administration structure the FEU apparently sees itself at the centre of operations, gaining an increasing grip on the LEA administrative web through the sensitive manipulation of its RCB network. And thirdly, within a finely wrought associated structure, the FEU recognizes that it is forced to enter into delicate political and economic relationships with such richly diversified bodies as the DES, MSC, DTI, and DoE. As a consequence of carrying out this supreme balancing act the FEU is often faced with the difficult task of trying to reconcile the conflicting external pressures coming from these widely disparate organizations, with the competing internal demands it places upon itself through its direct intervention within these qualtatively different structures.

None of this can be a cosy business; the maintenance of alliances and treaties in a fluctuating territorial landscape requires the keenest social and political acumen. Partly as a result of all this we see the FEU trying, on a theoretical level, to manage and reduce the very real tensions that do actually exist between 'education' and 'training'[32] and, on a practical level, attempting to achieve this by helping to blur the distinctions between the two at the top of the secondary school curriculum through its active support of TVEI and CPVE.

FEU: Pawn, knight or bishop?

According to its *Annual Report 1983–4* (p. 1) two of the FEU's original terms of reference framed in 1977 have constituted a repeated feature of its overall work. These, as will have been noted, can be summarized as: (1) 'helping' with curriculum experimentations; and (2) 'sharing' information. However, three of the remaining terms of reference had, (again according to the Report), been neglected. These terms can be understood as being to do with: (1) reviewing existing FE curricula; (2) identifying curricular overlap; and (3) determining a range of priorities for action following on from just such a series of reviews.

It may be argued however, that these particular terms of reference have now come very much to the fore in FEU thinking, and appear to dominate its future planning. Given the multiplicity of external agencies attempting to corner the education and training market with the 16–19 or 14–18 age range (depending upon the agency and its preferred policy), it is not surprising that the the FEU has suddenly become more expansionist in its practice, more rationalist in its approach, more conformist in its vision, and more prescriptive in its policies. For apart from attempting to maintain its high-profile image as a recently matured body independent of the DES, it is obliged to play this fiercely political chess game previously hinted at, as a knight with newly-acquired spurs engaged in polite combat both alongside and against the MSC's current role of ubiquitous queen and the DES's role of plodding king. In addition, having patched an alliance (for the purposes of CPVE) with BTEC and CGLI in their combined role as JBPVE, it finds itself having to bring them to heel in themushrooming vocational qualifications market[33]. The FEU's uneasy position has been clearly underlined by some of the statements contained within the *Interim Report* on the *Review of Vocational Qualifications in*

England and Wales (1985) issued jointly by the DES and the MSC. In determining what ought to be done in relation to the increasing spread of diverse vocational qualifications, the working group concluded that:

> machinery must be established to undertake more detailed analysis of existing qualifications, draw up a comprehensive blueprint for an improved structure, introduce it, and be held accountable for it. (p. 5)

A number of options as to which body shall be responsible for this machinery are, to date, being considered. One of them is to offer the whole package to 'an existing Government department or agency such as the Department of Education and Science (DES), the MSC or the Further Education Unit (FEU)' (p. 5). But, as has already been pointed out, the FEU, although a contender, is hardly able to match either the MSC or the DES in terms of political or financial power. However, it does possess a highly developed sense of educational pulse-taking, unlike the staid and traditionally bureaucratized DES, and the slickly bureaucratized but educationally blinkered MSC. The working group has been quick to recognize this:

> both the DES and the MSC already have expertise and strong contacts, but only in parts of the territory to be covered. The FEU has a high degree of expertise in the education field but no experience inthe training area or in acting as a regulatory or co-ordinating body. (*ibid.*, pp. 5–6)

In its response to this Interim Report the FEU has sought to clarify its current position in relation to the other main contenders and has seen a possible opening which would allow it to expand its operations. Within its response the FEU also incorporates a moderate rebuff of the working party's contention that it (FEU) lacks training expertise.

> The FEU, suitably augmented in terms of resources and remit would be willing and able to undertake the task. As the RVQ exercise is related to a greater degree of unification between education and industry-based qualifications, any agency will have to expand its expertise to cope with a new structure; and anyway the unit is not without experience in the training area.
> (FEU, 1985, *Response to the Review of Vocational Qualifications. Interim Report* p. 4)

In addition to its actual purposes, this response gives us a clearer indication of the 'vocationalists'' intentions, i.e., to achieve a 'greater degree of unification between education and industry-based qualifications'. Secondary education, further education, higher education? All three? The statement is ambiguous and one wonders to what extent it is a prediction of future policies.

In fairness, the FEU has acknowledge its own lowly knight's status and has contrived to raise itself publicly to bishop. One has only to read the 'Chairman's Foreword' for 1983–4 and 1984–5 respectively to note the change of tone from apologetic murmuring to confident declamation. In the 1983–4 Report the chairman stated rather self-effacingly that:

part of the energy of the Unit has been spent in trying to find more clarity in presentation and understanding. The readership of its publications could still be wider. (p. 1 *op. cit.*)

No such apologies in the 1984–5 'Foreword' where the chairman declared that:

the Unit for the first time established itself in a position of influence. The Unit spoke with authority on vocational preparation, mainstream vocational education, women in FE and FE in a multicultrual society. (p. viii, *op. cit.*)

The chairman characterized the FEU workings as 'expert and sensitive' whilst at the same time acknowledging its politically weak position. In a quaintly barbed closing paragraph the chairman averred that:

any revision of the structure of mainstream vocational education requires a greater level of political support than the FEU normally enjoys. (p. 2 *op. cit.*)

For the sake of the knight's survival, the FEU may be well advised to stick closely with the MSC's image of ubiquitous queen, instead of with the DES's counter image of the plodding and increasingly isolated king.

However, the situation may well not be as simple as all that. A recent article by Mark Jackson[34] suggests a murkier political depth to the whole issue than has just been intimated. According to Jackson, the FEU has perhaps miscalculated the strength of its possible connections with either the MSC or the DES, and is in danger of being cast aside by both. In addition to this, he sees the FEU being totally marginalized in the near future by yet another body which has begun to ascend the rungs of power and influence: the Further Education Staff College (FESC) at Coombe Lodge.

What is interesting here is that the present head of Coombe Lodge just happens to be Mr Geoffry Melling, an HMI who was the FEU's first director. Under Geoffrey Melling's direction Coombe Lodge now appears to be cornering an ever-larger proportion of the 'commissioned works' market operated by the MSC, with the FEU being left with an ever-smaller one.

What is of real importance however, is that (again according to Jackson), the FEU is in the business of roundly criticizing the FESC for adopting a too narrow and instrumentalist view of the FE curriculum. But for the FEU to assume the role of an erstwhile St George defending the concept of 'education' against a concept of 'training' wielded by the triple dragons of MSC, FESC and Industry is – as I hope to show by reference to its own model of curriculum development – a considerable irony.

In this desperate chess game of power then, the FEU, instead of moving up from knight to bishop, may well find itself ending up as a mere pawn, eventually being sacrificed through the mightier moves of others.

The FEU in action

In terms of its knowledge and experience of how curriculum innovation and development actually works in practice, the FEU is in advance of both the

DES and the MSC. By referring to Havelock's (1969)[35] analytical models which suggest how curriculum innovation and development operate either badly or well, it is plain to see that the FEU has learned from the past mistakes of others. Briefly, Havelock proposed three ways in which curriculum innovation is developed and then disseminated. Firstly, there is the 'Research, Development and Diffusion' (RDD) model, often referred to as the 'centre-periphery' or 'top-down' model. This approach to innovation and development was commonly used by the Schools Council in its early days, and the Humanities Curriculum Project (HCP) is probably one of the better known examples.

The model, imported from the United States and traced to its industrial and commercial roots rests on the 'invention' and meticuluous development of a project or set of prescriptive policies at a central point and then farmed out in an ordered and directive fashion to the periphery, in this case, the schools. Needless to say, in education this model has proved itself to be singularly unsuccessful, ill-suited as it is to the task in hand. This is because it rests on a purely technological and utilitarian view of teachers. The hidden assumption is that teachers are passive receivers at the edge of power, accepting packaged wisdom devised at the centre, and then acting as almost dehumanized agents transmitting this received wisdom on to their pupils. The model neglected to acknowledge the fact that education is fundamentally about values, meanings and beliefs being explored by teachers and pupils alike in a social institution.

It is not about the maintenance of a mere knowledge or skills factory where these things are simply transferred from one body to another. As this model repeatedly failed to deliver the goods, curriculum developers sought to find better ways and means of disseminating ideas and materials. As a result, Havelock identified the emergence of a second model; the 'Social Interaction' model. Here curriculum innovators and developers recognized the need for teachers to be directly or personally involved in some way with the policies or practices that were being recommended for adoption. This, consequently, meant a good deal of social interaction between 'innovators' and 'deliverers'. Hence the directives issuing from the centre were deliberately filtered through what are known as 'intermediate agencies'. Generally speaking these have tended to be teachers' centres or local colleges of further or higher education. Thirdly, Havelock identified what he saw as the 'problem solving' or 'periphery-centre' model. This completely moves the focus of importance from the centre to the periphery body, i.e. the school. Here, the school becomes its own newly defined 'centre' of self-diagnosed and self-directed change with what was originally the centre becoming sensitive, responsive and supportive to the school.

It can be argued that the DES has invariably adopted the first model of so-called 'innovation and development' by issuing a host of curriculum edicts from Elizabeth House and believing or assuming that teachers will assimilate and discharge their self-contained instructions accordingly. Certainly the number and variety of prescriptive and semi-prescriptive documents emanating from the centre has increased dramatically since 1979, and since 1981 it has been Sir Keith Joseph, more than any other Secretary of State since 1944, who has sought to impose or enforce particularly preferred modes of teaching and learning upon schools through the medium of either threatened or actual parliamentary legislation[36]. The MSC has tended also to adopt the first (RDD) model, principally, it would seem, as a consequence of its own self-imposed and diabolically rash timetabling procedures. As Maurice Holt has outlined, the speed at which the TVEI bolt was shot from the bow could not allow for the long-term rationalizing influence of a social interaction approach. However, its ability to make an impact on schools rests almost exclusively on the quantities of cash it is able to bring with it. When one considers that starting in September 1984 approximately 146 million pounds has been earmarked for spending on 19,760 students on TVEI schemes; and assuming this money is spent over the prescribed four-year period (14–18), it effectively means that each TVEI student will have benefited from having nearly seven and a half thousand pounds spent on him/her, in the form of straight cash, residential components, additional staffing and increased resources[37]. Contrast that with the paltry sum of approximately eighty four pounds spent over four years on every non-TVEI student[38].

Regional Curriculum Bases (RCBs) …

In realizing that it cannot compete either with such vast sums as those allocated to and by the MSC, or with the inherited political and social weight and status attached to the DES, the FEU has endeavoured to create alternative means of making an impact on education and training with its curriculum innovation and development policies. It has achieved this principally through the careful adoption of a well-oiled social interaction model founded on its Regional Curriculum Bases (RCBs) acting as intermediate agencies. According to the FEU (1984) publications, *The Regional Curriculum Base Initiative*, the RCBs:

> represent the first systematic attempt to create a regional network for the support of a specific area of curriculum development in FE. (p. vi, Preface)

The idea of establishing a Regional Curriculum Base was originally conceived in the West Midlands in 1979. A group of 16–19 year olds at the lower end of the academic ability range were identified as requiring a tailored education and training programme, the main elements of which would be: 'basic skills training, occupational skills sampling, general personal counselling and work experience' (*ibid.*, p. 5). It was felt that a staff training programme (to match this student training programme) was not only desirable but essential. The focus for this curriculum development and staff training package was the West Midlands Regional Curriculum Unit (WMRCU) established in January 1979. As a consequence of its increasing importance to local staff, the FEU in conjunction with the West Midlands Advisory Council for FE, and with the on-site assistance of staff at the FE Teacher Education Institution at Wolverhampton Polytechnic, set up the West Midlands Regional Curriculum Base in October 1980 with FEU financial 'pump-priming' support for a period of two years. The success of this project has led to the setting up of nine other RCBs throughout England and Wales on the same 'pump-priming' basis. In addition, each of the RCBs is located within, and connected to each of the ten Regional Advisory Councils for FE (RACs). Some have now become financially independent of the FEU, receiving funding from LEAs and the MSC alike, but all are still accountable, in one way or another, to the FEU. Each RCB's official remit is as follows:

> 1 to support curriculum development generally in the areas of vocational preparation;
> 2 to initiate and support staff development activities in areas of vocational preparation;
> 3 to create/develop a network of interested persons/institutions through-out the region;
> 4 to develop an information service and resource collection.
>
> (p. 1, *ibid.*)

The kinds of things on offer at, or coordinated by RCBs tend to vary but generally speaking they are in the form of: one-day conferences; workshops; short and long-term residential sessions; and awareness-raising events on themes such as 'Vocational Preparation', 'Multi-skills Workshops', 'Base Skills' and 'Profiling'. The RCBs are, however, monitored carefully by the FEU; since what they offer (in terms of staff training and curriculum development) should have 'compatibility with FEU curricular policies' (*ibid.*, p. 29). But our principal interest lies with the FEU's characterization of the future value RCBs may have in helping to 'vocationalize' the secondary school curriculum. As the concluding section of its publication states:

> new developments and challenges such as the Technical and Vocational Education Initiative (TVEI) and the Certificate of Pre-Vocational Education (CPVE) provide a welcome broadening of the activities of the Regional Curriculum Base to the Secondary Education arena, (and) it is hoped that the expreiences and expertise in staff development which are now starting to be accrued can be extended. (*ibid.*, p. 37)

Staff development

Staff development, through social interaction, is acknowledged to be the key to successful curriculum innovation and development; hence the emphasis in FEU projects and pamphlets on the notion of general staff development, improvement and training. This is usually in the form of what has come to be known as 'Curriculum-led staff development' using a 'cascade model' of implementation. Briefly, its logic can be reduced to the following:

1 *First* frame a set of curriculum policies at the centre (e.g. at the FEU).
2 *Second* explain the policies to the coordinators of intermediate agencies (e.g. RCBs).
3 *Third* have intermediate agency coordinators identify teachers/lecturers who are likely to be, or already known to be sympathetic to the kinds of policies which have been centrally conceived. (Much of the subsequent work is now carried out by the intermediate agency coordinators).
4 *Fourth* invite all interested parties to a series of awareness-raising events and workshops which are intended to outline the 'philosophy' or theoretical principles and purposes underlying the set of established policies.
5 *Fifth* have all the interested parties transform the policies' theoretical principles into practical curriculum materials.
6 *Sixth* invite selected personnel to a series of training sessions designed to equip them with the technique necessary to train others in the adoption of the curriculum policies and the deployment of the practical materials. This is known as 'Training the Trainers'.

This, basically, is what is meant by 'curriculum-led staff development': devise a curriculum policy; 'develop' staff in order that they will accept it; they will then 'develop' further staff in order that they in turn will then accept it and deploy it within their individual institutions. So through a kind of osmosis, brought about by social interaction and group membership, the policies become firmly absorbed into all connected institutions. Or, to change the analogy, parish priests are initiated into the revised curriculum order and then sent out as converted missionaries to preach the new gospel[39].

The importance of the RCBs as intermediate agencies, and the importance of social interaction as a means of getting people to do what you wish them to do, is not lost on the Chairman or the Board of Management at the FEU. As is claimed in the 'Commentary' in the *Annual Report 1984–5* there are to be: 'New styles of bulletins, executive summaries, few project reports and more face-to-face seminars' (p. 1).

Nevertheless, despite its comparatively subtle and wide-ranging successes in deploying this model of curriculum innovation and development with limited resources, (as against the bludgeoning success of the financially fat MSC), the FEU still is concerned at its failure to impose strict uniformity. Its downward thrust into schools via CPVE and TVEI, and its concern to unify the national system, particularly in terms of staff development, is evidenced by its Chairman's comment in one of its occasional *Newsletters*:

> Those projects which need a unified in-service policy across the schools and the FE sector are bound to include CPVE, profiling involvement in TVEI, and a long-term concern with teaching styles.
>
> (Owen, J.G. September, 1984, *Newsletter*)

And the key to this 'unified in-service policy' is control; a form of cybernetic control in danger of straitjacketing a whole system which paradoxically the FEU has assisted in loosening up and modernizing. FE staff, it would appear, need 'further development' if FEU curriculum policies are to have precisely the kind of institutional impact they were orginally designed to have.

> The gap between FEU messages and implementation shows how desperately systematic staff development is required throughout the FE system.
>
> (FEU, (1985), *Annual Report 1984–5* p. 1)

This point is emphasized in the case of the FEU's staff development programme for the implementation of CPVE. The FEU had commissioned 'external evaluators' to monitor and evaluate the various staff development courses which were in progress throughout the country's 104 LEAs. In the event, it turned out that the FEU had apparently wanted not 'democratic evaluators', but 'bureaucratic evaluators' (MacDonald, 1976)[40], or what Trow (1984)[41] calls 'policy analysts'. That is, persons who are in total agreement with the fundamental curriculum policies, and who are there to monitor any procedural problems which may interfere with the delivery of those policies. In the final 'debriefing' session at the FEU headquarters, both FEU officials and external evaluators were surprised to learn of a question mark being placed (by two schoolteachers) over the behavioural objectives model which underpins the CPVE. The documented response by an FEU official to this voicing of disquiet over the use of behavioural objectives, was: 'Obviously the programme needs systematizing and controlling![42]' In this respect the FEU exhibits a classic case of what Russell (1955)[43] termed the 'administrator's fallacy': the notion that society, or in this case the social institution of education, is a unified whole and can be 'systematized' according to a premeditated ideology and pre-planned model order[44].

Moreover, the FEU, in its strong desire to secure all of its curricular aims and objectives, has widened its staff development net to include all non-teaching staff as well. Its (1984) *Policy Statement* puts the case thus:

> If curriculum provision is accepted as the main object of the college, then sustained effort is needed beyond orientation/induction to keep *all* staff both aware of the rationale behind curriculum development and also alive to their own contribution. Support staff are no exception to this process and they are essential to the support system which is at the centre of our model of curriculum development.
>
> (FEU, (1984), *Staff Development for Support Staff in Further Education: Policy Statement*)

The key phrase is 'the rationale behind curriculum development'. Effectively this means the rationale shaped and fashioned by the FEU in terms of its own conception of the 'needs' it believes individuals, namely students, either have or ought to have. Staff development is necessary in order that students needs may be identified, described, classified and finally attended to within the boundaries of a so-called 'negotiated' curriculum. In order that this may be achieved, the FEU has first to identify and meet the needs of staff engaged in their new task of propounding the 'needs-based' pre-vocational and vocational ideology.

'Needs', 'skills' and 'curriculum design'

I say 'needs-based' because in the new pre-vocational and vocational parlance, the 'needs' of individuals are almost always defined in terms of 'skills' which they supposedly lack. Furthermore, these 'skills' (the word is now wholly synonymous with 'needs'), are generally of a kind which industrialists and politicians claim that society must be able to call upon in order for the economy to be kept afloat. Hence, in a kind of reverse logic, the 'needs' of industry (articulated in the public sphere of politics) are cleverly translated into the 'needs' of individuals (articulated in the public sphere of education)[45]. Once this single semantic feat is accomplished many other 'problems' can also be included in this reversed logic: the blame for the failure of industry can also be transferred to educationalists; and the blame for lack of economic renewal can be transferred to the unemployed. This is natural, in one sense, if a bureaucratic model of education as opposed to a professional model of education (Langford 1985)[46] is considered to be necessary. Langford defines the bureaucratic model of education as one which is governed and directed by persons outside of the actual profession. These are usually 'local or central government officials and politicians' (Langford 1985, p. 52). The professional model on the other hand, is on which is governed and directed by those who are actively engaged in the practice of education. For a bureaucratic model to be adopted, certain principles, policies and 'needs' have to be defined by influential bodies outside of the profession. Even a cursory analysis of the FEU curriculum model will reveal the importance the FEU attaches to such outside bodies; in this case to the collective body of industry.

The model[47] is effectively an updated version of Wheeler's 'wheel',[48] so beloved by past curriculum theorists. In essence, all we have is an inner circle intersected at the four points of the compass by four smaller circles containing, in clockwise fashion: 'Analysis of Needs'; 'Curriculum Design'; 'Implementation'; and 'Evaluation and Review'. Each of these is connected to a separate box, each of which in turn intersects an outer circle. Each box merely amplifies what is contained within the small circle. So, for example, the 'Analysis of Needs' in the small circle is amplified in its connected box so that it reads: 'Aims and Values of Learners, Teachers, Institution, Industry and Community'. And so on.

Now, on reading the model what becomes patently clear is that it is Industry's needs and influence that will outweigh the needs and influences of anybody else. According to the model 'Curriculum Design' is to be 'Industry centred', although it would perhaps be wrong to say that lip-service only is here paid to the notion of having curriculum 'Design' be 'Student Centred' as well.

However, in purely logical terms one wonders how it is at all possible to design a curriculum that is *both* 'Industry Centred' *and* 'Student Centred' (unless, of course, one does actually see the 'needs' of Industry being exactly equated with the 'needs' of individual students). The logic is fractured even further when one considers how it is possible to achieve a curriculum design which is also *both* 'Centrally Determined' *and* 'Negotiated'. At the end of the day, someone or some institutional body presumably has to make the final decision as to what may be included in the design and what may not. The fact that any representative of the teaching profession, responsible for the actual education and/or training of students, is missing from that right-hand box leaves one with the distinct impression that ultimately the curriculum design will be 'Centrally Determined' by whatever technocratic body is deemed responsible for centrally determining such matters. Moreover, it will be centrally determined according to the dictates of an Industry centred policy. For surely it is asking too much to assume that an individual student will have, in the classic phrase, 'parity of esteem' with industry when it comes to making a design claim, particularly given the theoretical boundaries of the model and the likely practical contexts governed by it?

The interchangeable 'needs/skills-based' curriculum espoused by the FEU is one which is fully endorsed by both government and industry for it clearly underlines their own preferred mode of educational thinking.

The object of education and training (now characterized by the hopes embedded in the extended YTS) is to have young people finally emerge who are to be:

> Fully competent in a particular job, to have acquired skills which can be transferred to other jobs, to have learnt how to apply competencies in unfamiliar stituations and to have increased his or her personal effectiveness.
>
> (Cassells, 1985)[49]

These new mantras: 'Acquired skills', 'transferred' or 'transferable skills' and 'applied competencies' – part of the common political and industrial linguistic scene – are fast gaining uncritical public acceptance, and the FEU seems fairly clear (as previously noted) about whose rhetoric it is prepared to adopt. *Basic Skills* (FEU, 1982) propounds the notion that 'the acquisition of basic skills' (p. xi) is an essential curriculum component. On one level one would not wish to dispute this; it is a favourite piece of fairly well understood jargon often deployed by HMI. But the new mythology which now surrounds the 'skills-based curriculum' is utterly byzantine in its complex hierarchy of mystification. The 1982 FEU publication *Basic Skills* apparently 'builds on the concept of core skills' which are, it just so happens, 'an elaborated definition of basic skills' (sic) p. xi). For an example of an 'elaborated definition' one need look no further than the FEU's set of 'Vocational Preparation Common Core Skills' (FEU 1982, *op cit*. pp. 45–54). These skills are grouped under twelve overall headings referred to as aims. These twelve are divided into sets known as objectives, numbering anything from six to nineteen per aim. Some of these sets are then subdivided into subsets of further, more specifically defined objectives until one is left with an overall list of approximately a hundred and thirty 'skills'. Then there are 'generic' skills; 'occupational' skills; 'skills across the curriculum'; 'process' and 'product' skills; 'service' skills and 'social' and 'life' skills. And finally, it is intended that students should progress from 'skill acquisition' through 'skill transfer' to eventual 'skill ownership' in which 'knowledge and understanding of principles' (FEU 1982, p. 114) are required[50].

So determined is it to follow and operate the 'skill-based curriculum' that the FEU has now advanced an even more bizarre set of 'skills'. In harking back to the comments of David (now Lord) Young (1982, 1985)[5] and those of his successor at the MSC, Bryan Nicholson,[52] the FEU has responded to this kind of populist appeal by staging a conference entitled 'Entrepreneurial Skills' in October 1985. In addition, it has begun publishing an *Enterprise Education Bulletin*, subtitled 'Delivering Entrepreneurial Skills' (no 1 January 1986). Coupled with this is a current research project rather despairingly billed as 'Entrepreneurship Education in Vocational Preparation – Materials Adaptation' (no 230). Education for entrepreneurship is very reminiscent of Protagoras' sophist view of what education ought to entail, and what its main object should be. Those of us not yet beguiled by the new vocationalism ought to beware. For this elastic concept of skill is subordinated to the final and most important concept in the set of new mantras: that of 'competency'.

'Competency' and its philosophical roots

Apparently, 'competency' can be simply defined as the 'knowledge, skills and attitudes required to perform a given task or act' (FEU 1982, *Competency in Teaching* p. 5). Competencies, like the skills they involve and depend upon, can be 'carefully identified' and 'stated in behavioural terms'. And, finally, the assessment of competence 'uses performance' as 'primary evidence, though the knowledge can be taken into account' (*ibid*, p. 5). The most fully articulated account of this view of education and training is to be found in the FEU publication (1984) *Towards a Competence-Based System,* which does, it must be admitted, acknowledge some of the many pitfalls associated with just such a view. Nonetheless, taken as an overall account of how education ought to be viewed, and how the curriculum needs to be considered, the 'skills and competence-based' approach requires some critical analysis. It needs to be traced back to its origins in order that a fuller understanding of what it means and what it entails, may be achieved. A detailed critical analysis is beyond the scope of this chapter; however, a brief survey of the key elements will be attempted.

It may be said that this 'skills–competence-based' approach has its roots in the twin movements of Rational Curriculum Planning (RCP) and Rational Curriculum Planning by Behavioural Objectives (RCPBO). These two movements (but particularly the latter), are underwritten by the fundamental philosophical belief that it is within the realms of possibility to determine the outcome of an event prior to its happening. It is therefore possible to predict and describe competencies prior to their performance. This belief is incorporated into a three-stage model of theory and practice supposedly applicable to any given field of human activity. Firstly, it is considered possible to agree on all pre-planned objectives; i.e. principles can be deliberately determined at the outset of an activity. Secondly, it is considered possible to agree on all the means by which the objectives can be secured; i.e. practices can be carefully formulated at a stage subsequent to the agreement on principles. And thirdly, it is considered possible to assess the final outcome of the activity; i.e. the performance (based on the principles and practices) can be acurately measured. This three-stage model is dependent upon a combination of the following five factors:

- a firm belief in science and objectivity;
- a dedication to efficiency;
- a determination to measure outcomes;
- an emphasis on observable performance;
- an ultimate concern with precision and specificity at all stages.

In philosophical terms this 'behavioural', view of human activity is essentially Millian in its conception. J.S. Mill's account of 'rational action' is similar to the three-stage model just discussed. First, get clear about 'ends'; second, hand the 'ends' over to science, for the scientist can tell us what the best means are for achieving the 'ends'. And third, simply act. This kind of account of human activity has found its most extreme expressions in military training[53]; industrial management[54]; and unfortunately once again, education.

Education has suffered this kind of onslaught before, and it isn't necessary to go right back to Protagoras in order to identify it. The ultra-rationalist and instrumental reasoning that now characterizes the FEU's perspective on the curriculum was abroad in the United States in the early part of this century, with the appearance on the educational scene of the American curriculum theorist, Franklin Bobbitt[55]. After nearly twenty years of administrative political wrangling over what should be included in public school syllabuses, Bobbitt's straightforward notion of 'scientific curriculum making' had obvious appeal. The directness and simplicity of his approach relieved the soul-searching; it effortlessly answered all the painful questions, and what is more, guaranteed the success of educational outcomes. As Bobbitt modestly states:

> The central theory is simple. Human life, however varied, consists in the performance of specific activities. Education that prepares for life is one that prepares definitely and adequately. for these specific activities. However numerous and diverse they may be for any social class, they can be discovered. This requires only that one go out into the world of affairs and discover the particulars of which these affairs consist. These will show the abilities, attitudes,

habits, appreciations, and forms of knowledge that men need. These will be numerous, definite, and particularized. The curriculum will then be that series of experiences which children and youth must have by way of attaining those objectives.

(Bobbitt 1918, p. 42)

What could be simpler? Life, according to Bobbitt, is merely a set of activities which, at the turn of a head, one can easily see being performed all around. All we need to do is list those performances which people need to be capable of in order to live a successful adult life, and then draft the list into a series of discrete objectives. What we end up with is an infinitely transferable blueprint for the curriculum. The trouble is, blueprints of heaven can often turn into maps of hell. As Oakeshott has pointed out, education is rather more to do with *conduct*, involving judgment, tradition, understanding and virtue, than with behaviour, involving the mere performance of prescribed skills[56].

An updated version of Bobbitt's theory is to be found in the preamble to the FEU's checklist of 'Common Core Objectives' which have already been mentioned:

The prescribed objectives are described in terms of a combination of observable performances to be expected of students and learning experiences to which they should be exposed.

(FEU 1981, *Vocational Preparation* p. 39)

The checklist itself is adapted from *A Basis for Choice*, and consists of the standard one hundred and thirty odd behavioural objectives. They make interesting reading. For example, under aim one: 'to bring an informed perspective as to the role and status of a young person in an adult society and the world of work', we find objectives 1.1, 1.5 and 1.6 being listed as: 'Describe a typical organizational structure of at least two different types of workplace or organization ...'; 'Describe the relevant trade union organizations within a particular firm or organization ...'; and 'Describe the basic management structure within a particular firm of organization ...' All this seems rather reminiscent of those dreary civics lessons in the early 1960s which achieved precious little other than a modicum of social control. Under aim three we discover a new form of gradgrindery; only this time it is not to do with the continual repetition of facts, but of experiences and performances. For example, objectives 3.2 to 3.5 read as follows: 'Experience the physical demands of some occupations ...'; 'Experience the manipulative demands of some occupations ...'; 'Experience the effect of working for an extended period of time between breaks ...'; and 'Perform tasks to a set standard and in a given time ...'

Some of the objectives hark more directly back to Bobbitt in terms of uncontentious practicality and style. Bobbitt, for example, listed some of the necessary abilities as being to do with 'checking up laundry slips'; 'building a camp fire', and 'selling one's automobile with profit to oneself'. Compare these with the FEU's objectives under aim eleven: '11.1, 'Be able to plan and prepare adequate meals.' 11.2, 'Use and maintain everyday machinery and equipment.' 11.3, 'Apply simple principles of health care, hygiene and physical fitness to their everyday lives.'

Aside from all the philosophical problems associated with compiling lists of objectives, there are the rather more obvious problems associated with the descent into trivia, both practical and linguistic. Take for example the FEU's pronouncement that it has constructed 'carefully designed prescriptors of performance'. Under the guise of extreme precision and high-toned seriousness, the FEU has tabled assessment procedures which allow for such absurdities as the following: apparently, 'can lay out a trolley in readiness for bedside treatment of patients' should be formally analysed and duly described as an example of 'decision-making planning' (FEU, 1984, *Towards a Competence-Based System.* p. 8). If I explained to my son's infant teacher that he had been engaged in a piece of 'decision-making planning' whereas in fact, he had merely put his toothbrush beside his evening milk-mug in readiness for cleaning his teeth, there is no doubt that I would be regarded with disbelief on a number of counts. The point is, there can be no end to this meaningless juggling of terms. This kind of linguistic exchange merely represents a brave, but somewhat dispirited managerial style underwritten by the desperate belief that something positive is being achieved. The potential crassness of it all has been well documented by Callahan (1965)[57] with reference to the constant cycle of efficiency drives occurring in the American education system whenever the economy dips into recession, or the US scientific and industrial image is tarnished, as was the case when Russia launched its sputnik.

Boyd H. Bode[58] writing in 1927 saw the immense problems associated with Bobbitt's view of the curriculum:

> The emphasis on specific objectives leads inevitably to the view that adult activities are the standards by which educational activities must be guided. As Bobbitt says: 'Education is primarily for adult life. Its fundamental responsibility is to prepare for the fifty years of adulthood, not for the twenty years of childhood and youth.' (1924). In other words, the emphasis on specific objectives justifies us in setting up adult activities as final patterns, and so to disregard the need of a progressive transformation of the pupils' experience in the direction of wider social insight. But since the need of a more flexible training cannot be entirely ignored, further 'objectives' are added, which turn out to be nothing more than pious admonitions. (p. 45)

There can be little doubt that the FEU is trading on Bobbitt's theory, and so Bode's comments are as relevant today as they were then. Take for example, another of the FEU's definitions of competence:

> Competence can be defined as: the possession and development of sufficient skills, knowledge, appropriate attitudes and experience for successful performance in life roles.
>
> (FEU 1984, *Towards a Competence-Based System*, p. 3)

'Bobbittry' is on the move again. Here. The dearth of imagination is self-evident. On one level the FEU's performance-based approach to the curriculum, concentrating as it does on the so-called 'needs' of adulthood, is repetitive, meaningless and trivial. On a much deeper level however, it is singularly instrumental, dangerously simplistic and plainly wrong. If there is a major curriculum problem today, as there certainly seems to be with the power, politics and language of vocationalism denting the weakened body of liberal education, then the FEU's answer is no answer at all. Bode offered a way out in the 1960s. Perhaps we ought to take note.

> The problem calls for historical perspective, for theory of mind, for insight into the educational significance of social institutions. (ibid., p. 58)

Curriculum 'deliberators' are at hand who can offer alternatives to the FEU model. To take one or two examples, Schwab (1969),[59] Reid (1978)[60] and Holt (1987)[61] concentrate on curriculum practicalities. Langford (1985)[62] details the significance of education as a social institution, while Jonathan (1985)[63] locates it within a modern philosophical context. What we do not need is a revival of Protagoras. Bobbitt's 'scientific curriculum making' served as a half-way house for the Sophist movement. This movement now resides at the FEU.

Although well-intentioned, the FEU has subscribed to the wrong model. And in doing so, finds that it has to rely on technocratic language, social interaction techniques, policy-led staff development, and administrative networking in order to achieve something that, at the end of the day, will not be worth having. 'Schools for success' are a fallacy. They may possibly provide the means to short-term gain, but only at the expense of long-term loss. Education, and hence the curriculum, is a problematic area, bound up as it is with values, meanings and beliefs. It cannot be reduced to lists of objectives, performances and skills. These merely provide quick and simple answers, whereas what is really needed is the framing of respectable questions. Right answers to wrong questions do not solve problems. After all, it may be argued that Socrates' moral dilemmas still provide a better model for education than do Protagoras' ethically neutered solutions.

Notes and references

1 Seale, D. (1984). 'FEU and MSC: two curricular philosophies and their implications for the Youth Training Scheme', in *The Vocational Aspect of Education*, vol. XXXVI, no. 93, pp. 3–10.
2 Pring, R. (1981). 'A basis for choice', in *Journal of Curriculum Studies*, vol. 13, no. 4 pp. 361–3.
3 see Holt, M. Chapter 9 in this volume.
4 The Certificate of Pre-Vocational Education (CPVE), launched in September 1985, is the 'new' 17–plus, which replaces the old Certificate of Extended Education (CEE). It is founded on the FEU document, *A Basis for Choice*, (1979), which displaced the *Keohane Report*, (1979).
5 It is interesting to note that the SCDC is the brainchild of Sir Keith Joseph, Conservative Secretary of State for Education, who abolished the Schools Council in 1984 despite the recommendation of the Trenaman Report (1981) to retain it, albeit in a modified form.

Instead Sir Keith announced in 1982 that he was intent upon setting up two separate bodies: the School Curriculum Development Committee (SCDC) and the Secondary Examinations Council (SEC). The former held its inaugural meeting on 6 January 1984; the latter on 23 May 1983. What is of particular importance however, is that both the Committee and the Council are centrally controlled by members appointed by Sir Keith himself. Unlike the unitary Schools Council for Curriculum and Examinations (1964–1984) the two new bodies are not governed in the main by the teaching profession.

6 Following the 1982 White Paper, *17 Plus: A New Qualification*, the JBPVE (Joint Board for Pre-Vocational Education) was founded on a joint basis by the City and Guilds London Institute (CGLI) and the Business and Technician Education Council (BTEC) with the remit of coordinating the CPVE.

7 See for example, DES, (1980), *A Framework for the School Curriculum;* DES, (1981), *The School Curriculum;* and DES, (1985), *The Organization and Content of the 5–16 Curriculum.*

8 See for example, Devon LEA, (1986), *Statutory Statement: The School Curriculum,* which states that in the Third Year of the secondary curriculum increased emphasis needs to be placed upon science and technology. There is no corresponding mention of either the expressive or creative arts.

9 See for example the Green Paper, (1985), *The Development of Higher Education into the 1990s,* (Command 9524), HMSO. Richard Hoggart (*TES,* 3.8.84, p. 10) sadly laments the rapid decline in status that is currently being accorded to the Arts.

10 Scrimshaw, P. (1983). *Educational Ideologies, Open University: Educational Studies, E204, Unit 2,* Open University Press.

11 Seminar: 'Progressing from vocational preparation' 19 February 1982, based on a FEU (1982) discussion document of the same title.

12 The FEU's 'enlightened definition' of skill is to be found in FEU, (1982), *Basic Skills.*

13 A short account relating the FEU's transition and development phase is to be found in DES, (1981), *Annual Report,* HMSO, Section 3, p. 20; and DES, (1983), *Annual Report,* HMSO, p. 19.

14 These categories have been gleaned from FEU, (1984), *Annual Report 1983–4,* pp. 3–10.

15 Much of this material has been distilled from FEU, (1985), *Annual Report 1984–5,* pp. 3–16. Again, use is made of the FEU's own categories which distinguish its works.

16 FEU publications in this area include: FEU, (1984), *Engineering Design;* FEU, (1984), *Robotic Arms;* and FEU, (1985), *Vocational Education and Training in Distribution.*

17 FEU publications in this area include: FEU, (1984), *Supporting and Developing Staff for IT;* FEU, (1984), *Computer Based Learning in FE;* and FEU, (1985), *Fifth-Generation Computers.*

18 Two of the most recent FEU publications in this area are: FEU, (1984), *Curriculum Development in the Education of Adults;* and FEU, (1984), *Consett.*

19 The publication by the FEU, (1985), of *Changing the Focus: Women and FE* is being followed by research project no. 302 entitled. 'Changing the Focus: Development of a Dissemination Strategy for the FEU Policy Statement on Women'. Research project no. 246 is entitled 'Raising Perceptual Awareness in Work with Young Women and Girls'.

20 As a result of the FEU's expertise in this area, the DES funded a major project which culminated in the joint publication (with the NFER) of FEU, (1985), *From Coping to Confidence.* Other publications include: FEU, (1981), *Students with Special Needs in FE;* FEU, (1984), *Routes to Coping;* and FEU, (1984), *Learning for Independence.*

21 See also FEU, (1983), *Policy Statement: Curriculum Development for a Multicultural Society,* in addition to: research project no. 219 'Towards a Non-Racist Curriculum'; no. 233 'Anti-Racist Curriculum Review and Staff Development – a Community Perspective'; and no. 234 'Anti-Racist Curriculum Review and Staff Development – a College Perspective'.

22 Education Management is, of course, an umbrella term for a variety of sub-topics: curriculum, finance, staffing etc. In curriculum terms the most significant FEU Education Management research project is 'Curriculum-Led Institutional Development' (project no. 116). With respect to funding, research project no. 299, 'Sources of Finance for FE' is an important work; and research project no. 310 'Staff Appraisal, Profiles and Continuing Personal Development' speaks for itself. Finally, two projects each with the intention of providing an overview of management concerns, are: 'Guidance and Support for Locally-Based

Management Development in Further Education' (Research project no. 258) and 'East Midlands Training in Education Management – Further and Adult Education'.

23 Following on from the White Paper, *Education and Training for Young People (April 1985)*, Tom King, the Conservative Secretary of State for Employment, announced the appointment of Oscar De Ville as Chairman of the RVQ Working Group. The principal aim of this Working Group is to 'recommend a structure of vocational qualifications in England and Wales'. (MSC/DES (1985), *Review of Vocational Qualifications. Interim Report. p. 9)*.

24 The establishment of this working party was first announced in the White Paper, (1985), *Better Schools*. It terms of reference are:

> To prepare drafts of national criteria against which pre-vocational and vocationally-oriented courses offered to pupils in compulsory secondary education will be appraised and monitored by the Secondary Examinations Council, including both single-subject or single-skill courses and grouped courses, within the framework of the curricular principles now under discussion between the Secretaries of State and local education authorities and having regard wherever appropriate to existing national criteria as approved by the Secretaries of State.
>
> (DES *Press Notice* dated 9 April 1985 p. 1)

25 See research project no. 294, 'Interactive Video in FE'.

26 See FEU, (1983), *Flexible Learning Opportunities*: and FEU, (1984), *Flexible Learning in Action*.

27 Soon to be published by the FEU: *Developing Numeracy Skills*.

28 The first phase saw the completion of a number of individual projects which were later summarized in the publication: FEU, (1983), *Computer Literacy: Parts 1 & 2*. (Now sold by Longmans Resources Unit under its updated title: *Computer Literacy: Units 1, 2, 3–4*). Other projects have included: 'Integration of Aims of Vocational Preparation into Foundation and Youth Training Schemes', (research project no. 105); 'Check List Development and Evaluation for Vocational Preparation Programmes', (research project no. 107), and 'A One-year Course of Vocational Preparation', (research project no. 111). Phase three, The Experimental College Network, began with Worthing College of Technology (research project no. 160). Its latest addition is Rumney College of Technology (research project no. 298).

29 For a snapshot view of the FEU's set of policies related to Staff Development the following research projects are of primary value: 'Staff development through Staff Learning Groups' (no. 224); 'Staff Development in a New Tertiary College' (no. 243); and 'Transition to CPVE – A Focus for College-wide Curriculum and Staff Development' (no. 260).

30 See pages 15–16 FEU, (1985), *Annual Report: 1984–5*.

31 These fourteen areas of concern are supported by the existence of ten formally constituted Advisory Committees and Working Groups operating in the following: curriculum; special needs; basic engineering; skills; new technology; adult education and training; education management; staff development for support staff; FEU/LEA consultation; and multicultural curriculum.

32 The 'education' versus 'training' debate has a long and convoluted history, (see pp. 151–172, 'The liberal and the vocational', chap. 7, in Silver, H. (1983), *Education as History*, Methuen). However, three papers offered at various points in the recent past are particularly interesting. They are: Wall, G.I. (1967), 'The concept of vocational education' in *Proceedings of the Annual Conference: Philosophy of Education Society of Great Britain*, pp. 51–66; Bell, G.H. (1981), 'Industrial culture and the school: some conceptual and practical isues in the schools–industry debate', in *Journal of Philosophy of Education*, vol. 15, no. 2, pp. 175–191; and Dearden, R.F. (1984), 'Education and training', in *Westminster Studies in Educatin*, vol. 7, pp. 57–66.

33 FEU. (1985). *Annual Report 1984–5*. 'FEU officers continue to support the CPVE Joint Board; although the FEU Board of Management felt it necessary in March 1985 to publish a brief statement working against the dangers of new qualifications undermining CPVE' (p. 3).

34 Mark Jackson, *TES*, (27.6.86), 'Quangos jostle for the pole position', p. 11.

35 Havelock, R. (1969). *Planning for Innovation through Dissemination and Utilization of Knowledge*. University of Michigan.

36 The best example of this is the White Paper, (1983), *Teaching Quality* which sets out to delimit both the ends and means of education within an instrumental or utilitarian framework. See Slater, F. *et al*, (1985), *The Quality Controllres*, Bedford Way Paper, no. 22, University of London Institute of Education, Methuen, for a substantial critique of this White Paper vision.

37 This sum is calculated on the basis of figures extracted from MSC, (1986), *TVEI Review '85: A Summary* (four-page pamphlet).

38 Figures based on the annual capitation grant allocated to a Plymouth secondary school of approximately five hundred pupils.

39 A detailed account of how this model works is to be found in: Grosch, P.D. (1985), 'Case study: some observations on theory and practice', unpublished M. Ed. thesis, University of Exeter, Appendix 3, pp. 211–239.

40 MacDonald, B. (1976), 'Evaluation and the control of education', in Tawney, D. (ed.), *Curriculum Evaluation Today: Trends and Implications*, Macmillan.

41 Trow, M. (1984). 'Researchers, policy analysts and policy intellectuals', in Husen, T. and Kogan, M. (eds.), *Educational Research and Policy*, Pergamon Press pp. 261–282.

42 See Grosch, P.D., *op. cit.*, p. 237.

43 Russell, B. (1955). *Authority and the Individual*. George Allen & Unwin, p. 116.

44 The same kind of point has been made by John Wilson who refers to this overall view as the Behaviourist Fantasy or BF, Wilson, J. (1979), *Fantasy and Common Sense in Education*, Martin Robertson Publishers, pp. 27–36.

45 An excellent philosophical account of this kind of argument is to be found in Jonathan, R. (1983), 'The manpower service model of education'. in *Cambridge Journal of Education*, vol. 13, no. 2, pp. 3–10.

46 Langford, G. (1985). *Education, Persons and Society: A Philosophical Inquiry*. Macmillan.

47 The FEU curriculum model is to be found in innumerable FEU documents. This one was taken from FEU, 1984, *Staff Development for Support Staff in Further Education: Policy Statement*, p. 5, FEU pamphlet.

48 Wheeler, D.K. (1967). *Curriculum Process*. University of London Press.

49 John Cassels, Director General of the National Economic Development Office, 13.6.85, *The Times*. In the same article John Cassels is quoted as saying that, 'Education and training must be geared to match the demand for more skills in British industry today'.

50 Much of the FEU work in this area is culled from some of the more opaque MSC documents such as: MSC, (1981), *Grouping of Skills Review; MSC, (1979), Grouping of Skills Sub-Project 1: Re-Deployment by Upgrading to Technician*; and MSC/DTP5 (1977), *Analytical Techniques for Skill Comparison: A Report describing some North American Approaches*. Another material sources has been the Institute of Manpower Studies (IMS) who have published five volumes on *Skills Needed for Young People's Jobs* (no date).

51 David Young, 'Helping the young help themselves', in *TES*, 26.11.82, and 'The lord of do-it-yourself solutions', in *The Guardian*, 25.2.85.

52 Bryan Nicholson has been reported as saying that, 'New curricula are required in education in order to lay the foundations of economic growth', *TES*, 12.7.85.

53 See for example, Miller, R.B. (1962), 'Analysis and specification of behaviour for training', in Glazer, R. (ed.), *Training, Research and Education*.

54 See for example, Taylor, F.W. (1947), *Scientific Management*.

55 Bobbitt, F., (1918). *The Curriculum*. Mifflin.

56 Oakeshott, M. (1967). 'Learning and teaching', in, Peters, R.S. (ed.), *The Concept of Education*, Routledge & Kegan Paul, p. 157.

57 Callahan, R.E. (1962). *Education and the Cult of Efficiency*. University of Chicago Press.

58 Boyd H. Bode, (1927). *Modern Educational Theories*, Macmillan, reprinted in *Curriculum Theory Network*, 5:1, (1975), pp. 39–59).

59 Schwab, J.J. (1969). 'The practical: a language for curriculum' in *School Review*, 78, pp. 1–24.

60 Reid, W. (1978). *Thinking About the Curriculum*. Routledge & Kegan Paul.

61 Holt, M. (1987). *Judgment, Planning and Educational Change*. London, Harper and Row.

62 Langford, G. (1985). *op. cit.*

63 Jonathan, R. (1985), 'Education, philosophy of education and context', in *Journal of Philosophy of Education*, vol. 19, no. 1 pp. 13–25.

CHAPTER 9

Beyond the new vocationalism

Maurice Holt

The root cause of the misconceptions and malfeasances described in this book is Britain's economic decline. By December 1982 British manufacturing production had fallen to the level at which it stood in 1967[1]. With growing unemployment, the education system was a convenient scapegoat for industry and politicians alike. The banner of skills and vocationalism had already been hoisted in James Callaghan's 1976 Ruskin College speech. It was a simple matter to instal the new doctrine through the powerful and non-accountable agency of the Manpower Services Commission. What might have been thought less simple, but which in the event turned out to be quite straightforward, was the enlistment of support for the vocabulary of skills and vocational preparation from the academic community. The result is that over The last five years, with the launching of YTS, TVEI and LPVE in quick succession, the language of the 'new vocationalism' has become a commonplace of staffroom discourse.

There is, however, absolutely no evidence to suggest that the new jargon has addressed fundamental issues to do with secondary education or, for that matter, with our industrial performance. In education these issues are plain enough, and brought sharply in focus by the contributions of Mike Golby and Bernard Barker. The knowledge-centred, examination-dominated curriculum of the grammar school has been applied uncritically to comprehensive schools. A form of education intended for 'academic' pupils (and celebrating, in any event, a peculiarly narrow view of intellect) has been applied, with alienating consequences, to pupils of all abilities.

Even so, it should be noted that schools have been remarkably successful, within this canon so warmly espoused by parents and politicians, in delivering examination results. Simon[2] has recorded the prodigious improvement made by schools over the last ten years, since comprehensive organization took hold. If getting jobs really were a matter of securing exam qualifications, youth unemployment would scarcely exist. But since there are so few jobs, it does: and it is politically expedient for the Prime Minister to describe education as 'a disaster'[3], and to argue that joblessness stems not from governmental infirmity but from an absence of work-related skills.

We can hardly be surprised if politicians regard attack as a form of defence, although the sustained vilification to which schools and teachers have been so unjustly treated bodes ill for our intellectual future as a nation and ought not to be forgotten, nor forgiven, too readily. But the fervour with which the doctrine of skills and vocationalism has been embraced is more serious, for two reasons. First, it embodies a rhetoric which is, as Barker puts it, 'almost meaningless for education'. And Jerry Wellington's inquiries suggest it has, in reality, as little meaning for employers: their needs 'are not framed in terms of skills'. To give the concept of a skill any durability, it is necessary to dress it up as a new, 'transferable' entity. The Further Education Unit has embarked on this strategy with great vigour, but the exercise – as Paul Grosch demonstrates – will not bear close scrutiny. The 'core skills' component of the YTS depends on the same device, orchestrated in this case by the Institute of Manpower Studies; but Ruth Jonathan shows with stark clarity that 'the Emperor still does not appear to have any clothes'.

And the rhetoric of skills is not merely meaningless: it diverts us in a most damaging way from the real task, which must be to develop a form of secondary education that will prepare our children, in Golby's words, to become 'good parents, full members of the community, thinking citizens and critical participants in an evolving democracy'. To be sure, the traditional grammar-school curriculum ill equips them for these tasks; but the pre-vocational skills-based curriculum is just as inept. As Barker observes, it amounts to little more than 'a retreaded "package" for slow learners'.

This is the second consequence of the skills bonanza – its inherent divisiveness. At a time when cohesion and commonality are so desirable – when the consequences of social and sectarian divisions are clearer than ever, and more harmful than ever – the last thing we should be introducing into schools is a form of curriculum which has repeatedly shown itself, whenever it has been tried, as one which reinforces distinctions between pupils by setting up the 'practical' alongside the 'academic'. Yet it is not inconceivable that at least some of those involved in this work are well aware of these consequences, and see them as desirable. Ranson[4] quotes from an interview with a DES official:

There has to be selection because we are beginning to create aspirations which increasingly society cannot match. In some ways this points to the success of education in contrast to the public mythology which has been created ... We have to select: to ration the educational opportunities to meet the job opportunities.

The reference here to the myth that schools have failed, when the reverse is demonstrably the case, is interesting too. And so is the view of another DES official interviewed by Ranson: 'If we have a highly educated and idle population we may possibly anticipate more serious social conflict. People must be educated once more to know their place'. This kind of social thinking, so characteristic of the mid-Victorians, hardly squares with the public rhetoric of an 'enterprise culture'. But if we should want to stigmatize part of the population by offering them an impoverished curriculum, the language of 'vocational preparation' is the simplest way to do it. The de Ville committee's proposal that a separate vocational qualification should be offered alongside GCSE does nothing to dispel these doubts. Neither does the government's determination to buttress the traditional grammar-school curriculum for the most 'academic' pupils by introducing a 'distinction' and 'merit' category into GCSE, and AS level at 18-plus as a further reinforcement to A-level.

In all these ways, skills and vocationalism not only deflect us from reinterpreting secondary education: they undermine attempts to give meaning to the notion of a common curriculum. But they fail too, as I have suggested, to treat the shortcomings of our industrial performance. Senker's study[5] of TVEI concludes that:

> If is difficult to make a case for technical education in schools on straightforward economic grounds. Japanese 'failure' to incorporate significant elements of technical education in school curricula does not seem to have impaired their country's economic performance. The Japanese school curriculum is very broad. Engineering as such is not taught in Japanese schools ... The TVEI is unlikely to contribute directly, even in the long run, to the fundamental ... problems which afflict Britain in this era of rapid technological change.

The point is made more generally in Ollerenshaw's perceptive and authoritative survey of education and industry[6]:

> Wherein does any potential threat of manpower planning lie? It lies in too narrow or too early specialization in school or in further or higher education in subject disciplines which ... do not form a sound or broad enough base for rapidly changing types of employment ... It lies in any too-detailed attempts to match courses to current employment needs which may later collapse ... It lies in uniformity, in centrally administered and adjudicated examination ... It lies in trying to manipulate the education system to meet forecast manpower requirements ...

What is particularly interesting about Ollerenshaw's list is that all these threats to industrial health are current policy, and some of them are in favour with other political parties the effect of 'voc-prep' is to foreshorten a broad education from 11, the new CTCs imply a reinstatement of the 11–plus; so that it ends at 14, not 16; the rhetoric of the 154–18 curriculum narrows and prematurely specializes; YTS and CPVE both gear the post–16 curriculum to current employment needs, through their close linkage with industrial training; the new GCSE examination at 16–plus will be nationally controlled through its grade criteria; the manipulation of further and higher education to meet currently perceived needs is now a major objective of MSC and DES planning as Large has noticed[7]:

> The essential point about the huge investments in higher education in Japan, Singapore, South Korea and the rest is that they are aimed not merely at meeting the narrow, cannon-fodder demands for particular (and perhaps short-lived) technical skills; they seek to produce multi-disciplinary graduates, ready to handle the kaleidoscopic shifts of information-based economies.

Several observers have noted that government policies incline towards a West German model of education and training. And the political lobby which argues that an 'anti-industrial culture' exists in Britain – which methods such as 'Education for Capability', with its emphasis on the German concept of *technik* as the missing element in our schools, would allegedly eliminate – draws support from the same source. It is very evident that the MSC seeks to move in this direction, for the IMS report *Competence and Competition* (1984) took pains to emphasize the merits of West German arrangements. It needs to be said that not only is much of this advocacy based on a misconception; it is also the case that the West Germans are beginning to doubt whether their model – which is, after all, as old as this century – gives them the flexibility modern economies need, and which that of Japan clearly possesses.

In the short term, German approaches largely remove 16–18 year olds from the unemployment register. But their 'dual system' links the workplace with a broadly-based education in the *berufsschulen* – a very different matter from the impoverished offerings of the MSC 'core skills' programme. The Germans have a concept of 'formation', of 'combined education and training of the whole person'[8] which imposes vastly increased costs upon German industry. German industrialists have come to see the economic benefits of this. In the UK, training during employment is a low priority on which very small sums are spent. Moreover, British firms are a byword for philistine shortsightedness – even the director of the MSC has had to resort to shaming them into some kind of training activity[9]. As Clive Seale points out, 'The CBI position on the curriculum of the YTS allows little room for liberal educational principles'.

It is unlikely that British industry could now find the money to finance a German-style 'formation' system, even if it had the will to do so. And German doubts about the future efficiency of their system surfaced when, at an international conference, their team:

> spoke of an uphill struggle against the divisiveness of their system, which provides excellent vocational education for the majority but cuts them off from the academic few ... They voiced fears that neither (group) is being prepared for a changing world[10].

But the Germans have, of course, made little progress towards a system of comprehensive schools; it seems sad that rather than build on this national asset, we are being urged to support policies which can only reinforce divisiveness.

What is less generally known, though, is that *technik* has no place in the German school curriculum. Hörner remarks: 'The alleged "third culture" (*Technik*) either does not appear at all on the West German secondary school curriculum or is merely allotted an entirely marginal position.[11]' West German industrial success owes nothing to the vocational strategies being urged on British schools by the MSC, the FEU and the 'Education for Capability' movement: 'Primary and secondary education in the Federal Republic of Germany has ... stressed that learning at school is to be free of all economic ends or purposes' (Hörner). This may come as a surprise, enjoined as we are by the 1985 White Paper, *Better Schools*, that 'It is vital that schools should always remember that preparation for working life is one of their principal functions' (para. 46).

The reason for this seeming neglect is not that the West Germans despise technology: quite the reverse. They recognize that it is not only different from science, but a demanding intellectual activity for professional courses at degree level. Advanced technical education in the German *Technische Hochschule*, as Hörner points out, differs from that offered in English polytechnics and colleges by its freedom from vocational concerns and its academic parity with traditional arts and science courses. The lesson for us here is clear: nothing is to be gained by pretending that watered-down, science-linked 'technology' courses 14–16 advance the purposes of either education or industry.

In any event, even the *Technische Hochschulen* are now showing their age – as, indeed, is the divided West German system. Now often rechristened as *Technische Universitaten* to enhance their status, growth in engineering students has still been outstripped, James[12] points out, 'by the growth in student numbers for social sciences and economics'. As regards British admiration for Germany's dual system, James offers a word of warning:

> Unfortuantely, there is a large element of myth about this picture. The apprenticeship system is a rather odd relic of an odd past, and is far from being a purpose-built tool to handle the microchip ... In short, Germany has been training the young to repair fridges and cars in a customer society, but not really to service a technical revolution ... During the past 15 years, Germany has lost more jobs than Britain ... Many German businessmen are seriously worried by the implications of Germany's failure to adjust technical training to new circumstances.

Yet this 'odd' and outdated system seems to monopolize the thinking of the government, the MSC and the DES. And it is a system, with its compliant public acceptance of a division of pupils into different categories, which derives from a much more authoritarian society than Britain's[13]. Our political masters seem to have forgotten that the idea of the 11–plus eventually became so repugnant to the polity that it was a prime political issue. They have forgotten, too, that in the 11–16 common school linked to the 16–19 tertiary college we have developed our own British solution, and an infinitely better one.

But such a solution requires an altogether more hard-headed view of technology as *technik* than the soft options masquerading under the banner of technology in TVEI 14–16 courses. It must build on physics and mathematics, which are the appropriate pre-university preparation for it[14]. There is, though, great virtue in the quite different argument that a design-based techno-aesthetic course should be a core component. Such courses, linking crafts with plastic and graphic art and kept well clear of misleading and pretentious associations with school science, treat technology in a broad, liberal sense altogether appropriate for the 11–16 curriculum. Their justification has everything to do with education, and nothing to do with vocational ends. It is regrettable that HMI have plumped for scientized school technology, despite its absence from the curriculum of German and Japanese schools and the poor educational case for it.

In technology as in other school subjects, there is a confusion of purpose once educational considerations are pushed aside in the urge to be 'relevant'. Sir Keith Joseph has done much harm with his assertion that

> What is taught needs to be more obviously applicable to the real world that the young see and will see about them. One very direct example of this approach has been the TVEI but the approach needs also to colour the primary curriculum, teacher training and examinations[15].

We can agree that the learning encounter devised by the teacher must have *connectedness* with the pupil's state of mind; otherwise it will be merely inert, decontextualized knowledge of the kind which features prominently in the grammar-school curriculum. But the test – as Barker's discussion bears out – is to do both with *what* is taught and *how* it is taught. Writing an ode to a tractor may be very relevant to the real world of a country primary school, yet very boring. Discussing dinosaurs is quite irrelevant in the modern world, yet can be totally enthralling. This is not to say that content is unimportant, that only process matters – a view which is fashionable but absurd. It is to assert that both matter, and both depend on the professional judgment of teachers rather than imposed and misleading doctrines – whether these doctrines emanate from government ministers, captains of industry or, for that matter, educationists.

The Joseph doctrine of relevance leads to a further misconception, since it implies that the educational encounter is to be derived from an analysis of whatever activity is to be classed as 'relevant'. Much of the appeal of vocationalism stems from its evident preoccupation with what is 'relevant', but attempts to put pedagogical flesh on the rhetorical bones inevitably lead to the kind of banalities set forth by writers like Charters and Bobbitt in the US during the 1920s. Bode's masterful annihilation of this approach should be compulsory reading for anyone contemplating it[16], and certainly for the FEU: its whole 'voc-prep' philosophy, as Paul Grosch makes clear, is pure Bobbitry, and it is extraordinary that a view of education discredited fifty years ago should be so naively embraced today. Our reluctance to choose politicians and administrators with a sense of historical perspective means that we often, as taxpayers, indulge them in the expensive luxury of making the same mistakes again and again. Stone[17] makes this point tellingly, in discussing the vocational attack on the liberal tradition of Scottish education at the turn of the century:

The utilitarians won, of course; and the irony at the end of all this should be spelled out: we are now less literate than we were in 1900, and I suspect that we have relatively fewer skills than we had in 1870, when the educational debate got under way.

Richard Smith's study of the DES-funded Teacher Education Project shows the dangers of applying the doctrine of 'relevance' to teacher training – a specific item on Sir Keith Joseph's 1983 list, subsequently given the full treatment in the White Paper, *Teaching Quality*, (1984). It is said that Sir Keith regards this wonderfully wrong-headed document as his greatest achievement in office: certainly the urge to base the training course on what is 'relevant' to classroom experience is evident on every page. It is the great merit of Smith's chapter that it turns the argument of relevance on its head. For he shows that attempts to define teaching as a series of learnable, relevant skills, far from appealing to our common sense, fly in the face of it:

> It is so obvious that personality and character are crucially important in teachers that the point would not be worth making were it not that too much emphasis on skills is effectively a denial of it.

More generally, we may say that talk of 'relevance' is a superficially beguiling way of dismissing education as an instrumental activity. The education of teachers is only worth doing if it relates directly to their work in classroom; the education of pupils must similarly relate exclusively to what can be justified as worth knowing in the 'real world'. It is a view dismissive not only of education, but also of those who are to be educated. For they are viewed not as *ends*, themselves capable of acting as moral agents, and therefore to be equipped as such; they are rather *means*, functionaries who will demonstrate their skills in the classroom, pupils who will possess the required range of competencies. Because it is a diminished view of the educational encounter, it lends itself to the reductionism of skills, and to such futile exercises as the attempt to separate skills from knowledge, attitudes and values. Wellington's discussion is helpful here; and it should be noted that the HMI 'Red Book' series, while showing an admirable concern for a broad core 'entitlement curriculum' 11–16, entirely misses the point of such a programme by insisting that it can be fragmented in this way. The same tedious litany of 'knowledge, skills, attitudes and values' is prominent in other HMI publications[18] and confirms one's suspicions that senior HMI have succumbed to the virus *technocraticus managerialis*. The cure is long and painful. Fortunately most teachers are immune.

Their immunity is guaranteed by their implicit understanding that education is more than a collection of competencies: it is, in Oakeshott's phrase, about helping pupils to 'make something of themselves'. The enterprise of education is not primarily to do with knowledge, and it is unfortunate that HMI, in their 'Red Book' prescriptions, have allowed epistemology to dominate their thinking. Of course content matters, and it needs to be broadly based if pupils are to acquire the capacity to act rationally; but it is only a means to this end, which depends primarily on the art of judgment. Education is essentially a practical and moral enterprise, and we can endorse Smith's conclusion: 'It looks as though "virtues" rather than "skills" should be at the heart of our conception of a good teacher'. And there is a symmetry between teacher and taught: teachers need to be moral agents in order that their pupils should learn how to become moral agents too.

Golby's point in his opening chapter is on all fours with this view: 'school is primarily about the virtues of the considered life'. And one might add, with Socrates, that 'the unexamined life is not worth living'. Education, in language of skills and vocationalism, no more addresses these moral principles than it does in the grammar–school language of knowledge and examinations. To substitute skill for knowledge is only to pass from one side to the other of the same counterfeit coin. Neither a purely vocational nor a purely epistemological approach can constitute a basis for an educational programme.

From the evidence discussed here, however, it would appear that the two approaches beget each other: the 1943 Norwood report's division into the academic on the one hand, and the technical and practical on the other, might perhaps be regarded as the acceptance of the inevitable. Each is parasitic on the other: the academic curriculum leading to GCSE bears a symbiotic relationship with the vocational curriculum leading to a form of CPVE at 16–plus. This innate bipartism has been accurately captured by Sir Keith Joseph:

> A balance (has) to be achieved between the values of the broad liberal tradition on the one hand, and the tradition of useful education on the other ... I do not deplore this (liberal) tradition at all: it is vital for the preservation and enrichment of our culture ... But I do deplore the one-sidedness and dominance of that tradition.[19]

So de we, in this book: but to suppose that some mix of the 'old humanist' tradition with the 'industrial training' model will produce sound 'public education' (to use Raymond Williams's terms) is like trying to make yoghourt from stirring chalk and cheese.

The tragedy of construing the secondary curriculum in this way is that it commits us to a sterile and misconceived dualism: our children are to be yoked for ever alongside each other in an unnecessary and destructive misalliance, like characters in a Greek tragedy. As Wellington reminds us, Huxley had the vision half a century ago to perceive this, and argue that 'technical education should become more liberal, and academic education a more adequate preparation for everyday life'.

Huxley was surely right to point towards a single, unified form of curriculum which could learn from the errors of these two malformations. But to believe that this unity can be achieved by more of one and less of the other misses the point that neither ingredient is equal to the task. Furthermore, it is to suppose that we should seek some kind of blend, when what is really needed is a fresh synthesis. Education as an ethical and political enterprise – and secondary education for all for life in modern society cannot settle for less – must address precisely those practical and moral issues which inspired the Greeks to invent liberal education. It is our peculiarly British tragedy that we fostered, in the last century, a perverted form of liberal education in our public schools and took it as the basis of secondary education under the 1904 Regulations for grammar schools. Instead of preparing pupils, as Aristotle had argued, for the active tasks of the moral agent, the curriculum esteemed knowledge as non-negotiable and absolutely determined, to fit them for the passive role of the moral judge[20].

But it is of the essence of liberal education that it must be reinterpreted in every age, and it is precisely this task which we must address ourselves to now. As Golby has pointed out, our obsession with skills and vocationalism is incompatible with educational concerns, and has diverted us from these important matters. It has led to official publications invested with central authority, yet offering 'no discernible view of curriculum design'. It has generated an empty-headed rhetoric and closed our minds to consideration of such possible realities for our children as 'education for a workless future'. It has led to many millions of pounds being spent, through the TVEI, on a handful of pupils in a divisive fashion which reinforces locker-room prejudice against intellectual inquiry and for new technology, but leaves untouched any consideration of the real issues for secondary education. And in higher education, the instrumentalism of the vocationalists has damaged teacher education, distorted funding for degree courses and given the seal of approval to a short-sighted and economically unsound approach to manpower planning.

Much of this lost ground cannot be recovered. But if we can recover our vision of liberal education, and place a concept of the virtues at the heart of the school curriculum, we can turn our present uncertainties and tribulations to good accout. There will be no easy answers: much discussion and deliberation lie ahead[21]. But we can no longer evade the task.

Notes

1 Quoted in Glover, I.A. (1985), 'How the West was lost? Decline in engineering and manufacturing in Britain and the United States', *Higher Education Review*, summer.
2 Simon, B. (1984). 'Comprehensives show steady improvement', *Marxixm Today*, autumn.
3 Mrs Thatcher's disdain for the maintained sector is chronicled in Wolpe, A. and Donald, J. (1983), *Is Anyone Here from Education?*, Pluto Press.
4 Ranson, S. (1985). 'Towards a tertiary tripartism: new codes of social control and the 17–plus', in Broadfoot, P. (1984), (ed.), *Selection, Certification and Control*, Falmer.
5 Senker, P. (1986). 'The TVEI and UK economic performance – an initial assessment', *Journal of Education Policy*, vol. 1, no. 4.
6 Ollerenshaw, Dame K. (1985). 'Manpower planning – the threat or spur to education', *Third Willis Jackson Lecture, BACIE*, (16 Park Crescent, London W1n 4AP).

7 Large, P. (1985). 'The Thatcher years of wasted brain power', *Guardian*, 10 April

8 The phrase is taken from a perceptive article by Stuart Maclure: Maclure, S. (1985), 'An industrial education lesson for the UK?', *The Times Educational Supplement*, 1 February.

9 'The MSC's management has fired another big salvo in its campaign to shame employers into spending more on training': *The Times Educational Supplement*, 13.6.86.

10 Jackson, M. (1985). 'Germans raise doubts about their system', *The Times Educational Supplement*, 1 February.

11 Hörner, W. (1985). '"Technik" and "Technology"; some consequences of terminological differences for educational policy-making', *Oxford Review of Education*, vol. 11, no. 3.

12 James, Harold (1985). 'The disillusioned apprentices', *The Times,* 13 December.

13 A fascinating study of anthropological differences stemming from family patterns, which describes those of Germany as 'authoritarian' and those of England as 'absolute nuclear', is given in Todd, E. (1985), *The Explanation of Ideology*, Oxford, Blackwell.

14 Just as a spurious form of 'technology' makes little contribution to the 11–16 curriculum, so the invention of GCE advanced level courses in 'engineering' and 'computer technology' may do more harm than good in the 16–19 curriculum. The University of Manchester Institute of Science and Technology makes it clear that entrants to its Department of Computer Science are best prepared by taking A-levels in physics and mathematics.

15 From a speech given to the Council for Local Education Authorities (CLEA) on 15 July, 1983.

16 Boyd H. Bode (1927). *Modern Educational Theories*, Macmillan, reprinted in *Curriculum Theory Network* 5:1, (1975), pp. 39–59.

17 Stone, Norman (1986). 'Energy and education', book review in *The Sunday Times*, 28 December.

18 For example, in DES/HIM, (1985), *The Curriculum from 5 to 16*, HMSO.

19 As reported in *The Times Higher Education Supplement*, 14 March 1986.

20 The argument is lucidly set out in Reid, W.A., (1980), 'Democracy, perfectability and the battle of the books: thoughts on the conception of liberal education in the writings of Schwab', *Curriculum Inquiry*, vol. 10, no. 3.

21 These issues are taken further in Holt, M. (1987), *Judgment, Planning and Educational Change*, London, Harper and Row.

Contributors

Bernard Barker is Head of Stanground Comprehensive School, Peterborough.

Michael Golby is Senior Lecturer in Curriculum Studies at the School of Education, University of Exeter.

Paul Grosch is a Research Student at the School of Education, University of Exeter.

Maurice Holt is Principal Lecturer in Curriculum Studies at the St Mark and St John College of Higher Education, Plymouth.

Ruth Jonathan is Senior Lecturer in Education at the Department of Education, Edinburgh University.

Clive Seale was a Research Officer at Garnett College London, and now works for the Institute of Social Studies in Medical Care.

Richard Smith is Lecturer in Education at the School of Education, University of Durham.

Jerry Wellington is Lecturer in Education in the Division of Education, University of Sheffield.

Index